REWRITING WORK

Foundations and Innovations in Technical and Professional Communication

Series Editor: Lisa Melonçon

Series Associate Editor: Sherena Huntsman

The Foundations and Innovations in Technical and Professional Communication series publishes work that is necessary as a base for the field of technical and professional communication (TPC), addresses areas of central importance within the field, and engages with innovative ideas and approaches to TPC. The series focuses on presenting the intersection of theory and application/practice within TPC and is intended to include both monographs and co-authored works, edited collections, digitally enhanced work, and innovative works that may not fit traditional formats (such as works that are longer than a journal article but shorter than a book).

The WAC Clearinghouse and University Press of Colorado are collaborating so that these books will be widely available through free digital distribution and low-cost print editions. The publishers and the series editors are committed to the principle that knowledge should freely circulate and have embraced the use of technology to support open access to scholarly work.

Other Books in the Series

REWRITING WORK

Edited by Lora Anderson

The WAC Clearinghouse
wac.colostate.edu
Fort Collins, Colorado

University Press of Colorado
upcolorado.com
Denver, Colorado

The WAC Clearinghouse, Fort Collins, Colorado 80523

University Press of Colorado, Denver, Colorado 80203

ISBN 978-1-64215-212-8 (PDF) | 978-1-64215-213-5 (ePub) | 978-1-64642-616-4 (pbk.)

DOI 10.37514/TPC-B.2023.2128

Produced in the United States of America

Library of Congress Cataloging-in-Publication Data

Names: Anderson, Lora, 1963– editor.
Title: Rewriting work / edited by Lora Anderson.
Description: Fort Collins, Colorado : The WAC Clearinghouse ; Denver, Colorado : University Press of Colorado, 2024. | Series: Foundations and innovations in technical and professional communication | Includes bibliographical references.
Identifiers: LCCN 2023056539 (print) | LCCN 2023056540 (ebook) | ISBN 9781646426164 (paperback) | ISBN 9781642152128 (adobe pdf) | ISBN 9781642152135 (epub)
Subjects: LCSH: Business writing. | Communication of technical information.
Classification: LCC HF5718.3 .R49 2024 (print) | LCC HF5718.3 (ebook) | DDC 808.06/665—dc23/eng/20240131
LC record available at https://lccn.loc.gov/2023056539
LC ebook record available at https://lccn.loc.gov/2023056540

Copyeditor: Meg Vezzu
Designer: Mike Palmquist
Series Editor: Lisa Melonçon
Series Associate Editor: Sherena Huntsman

The WAC Clearinghouse supports teachers of writing across the disciplines. Hosted by Colorado State University, it brings together scholarly journals and book series as well as resources for teachers who use writing in their courses. This book is available in digital formats for free download at wac.colostate.edu.

Founded in 1965, the University Press of Colorado is a nonprofit cooperative publishing enterprise supported, in part, by Adams State University, Colorado State University, Fort Lewis College, Metropolitan State University of Denver, University of Alaska Fairbanks, University of Colorado, University of Denver, University of Northern Colorado, University of Wyoming, Utah State University, and Western Colorado University. For more information, visit upcolorado.com.

Land Acknowledgment. The Colorado State University Land Acknowledgment can be found at https://landacknowledgment.colostate.edu.

■ Contents

This book is dedicated to Mary Beth Debs.

REWRITING WORK

Introduction

Lora Anderson

UNIVERSITY OF CINCINNATI

Collaboration between academics and practitioners of technical and professional communication (TPC) came into existence because of the needs of businesses and government for a particular set of writing skills (Dicks, 2002). As such, the academic field of TPC historically has maintained a strong connection to workplace writing practices in both our pedagogy and research efforts. Our academic programs speak to this connection with a high value placed on internships, service learning, and pedagogy that emphasizes workplace skills such as multimedia writing and design. This connection is also clearly visible in the research presented in edited collections, single-authored books, and journal articles on workplace writing in the 1990s and early 2000s (e.g., Brumberger, 2007; Dias et al., 1999; Henry, 2000; Lentz, 2013; Leyden, 2008; Schneider & Andre, 2005; Spilka, 1993 Sullivan & Dautermann, 1996).

Despite this sustained scholarly engagement, however, the connection between academic research and workplace practices can be fraught. Challenges in making clear connections between academic and practitioners' work and working as collaborators include academic tenure requirements (i.e., the need for publishing in scholarly venues), difficulty with finding grant funding for projects, and opposing timelines and goals (Mirel & Spilka, 2002). Kirk St.Amant and Lisa Melonçon (2016) add the additional challenge of agreeing on what constitutes research and what questions should be asked. Some have viewed these challenges as so significant that the academic world and the world in which TPC is practiced have been characterized as different cultures (Boettger & Friess, 2016; Dicks, 2002).

In a section devoted to revising the relationships between industry and academic in Barbara Mirel and Rachel Spilka's 2002 edited collection, R. Stanley Dicks outlines the significant challenges he sees as getting in the way of technical communication practitioners and scholars successfully collaborating: 1) the perception of information, 2) writing styles, 3) views on collaboration, 4) assumptions about employment, 5) workload expectations, 6) power issues, 7) trust, 8) philosophical leanings, and 9) reward systems. Such differences have been seen by more recent scholars as so divided that Ryan K. Boettger and Erin Friess (2016) give a nod to the 1992 book *Men Are from Mars, Women Are from Venus: The Classic Guide to Understanding the Opposite Sex*, using the planets to characterize the divide between TPC academia and workplace. Similar to earlier scholars, Boettger and Friess (2016) lay the blame on the publication requirements of academics and say that these fundamental needs for career advancement result

DOI: https://doi.org/10.37514/TPC-B.2023.2128.1.3

in academics and practitioners seeming to be from different planets. In their analysis of professional and academic publishing forums over a 20-year period, they found evidence that these "cultures" remain as siloed as ever despite efforts to create crossover in publication venues and publication content, such as the Practitioner Takeaways in *Technical Communication*, the journal that published Boettger and Friess' study.

Perhaps because of these perceptions, much early workplace writing research was conducted as ethnography (e.g., Beaufort, 1999; Dautermann, 1997; Doheny-Farina, 1986; Hannah & Simeone, 2018; Henry, 2000; Katz, 1998; Smart, 2006; Winsor, 2003)—a methodology conducted in specific settings and focused on identity constructions of insiders and outsiders. As such, many of the studies focus on the identity of "newcomer" to the workplace and how they "assimilate" to a specific workplace culture. Representative of this work are Patrick Dias, Aviva Freedman, Peter Medway, and Anthony Par's (1999) study of academic and professional workplace contexts, Jennie Dautermann's (1997) *Writing at Good Hope: A Study of Negotiated Composition in a Community of Nurses*, and Jim Henry's (2000) *Writing Workplace Cultures: An Archaeology of Professional Writing*. In Patrick Dias, Aviva Freedman, Peter Medway, and Anthony Par's 1999 book *Worlds Apart: Acting and Writing in Academic and Workplace Contexts*, the authors report on an ethnographic seven-year multisite comparative study of writing in different university courses and matched workplaces. They note the difficulty of newcomers to workplace settings mainly due to ideological interests represented in the genres of these workplaces. Jim Henry's (2000) *Writing Workplace Cultures: An Archaeology of Professional Writing*, also using an ethnographic approach, grew out of a graduate course he was teaching and was targeted to both teachers of TPC and "their workplace colleagues" (pp. xi-xii). His study involves 83 workplace ethnographies spanning a period of seven years. While positioned from a composition perspective, Henry himself spent time as a technical writer in the railroad industry. He uses the metaphor of archaeology to characterize his book: "an archaeology, in which researchers' findings and researchers' self-representations figure as so many shards to be scrutinized by readers according to their own theoretical frames and local contexts" (p. 11). Jennie Dautermann (1997) substitutes the notion of cultures with discourse communities in *Writing at Good Hope: A study of Negotiated Composition in a Community of Nurses*; nonetheless, she employs the ethnographic methods of participant observation and interviews. Drawing on Norman Denzin's (1989) descriptive realism, she sees the writers in the setting she studies as making "attempts to allow the world being interpreted to interpret itself" (p. 25).

Despite the rich history of ethnographic workplace studies, Carl Herndl (1995) firmly states that workplace studies of TPC tended toward the descriptive rather than critical due largely to the research methods we borrowed from anthropology. The result of this methodology, he argues, is the reproduction of the culture's dominant discourse such as that explored by Joanne Yates' (1989) foundational text *Control through Communication: The Rise of System in American Management*, which details how management control was established through internal communications in the railroad and manufacturing firms from the mid-1800s to early 1900s, and Dorothy A. Winsor's (2003) examination of power structures between engineers and technicians as represented in writing genres at an engineering center.

Since such critiques of workplace writing research methods, scholars have responded to Bernadette Longo's (2006) call to not limit themselves to working "within the walls of one organization" (p. 113). The response has resulted in workplace studies growing beyond ethnography to using a broad range of methods to study workplace writing and foster the relationships between academics and practitioners. Elisabeth Kramer-Simpson (2018), for example, uses an empirical study on the role of industry mentors and academic internship coordinators in teaching TPC students. In their work with gender and feminism in business, technical, and workplace writing studies, Kate White and colleagues (2016) provide a study based on a metanalysis of journal issues. Others have undertaken a variety of methods to study workplace writing, as Melonçon and St.Amant (2019) outline.

But place still matters, and myself and the contributors in this volume make the argument that it matters now as much as it did when we largely studied workplace writing through ethnography. Place is important in two ways. First, it has implications for questions of identity that reach beyond the identities of insider or outsider. Second, place has become a critical factor in how we get work accomplished. I echo Claire Lauer and Eva Brumberger's (2019) call for redefining writing so that it works for a "responsive" workplace (p. 635), but here I extend it to workplace writing research, which has a primary goal to understand how groups of people create knowledge and make their worlds functional and coherent through written language. As such, the goal of this collection is to provide research into 21st-century workplaces in order to capture some of the evolutions that we've seen in the work*place*, workplace writing, and writers' identities. To do so, the chapters in this collection address workplace writing largely through two questions: How do we fit in? How do we adapt? These questions have not been applied mutually exclusively because they are, of course, intertwined, but for the purposes of this volume, I approach the question of how we fit in as a question of identity and how our identity shifts as we adapt to changes in technology and changes in the spaces in which work gets done.

■ Identities and TPC

Identity issues in TPC are related to both the identity of the field and the identity of individuals working in the area and scholars in the discipline. The identity of TPC as a field can be a slippery concept. Rachel Spilka (2002) and James M. Dubinsky and Kristen Getchell (2021) have argued that this crisis of identity is related to our struggle to define the field in a uniform way. For Dubinsky and Getchell (2021), this struggle is visible in the various names TPC faculty have used to describe their work:

> Since the mid- to late-1980s, English department faculty who teach and research in what has come to be called professional communication (PC), professional and technical communication (PTC), or technical and PC (TPC) have struggled to define its disciplinary boundaries or adequately describe the fields that compose or exist within it. (p. 434)

Lisa Meloncon and Joanna Schreiber (2022), on the other hand, argue that "the field [TPC] is comprised of various components that must be reflected upon from time to time in order to maintain a sustainable and flexible identity" (p. 4). This ability to maintain a flexible identity is critical for workplaces and writing to be responsive.

TPC scholarship has often addressed the need for this flexibility and responsiveness in conversations about defining the role of the technical communicator in the workplace by relating the role to what the future of the field itself looks like (e.g., Albers, 2005; Giammona, 2004; Mehlenbacher, 2013; Pringle & Williams, 2005), the changing nature of our expertise (e.g., Carliner, 2001; Durack, 2003; Hayhoe, 2007; Mogilevsky, 1968), and our status (e.g., Slack et al., 1993; Spilka, 2002; Wilson & Wolford, 2017). Essays concerned with the future of TPC often have the explicitly stated goal of predicting the direction of the field in light of technological changes that impact the work of technical writing and communication. In Michael J. Albers' introduction to his 2005 *Technical Communication* special issue entitled "The Future of Technical Communication," for example, he states, "For this special issue, I was looking for forward-looking articles that consider how technology is changing the technical communication field and how those changes will affect the profession" (p. 267). Barbara Mirel and Rachel Spilka's (2002) edited collection uses the connections and tensions between our academic field and practitioners to forecast the directions of technical communication in the 21st century.

Many of the technological changes have resulted in a broadening of our definition of what technical writing work is. Miles A. Kimball (2017) notes people generally think of instructions when thinking about what a technical communicator produces. George F. Hayhoe (2007) states that when technical communication first emerged as a profession in the 1940s, the job was solely defined as technical writing, writing that included producing documents such as proposals, and procedures. Over time, Hayhoe (2007) continues, technical communication became referred to as an "umbrella profession because it subsumes a great variety of tasks" (p. 281), including usability expert, content management specialist, and web designer. Hayhoe's assessment is echoed by David Wright et al. (2011):

Over time, we have predicted that the future technical communicator needs to be skilled as writer, editor, graphic artist, software
specialist, usability specialist, multimedia developer, database manager, information designer, knowledge manager, programmer, corporate executive, and subject matter expert while being versed in
a variety of disciplines, including health care, finance, electronics,
international business, and foreign language. (pp. 447–448)

This explosion of roles and settings over time also created a need for new ways
to talk about individual identities. Historically, our disciplinary identity crisis has
fueled research with tenacious ties to ideas about knowledge, agency, and power
around the question of who we are as individual writers. Leading such discussions of agency, power, and status is Jennifer Daryl Slack and colleagues' 1993
article "The Technical Communicator as Author: Meaning, Power, Authority," in
which the authors link the role of technical communicators to the communication process itself. In the article, they outline three views of the communication
process which suggest different "places" for the technical communicator: 1) the
transmission view, 2) the translation view, and 3) the articulation view. They characterize these views as follows:

The transmission view can be delimited in terms of a concern, for
the most part, with the possibilities and problems involved in message transmission, that is, in conveying meaning from one point
to another. The second—what we will call the translation view of
communication—can be understood in terms of a primary concern with the constitution of meaning in the interpretation and
reinterpretation of messages. The third—what we will call the
articulation view of communication—can be grasped as a concern
principally with the ongoing struggle to articulate and rearticulate
meaning." (Slack et al.,1993, p. 14)

Over a decade later, in the introduction to volume one of the landmark
two-volume collection entitled *Power and Legitimacy in Technical Communication*, edited by Teresa Kynell-Hunt and Gerald J. Savage, Savage (2004) states
that identity "goes beyond identifying characteristic skills and knowledge of the
field" to

prioritizing kinds of knowledge and skills involves defining a set
of professional values and beliefs, determining what constitutes
knowledge, what methodologies are acceptable for the research
that produces knowledge in the fields, and what ethical principles
apply to the application of our knowledge. (p. 3)

Discussions about the role of technical communicators have also focused on
agency and status. The title of Dorothy Winsor's (2003) book *Writing Power:*

Communication in an Engineering Center clearly communicates our interests in power. Winsor addressed her underlying questions of how work gets done and what orders work at complex organizations through an examination of how power, generic texts, and knowledge interact. Using genre theory, she says that some of the tools organizations use are genre texts, and she argues that the work order is a genre text, which the company she calls AgriCorp uses to get work done by allowing technicians and engineers to work together to realize organizational goals and produce knowledge.

Identity discussions have also focused on the connection to expertise (e.g., Andersen, 2014; Clark & Andersen, 2005; Conklin, 2007; Giammona, 2004; Hart-Davidson, 2013; Kynell-Hunt & Savage, 2003, 2004; Longo, 2000; Wilson & Wolford, 2017; Winsor, 2003). Some of this work is grounded in conversations about the state of research in the field generally (e.g., Albers, 2016; Blakeslee & Spilka, 2004; McNely et al., 2015; Melonçon & St.Amant, 2019; St.Amant & Melonçon, 2016) or professionalization of the field (e.g., Davis, 2004; Savage, 1999, 2004; Spilka, 2002). Most pertinent to this volume is the scholarship that discussed TPC identities as symbolic analysts, knowledge workers, discourse workers, and entrepreneurs. Johndan Johnson-Eilola (1996) initially brought Robert Reich's (1991) concept of the symbolic analyst to the forefront in TPC literature. He uses the role of symbolic analysts to relocate the value of technical communicators' work in the post-industrial age, arguing that symbolic analytic workers rely on skills in abstraction, experimentation, collaboration, and system thinking to work with information across a variety of disciplines and markets. Building on Reich, he elsewhere describes how symbolic analysts "tend to work online, either communicating with peers (they rarely have direct organizational supervision) or manipulating symbols" (Johnson-Eilola, 2005, p. 28).

Greg Wilson (2001) similarly argues for the use of the phrase "symbolic analysts":

> Technical communicators who function as symbolic analysts may never fully escape the less glamorous aspects of technical communication, but they will be able to increase their value to the company, their job satisfaction, the efficiency of their company's technical communication, and their power to shift conceptual structures. They must, however, get out of the cubicle and articulate themselves as invaluable to the function of the company, explaining that the company's product is information, in that today the product is secondary to how people understand the product. (p. 84)

In describing networked writing practices, Stacey Pigg (2014) also asserts that many of those working in these environments fit Reich's (1991) definition of the "symbolic analyst" whose work involves creative and critical thinking as well as managing complex information. Other scholars have employed the nomenclature of knowledge worker or discourse worker. Theorizing knowledge work that occurs outside of traditional work/office spaces, Clay Spinuzzi et al. (2019) identify the people working in coworking spaces as "independent knowledge workers" (p. 112). Pigg (2014) also uses this phrase (as well as the phrase "symbolic analyst") to describe the distributed work of the informants in her study of social media and digital participatory writing environments. In their discussion of knowledge work, Greg Wilson and Rachel Wolford (2017) situate their re-theorizing of technical communicators as post-postmodern discourse workers through Jim Henry's (2006) definition of discourse worker as well as Slack et al.'s (1993) technical communicator as author and Michael J. Salvo's (2006) postmodern expert, an expert with the added responsibilities of "helping educate and prepare those interested and invested in the solution to be able to effectively engage dominant exercises of power" (p. 225). Wilson and Wolford's proposed post-postmodern discourse workers would similarly understand their economic relationship to institutions in ways that would help them shape discourse within these institutions.

As economic structures and institutions became more fragmented and global in nature, the word "entrepreneur" gained cache as a descriptive term for TPC workers. In his introduction to the special issue of the *Journal of Business and Technical Communication* called "Rhetoric of Entrepreneurship: Theories, Methodologies, and Practices", Spinuzzi (2017) defines entrepreneurship as "roughly, the process of discovering and conceptualizing problems and then solving those problems with innovative solutions" (p. 276). In his own special issue introduction for the same journal, Steven Fraiberg (2021) argues that globalization has shifted toward an entrepreneurial economy, one made up of systems that "comprise a complex and ever shifting array of venture capitalists, start-up entrepreneurs, accelerators, coworking spaces, meetups, conferences, and a range of other actors, activities, events, and spaces" (p. 176). Brenton Faber and Johndan Johnson-Eilola (2002) similarly focus on the global marketplace and assert that to compete in a global marketplace, technical communicators must become knowledge producers rather than merely product producers. Other scholars have used the entrepreneur identity as a way to address specific issues in TPC. Ben Lauren and Stacey Pigg (2016), for example, offer an entrepreneurial model as a way to address the divide between, "describing how TC entrepreneurs access, learn, and disseminate relevant information" (p. 300), and Natasha N. Jones (2017) examines the rhetorical narratives of Black entrepreneurs in work that "legitimizes knowledge making beyond the dominant disciplinary domains" (p. 344).

■ How We Adapt: Places of Work

As Henry (2006) notes, the nature of the workplace has changed dramatically since the writing of Lee Odell and Dixie Goswami's (1985) *Writing in Nonacademic Settings*. Broadly speaking, the greatest change in location is that from agricultural pursuits to "white-collar office workers" (Light, 1988, p. 20). In his characterization of 20th-century U.S. economy, Henry (2006) talks about the innovation of the assembly line, which allowed for mass production of goods, and Frederick W. Taylor's (1911) scientific management principles, principles that had impacts for workplace writing practices. Yates also says: "Systemic management as it evolved in the late nineteenth and early twentieth centuries was built on an infrastructure of formal communication flows: impersonal policies, procedures, and processes, and orders flowed down the hierarchy" (1989, p. 20). In this introduction's section on identities, this is clear, especially in the scholarship on distributed work—work that "splices together divergent work activities (separated by time, space, organizations, and objectives) and that enables the transformations of information and texts that characterize such work" (Spinuzzi, 2007, p. 265) and globalization.

By the 1950s, offices were designed for more flexibility, but workers still sat in rows of desks, which were replaced in the 1960s with the "action office," which "included a variety of work settings for staff, increased freedom of movement, and greater privacy when working with the ability of workers to personalize their space" (Marhamat, 2021, n.p.). The 1970s continued the open-office trend until the cubicle era of the 1980s. As workers became more mobile in the 1990s and the cell phone became ubiquitous, workers began to have flexibility in terms of remote work. This flexibility led to the rise of open plans, lounges, cafés, and other co-working spaces, and employees were no longer tied to their desks beginning in 2000 (Marhamat, 2021).

This trend continued in the next decades, but the preference for remote work solidified under public health measures taken as the COVID-19 pandemic began. As my state (Ohio) went into lockdown due to COVID in March 2020, I Zoomed with coworkers and colleagues who were working in laundry rooms, cars, and dining rooms. I watched the random cat cross a keyboard, heard a dog bark at a mail truck (usually mine), and witnessed kids in all stages of dress in people's backgrounds. Eventually, we became very good at trying to make these spaces "look" professional, using Zoom virtual backgrounds of bookcases filled with volumes of texts and fake office spaces. In TPC, Jennifer Bay and Patricia Sullivan (2021) specifically look at what the shift to remote work means in terms of researching what home-based workplace writing looks like and argue "the collapse of traditional work–life boundaries might allow for a renaissance of feminist research methods in technical and professional communication" (p. 168).

The way we worked during lockdown and the more long-lasting changes these practices have created attest to the fact that the only real constant is change, and this adage applies to workplace writing practices, definitions of workplace, and, as a result, the way we research and think about our field. This experience reinforced my sense of how important and fluid our definitions for writing workplaces can be in TPC. As such, the very nature of TPC work, both as a discipline and a profession, requires constant re-engagement. Our work experiences during the pandemic and these reflections on them highlight the need to continually engage with, question, and redefine what the work of technical communication is and where it is done so that our pedagogy is relevant and our research is valuable to ourselves, our students, and technical communication practitioners.

■ The Chapters

This volume takes up the call to pay attention to work*place* for the activities of TPC practitioners, acknowledging that the work of these individuals "requires activities such as locating and constructing rhetorical spaces (virtual and physical) to support multiple writing tasks" (Pigg, 2014, p. 69). The chapters in this collection address TPC identities, what places or spaces qualify as writing workplaces, and how they impact identities and ideas about expertise.

Jeremy Rosselot-Merritt and Janel Bloch's chapter, "Common Thread, Varied Focus: Defining *Workplace* in Technical and Professional Communication," sets up the work in the later chapters through an analysis of a large sample of published workplace-oriented TPC research from 1980–2019. In this chapter, the authors provide an extended snapshot into how the idea of *workplace* has evolved over time in TPC. Similar to Lisa Melonçon and Joanna Schreiber (2022), the authors establish that, while TPC has historically been tied to engineering, computer science, and scientific fields, the discipline now includes a range of industries, organizations, sites, and locations. Rosselot-Merritt and Bloch acknowledge that one of the challenges of such a diverse field is the risk of diluting its collective identity in ways that might lead to missed opportunities to expand TPC's practical application and prospects for scholarly research. Their meta-analysis of 150 peer-reviewed articles, book chapters, and full-length books draws attention to several challenges for TPC relating to "construct conceptualization, research sustainability, professional identity, and the relationship between academic study and professional practice."

In "Emphasizing Place in Workplace Research," Lisa Melonçon argues that TPC work is no longer fixed in terms of place. Grounding her argument in work in cultural geography and rhetorical theory, she offers the concepts of geo-rhetoric and micro-contexts to focus specifically on the material impacts of place on workplace writing to give it a *geography*. The chapter then moves to put these concepts into practice by drawing on data from a two-year ethnographic study that examined the knowledge management and writing practices of a mid-size organization in the Midwest.

Lance Cummings' chapter, "Understanding 21st-Century Workplace Writing Communities: An Ethnomethodological Study of *Phatic* Communication in Large Corporations," focuses on the nature of several hierarchical shifts of workplace writing to accommodate work that is fast-paced and constantly in flux. Cummings reports on an ethnomethodological study to argue that this shift has created deeper writing communities and networks and that understanding how writers create and maintain networks, both in-house and abroad, is crucial to our understanding of 21st-century workplace writing and how to prepare students for the human side of technical communication.

Of course, workplace writing in the 21st century goes beyond words, as Brian Fitzpatrick and Jessica McCaughey's chapter on freelancers suggests. The authors re-envision the idea of "newcomer" through Jean Lave and Etienne Wenger's (1991) Community of Practice by examining the writing demands placed on freelance and gig workers through two case studies drawn from a larger pool of interviews with full-time freelancers: an illustrator and a television commercial director. Their research questions center around what differentiates the writing and communication of these workers from that of professionals in more traditional full-time employment situations, as well as how these workers navigate the changing contexts of "workplace" and "workplace writing."

Focusing on TPC identities, in "Writer Identity, Literacy, and Collaboration: 20 Technical Communication Leaders in 2020," Ann Hill Duin and Lee-Ann Kastman Breuch examine how the TPC workplace has evolved and the literacies TPC practitioners need through interviews with 20 TPC industry leaders—members of their program's Technical Communication Advisory Board. Their results note a growing importance of writer identity, sociotechnological literacies, and collaboration. Because their study was conducted during the COVID-19 lockdown, their interviewees also had the opportunity to address how TPC practitioners might best prepare for remote work, strategic roles, and building of the profession.

Mark A. Hannah and Chris Lam's chapter also adds to the TPC scholarship on collaboration (e.g., Debs, 2002; Henry, 2006; Kohn, 2015; Spinuzzi, 2012; Walton et al., 2019). In their chapter, "Melding Expertise: Developing a Relational, Competency Model for Performing Work in Complex Workplace Collaborations," Hannah and Lam use a case study of a TPC practitioner working on a multi-expertise workplace team of geoscientists to make observations about what kinds of skills, competencies, and training TPC practitioners may need in highly technical, multi-expertise workplace teams. They offer a "model of 'functional flexibility'" and illustrate its use in an organizational context that involves the features of contemporary workplace contexts."

The final chapter addresses identity, place, and product through a study on workplace writing skills. In "Entry-Level Professional Communicators in the Workplace: What Job Ads Tell Us," Kelli Cargile Cook, Bethany Pitchford, and Joni Litsey report on a content analysis of job ads to extend the work of Eva Brumberger and Claire Lauer (2015), Sally Henschel and Lisa Meloncon (2014), and Meloncon and Henschel (2013) and provide insights into the professional communication workplace and illuminate the expectations these employers have for professional communicators.

▌ Thoughts on Future Directions of Workplace Writing Research

The work in this collection is designed to contribute to the scholarship of workplace writing studies by capturing some of the evolutions that we have seen in workplace writing in the last decades. As technologies and work spaces continue to change and the TPC practitioner continues to need to adapt, there are many opportunities for more of this research. Although ethnographic studies are more difficult to conduct in contemporary workplaces due largely to time constraints, studies that use contextual inquiry could be a useful method. Spinuzzi (2000) defined contextual inquiry (CI) as a field method oriented to design and "dedicated to divining the underlying work structure of a given workplace and standardizing the work structure in ways that increase the system's efficiency and the individual's control and happiness" (p. 424). He continued that CI was designed to promote radical change "because it involves manipulating the underlying work structure rather than the artifact" (p. 425).

Other types of longitudinal studies, such as the one Jeremy Rosselot-Merritt and Janel Bloch offer in this volume, would also be useful. For example, many researchers examine the question of how to best prepare our students for the workplace through some type of skills analysis, such as the one Kelli Cargile Cook, Bethany Pitchford, and Joni Litsey offer in this volume, and work published about visual and design skills TPC practitioners use in the workplace (e.g., Brumberger, 2007; Carliner, 2001). A longitudinal study or one that provides a historical perspective could be of great value to TPC scholars and program administrators alike. As a way to continue to try to better link workplace practices to academic study, more research published by teams of academics and practitioners would also be of value.

All of this is to say that our work in workplace writing research is far from done.

▌ References

Albers, Michael J. (2005). Introduction: The future of technical communication. *Technical Communication, 52*(3), 267–272.

Albers, Michael J. (2016). Improving research communication. *Technical Communication, 63*(4), 293–297.

Andersen, Rebekka. (2014). Rhetorical work in the age of content management: Implications for the field of technical communication. *Journal of Business and Technical Communication, 28*(2), 115–157. https://doi.org/10.1177/1050651913513904.

Bay, Jennifer & Sullivan, Patricia. (2021). Researching home-based technical and professional communication: Emerging structures and methods. *Journal of Business and Technical Communication, 35*(1), 167–173. https://doi.org/10.1177/1050651920959185

Beaufort, Anne. (1999). *Writing in the real world: Making the transition from school to work.* Teachers College Press.

Blakeslee, Ann M. & Spilka, Rachel. (2004). The state of research in technical communication. *Technical Communication Quarterly, 13*(1), 73–92. https://doi.org/10.1207/S15427625TCQ1301_8

Boettger, Ryan K. & Friess, Erinn (2016). Academics are from Mars, practitioners are from Venus: Analyzing content alignment within technical communication forums. *Technical Communication, 63*(4), 314–327.

Brumberger, Eva. (2007). Visual communication in the workplace: A survey of practice. *Technical Communication Quarterly, 16*(4), 369–395. https://doi.org/10.1080/10572250701380725.

Brumberger, Eva & Lauer, Claire. (2015). The evolution of technical communication: An analysis of industry job postings. *Technical Communication, 62*(4), 224–243.

Carliner, Saul. (2001). Emerging skills in technical communication: The information designer's place in a new career path for technical communicators. *Technical Communication, 48*(2), 139–144.

Clark, Dave & Andersen, Rebekka. (2005). Re-negotiating with technology: Training towards more sustainable technical communication. *Technical Communication, 52*(3), 289–301.

Conklin, James. (2007). From the structure of text to the dynamic of teams: The changing nature of technical communication practice. *Technical Communication, 54*(2), 210–231.

Dautermann, Jennie. (1997). *Writing at Good Hope: A study of negotiated composition in a community of nurses.* Ablex.

Davis, Marjorie T. (2004). Shaping the future of our profession. In Teresa Kynell-Hunt & Gerald J. Savage (Eds.), *Power and legitimacy in technical communication: Volume II Strategies for Professional Status* (pp. 75–86). Baywood Publishing Company, Inc.

Debs, Mary Beth. (1993). Corporate authority: Sponsoring rhetorical practice. In Rachel Spilka (Ed.), *Writing in the workplace: New research perspectives* (pp. 158–170). Southern Illinois University Press.

Denzin, Norman K. (1989). *Interpretive interactionism.* Sage.

Dias, Patrick, Freedman, Aviva, Medway, Peter & Par, Anthony. (1999). *Worlds apart: Acting and writing in academic and workplace contexts.* Lawrence Erlbaum Associates.

Dicks, R. Stanley. (2002). Cultural impediments to understanding: Are they insurmountable? In Barbara Mirel & Rachel Spilka (Eds.), *Reshaping technical communication: New directions and challenges for the 21st century* (pp. 7–25). Lawerence Erlbaum Associates.

Doheny-Farina, Stephen. (1986). Writing in an emerging organization: An ethnographic study. *Written Communication, 3*(2), 158–185. https://doi.org/10.1177/0741088386003002002.

Dubinsky, James M. & Getchell, Kristen. (2021). The disappearance of business communication from professional communication programs in English departments. *Journal of Business and Technical Communication, 35*(4), 433–468. https://doi.org/10.1177/10506519211021466.

Durack, Katherine T. (2003). From the moon to the microchip: Fifty years of technical communication. *Technical Communication, 50*(4), 571–584.

Faber, Brenton & Johnson-Eilola, Johndan. (2002). Migrations: Strategic thinking about the future(s) of technical communication. In Barbara Mirel & Rachel Spilka (Eds.), *Reshaping technical communication: New directions and challenges for the 21st century* (pp. 135–148). Lawerence Erlbaum Associates.

Fraiberg, Steven. (2021). Introduction to special issue on innovation and entrepreneurship communication in the context of globalization. *Journal of Business & Technical Communication, 35*(2), 175–184. https://doi.org/10.1177/1050651920979947.

Giammona, Barbara. (2004). The future of technical communication: How innovation, technology, information management, and other forces are shaping the future of the profession. *Technical Communication, 51*(3), 349–366.

Hart-Davidson, William. (2013). What are the work patterns of technical communication? In Johndan Johnson-Eilola & Stuart A. Selber (Eds.), *Solving problems in technical communication* (pp. 50–74). University of Chicago Press.

Hannah, Mark A. & Simeone, Michael. (2018). Exploring an ethnography-based knowledge network model for professional communication analysis of knowledge integration. *IEEE Transactions on Professional Communication, 61*(4), 372–388.

Hayhoe, George. F. (2007). The future of technical writing and editing. *Technical Communication, 54*(3), 281–282.

Henry, Jim. (2000). *Writing workplace cultures: An archaeology of professional writing.* Southern Illinois University Press.

Henry, Jim. (2006). Writing workplace cultures—Technically speaking. In J. Blake Scott, Bernadette Longo & Katherine V. Wills (Eds.), *Critical power tools: Technical communication and cultural studies* (pp. 199–218). SUNY Press.

Henschel, Sally & Melonçon, Lisa. (2014). Of horsemen and layered literacies: Assessment instruments for aligning technical and professional communication undergraduate curricula with professional expectations. *Programmatic Perspectives, 6*(1), 3–26.

Herndl, Carl. (1995). The transformation of critical ethnography into pedagogy: Or the vicissitudes of traveling theory. In A. Duin & C. Hansen (Eds.), *Multidisciplinary research on workplace writing: Challenging the boundaries* (pp. 17–34). Lawrence Erlbaum.

Johnson-Eilola, Johndan. (1996). Relocating the value of work: Technical communication in a postindustrial age. *Technical Communication Quarterly, 5*(3), 245–270.

Johnson-Eilola, Johndan. (2005). *Datacloud: Toward a new theory of online work.* Hampton Press.

Jones, Natasha N. (2017). Rhetorical narratives of Black entrepreneurs: The business of race, agency, and cultural empowerment. *Journal of Business and Technical Communication, 31*(3), 319–349. https://doi.org/10.1177/1050651917695540.

Katz, Susan M. (1998). *The dynamics of writing review: Opportunities for growth and change in the workplace.* Ablex Publishing.

Kimball, Miles A. (2017). The golden age of technical communication. *Journal of Business and Technical Communication, 46*(3), 330–358. https://doi.org/10.1177/0047281616641927.

Kohn, L. (2015). How professional writing pedagogy and university–workplace partnerships can shape the mentoring of workplace writing. *Journal of Technical Writing and Communication, 45*(2), 166–188. https://doi.org/10.1177/0047281615569484.

Kramer-Simpson, E. (2018). Moving from student to professional: Industry mentors and academic internship coordinators supporting intern learning in the workplace. *Journal of Technical Writing and Communication, 48*(1), 81–103. https://doi.org/10.1177/0047281616646753.

Kynell-Hunt, Teresa & Savage, Gerald J. (Eds.). (2003). *Power and legitimacy in technical communication Volume 1.* Baywood.

Kynell-Hunt, Teresa & Savage, Gerald J. (Eds.). (2004). *Power and legitimacy in technical communication volume 2.* Baywood.

Lauer, Claire & Brumberger, Eva. (2019). Redefining writing for the responsive workplace. *College Composition and Communication, 70*(4), 634–663.

Lauren, Benjamin & Pigg, Stacey. (2016). Toward multidirectional knowledge flows: Lessons from research and publication practices of technical communication entrepreneurs. *Technical Communication, 63*(4), 299–313.

Lave, Jean & Wenger, Etienne. (1991). *Situated learning: Legitimate peripheral participation.* Cambridge University Press.

Lauer, Claire & Brumberger, Eva. (2019). Redefining writing for the responsive workplace. *College Composition and Communication, 70*(4), 634–663. https://doi.org/www.jstor.org/stable/26772588.

Lentz, Paula. (2013). MBA students' workplace writing: Implications for business writing pedagogy and workplace practice. *Business and Professional Communication Quarterly, 76*(4), 474–490. https://doi.org/10.1177/1080569913507479.

Leyden, Jon A. (2008). Novice and insider perspectives on academic and workplace writing: Toward a continuum of rhetorical awareness. *IEEE Transactions on Professional Communication, 51*(3), 242–263. https://doi.org/10.1109/TPC.2008.2001249.

Light, Walter. (1988, February). How the workplace has changed in 75 years. *Monthly Labor Review, 111*(2), 19–25.

Longo, Bernadette. (2000). *Spurious coin: A history of science, management, and technical writing.* State University of New York Press.

Marhamat, Bobby. (2021,September 10). Workplaces have changed – And it's time they change again. *Forbes.* https://www.forbes.com/sites/forbesbusinessdevelopment council/2021/09/10/workplaces-have-changed--and-its-time-they-change-again/?sh=55913e5075bf.

McNely, Brian, Spinuzzi, Clay & Teston, Christa. (2015). Contemporary research methodologies in technical communication. *Technical Communication Quarterly, 24*(1), 1–13. https://doi.org/10.1080/10572252.2015.975958.

Mehlenbacher, Brad. (2013). What is the future of technical communication? In J. Johnson-Eilola & S. A. Selber (Eds.), *Solving problems in technical communication* (pp. 187–208). University of Chicago Press.

Melonçon, Lisa & Henschel, Sally. (2013). Current state of US undergraduate degree programs in technical and professional communication. *Technical Communication, 60*(1), 45–64.

Melonçon, Lisa. & Schreiber, Joanna. (2022). Introduction: Promoting a sustainable collective identity for technical and professional communication. In Lisa Melonçon & Joanna Schreiber (Eds.), *Assembling critical components: A framework for sustaining technical and professional communication* (pp. 3–16). The WAC Clearinghouse; University Press of Colorado. https://doi.org/10.37514/TPC-B.2022.1381.

Melonçon, Lisa & St.Amant, Kirk. (2019). Empirical research in technical and professional communication: A 5-year examination of research methods and a call for research sustainability. *Journal of Technical Writing and Communication, 49*(2), 128–155. https://doi.org/10.1177/0047281618764611.

Mirel, Barbara & Spilka, Rachel (Eds.). (2002). *Reshaping technical communication: New directions and challenges for the 21st century.* Lawrence Erlbaum.

Mogilevsky, Michael. (1968). The changing role of the technical writer in the 1970s. *Journal of Business Communication, 5*(2), 38–51. https://doi.org/10.1177/002194366805 0500205.

Odell, Lee & Goswami, Dixie. (1985). *Writing in nonacademic settings*. The Guilford Press.

Pigg, Stacey. (2014). Coordinating constant invention: Social media's role in distributed work. *Technical Communication Quarterly, 23*(2), 69–87. https://doi.org/10.1080/105722 52.2013.796545.

Pringle, Kathy & Williams, Sean D. (2005). The future is the past: Has technical communication arrived as a profession? *Technical Communication, 52*(3), 361–370.

Reich, Robert B. (1991). *The work of nations: Preparing ourselves for 21st-century capitalism*. Vintage Books.

Salvo, Michael J. (2006). Rhetoric as productive technology: Cultural studies in/as technical communication methodology. In J. B. Scott, B. Longo & K. V. Wills (Eds.), *Critical power tools: Technical communication and cultural studies* (pp. 219–240). SUNY Press.

Savage, Gerald J. (1999). The process and prospects for professionalizing technical communication. *Journal of Technical Writing and Communication, 29*(4), 355–381. https://doi.org/10.2190/7GFX-A5PC-5P7R-9LHX.

Savage, Gerald J. (2004). The process and prospects for professionalizing technical communication. In T. Kynell-Hunt & G. J. Savage (Eds.), *Power and legitimacy in technical communication: Volume I The Historical and Contemporary struggle for professional status* (pp. 137–165). Baywood Publishing.

Schneider, Barbara & Andre, Jo-Anne. (2005). University preparation for workplace writing: An exploratory study of the perceptions of students in three disciplines. *International Journal of Business Communication, 42*(2), 195–218. https://doi.org/10.1177 /0021943605274749.

Slack, Jennifer Daryl, Miller, David James & Doak, Jeffrey. (1993). The technical communicator as author: Meaning, power, authority. *Journal of Business and Technical Communication, 7*(1), 12–36. https://doi.org/10.1177/1050651993007001002

Smart, Graham. (2006). *Writing the economy: Activity, genre and technology in the world of banking*. Equinox Publishing.

Spilka, Rachel. (1993). *Writing in the workplace: New research perspectives*. SIU Press.

Spilka, Rachel. (2002). Becoming a profession. In B. Mirel & R. Spilka (Eds.), *Reshaping technical communication: New directions and challenges for the 21st century* (pp. 97–100). Lawerence Erlbaum Associates.

Spinuzzi, Clay. (2000). Investigating the technology-work relationship: A critical comparison of three qualitative field methods. Proceedings of IEEE professional communication society international professional communication conference and Proceedings of the 18th annual ACM international conference on Computer documentation: technology & teamwork, 419–432.

Spinuzzi, Clay. (2007). Guest editor's introduction: Technical communication in the age of distributed work. *Technical Communication Quarterly, 16*(3), 265–277. https://doi.org /10.1080/10572250701290998.

Spinuzzi, Clay. (2012). Working alone together: Coworking as emergent collaborative activity. *Journal of Business and Technical Communication, 26*(4), 399–441. https://doi .org/10.1177=1050651912444070.

Spinuzzi, Clay. (2017). Introduction to the *JBTC* Special Issue on the rhetoric of entrepreneurship: Theories, methodologies, and practices. *Journal of Business and Technical Communication, 31*(3), 504–507. https://doi.org/10.1177/1050651917695537.

Spinuzzi, Clay, Bodrožić, Zlatko, Scaratti, Guisppe & Ivaldi, Silvia. (2019). "Coworking is about community": But what is "community" in coworking? *Journal of Business and Technical Communication, 33*(2), 112–140. https://doi.org/10.1177/1050651918816357.

St.Amant, Kirk & Melonçon, Lisa. (2016). Reflections on research: Examining practitioner perspectives on the state of research in technical communication. *Technical Communication, 63*(4), 346–363.

Sullivan, Patricia & Dautermann, Jennie. (Eds.). (1996). *Electronic literacies in the workplace: Technologies of writing*. National Council of Teachers of English, and Computers in Composition.

Taylor, Frederick W. (1911). *The principles of scientific management*. Harper & Brothers.

Walton, Rebecca, Moore, Kristen & Jones, Natasha. (2019). *Technical communication after the social justice turn: Building coalitions for action*. Routledge.

White, Kate, Rumsey, Suzanne Kesler & Amidon, Stevens. (2016). Are we "there" yet? The treatment of gender and feminism in technical, business, and workplace writing studies. *Journal of Technical Writing and Communication, 46*(1), 27–58. https://doi.org/10.1177/0047281615600637.

Wilson, Greg. (2001). Technical communication and late capitalism: Considering a postmodern technical communication pedagogy. *Journal of Business and Technical Communication, 15*(1), 72–99. https://doi.org/10.1177/1050651901015000104.

Wilson, Greg & Wolford, Rachel. (2017). The technical communicator as (post-postmodern) discourse worker. *Journal of Business and Technical Communication, 31*(1), 3–29. https://doi.org/10.1177/1050651916667531.

Winsor, Dorothy A. (2003). *Writing power: Communication in an engineering center*. SUNY Press.

Wright, David, Malone, Edward A., Saraf, Gowri G., Long, Tessa B., Egodapitiya, IrangiK. & Roberson, Elizabeth M. (2011). A history of the future: Prognostication in technical communication. *Technical Communication Quarterly, 20*(4), 443–480. https://doi.org/10.1080/10572252.2011.596716.

Yates, JoAnne. (1989). *Control through communication: The rise of system in American management*. The Johns Hopkins University Press.

1. Common Thread, Varied Focus: Defining Workplace in Technical and Professional Communication

Jeremy Rosselot-Merritt
CARNEGIE MELLON UNIVERSITY

Janel Bloch
NORTHERN KENTUCKY UNIVERSITY

Abstract

Despite a strong, long-standing connection between the workplace and technical and professional communication (TPC) as a practical field, workplace-oriented scholarship in TPC has demonstrated significant variability in how the workplace is conceptualized. What's more, many of those concepts have been implicit, with no unified or codified parameters for the workplace as an object of inquiry in TPC scholarship. In this chapter, the authors perform a metasynthesis of workplace-oriented scholarship spanning approximately four decades, examining how scholars have researched and written about the workplace conceptually, methodologically, theoretically, and philosophically. Noting specific trends, patterns, and challenges in their findings, the authors argue for a working definition of workplace in TPC designed for long-term applicability and relatability to both academics and practitioners.

Keywords

workplace, definition, technical and professional communication, practitioner, history, work context

Technical and professional communication (TPC) pedagogy and scholarship are inherently related to the workplace. However, what exactly does the concept of *workplace* entail? Despite being a common thread in pedagogy and research, no unifying notion of *workplace* as a construct of study in TPC exists. Likely every scholar, student, and practitioner asked would give a definition of *workplace* reflecting different philosophical and functional underpinnings. It is difficult to conduct sustainable (Melançon & St.Amant, 2019) workplace research without agreeing on the contexts being studied.

Therefore, in addressing the following research questions, this chapter seeks to conceptualize the *workplace* construct as it has evolved in TPC, leading to a tenable definition for use in TPC scholarship and pedagogy:

- How have sites of workplace research in TPC evolved over time?
- What key parameters of *workplace* are common to the discipline?
- How might TPC scholars contextualize workplace research in ways that help strengthen the connections between academia and practitioners?

Through an analysis of a large sample of published workplace-oriented TPC research from 1980–2019, this chapter traces the notion of *workplace* through multiple moments in TPC's evolution. This analysis provides the basis for a definition of *workplace* that can build cohesive parameters for future TPC workplace-oriented scholarship and further the conversation regarding how TPC research, pedagogy, and practice can align and synergize (St. Amant & Melonçon, 2016b). In advancing a definition of *workplace* that can help fill practical gaps, this chapter suggests ways in which TPC researchers can both conceptualize work contexts and better address the needs of the workplace as it evolves.

Workplace and TPC: A Long-Standing Relationship in Academic Study and in Practice

TPC has always been associated with addressing workplace needs. Well before its emergence as a distinct field of practice with corresponding job titles and full-time employment opportunities, TPC served engineering students needing writing skills. By 1899, some engineering schools had separate English departments (Connors, 1982/2004). Textbooks and handbooks specifically devoted to technical writing also began to appear. For example, Samuel Chandler Earle's (1911) *The Theory and Practice of Technical Writing* focused on teaching engineers the "logical structure" (p. vii) of typical types of writing (e.g., descriptions, narratives, directions), pointing out in its preface that such a book was needed because an engineer uses "a form of expression no less special than that of the lawyer, the novelist, or the poet" and "needs special training in writing, over and above all that he may get in general composition" (p. vi). Earle's (1911) text also covered "practical applications" such as "addressing general readers" and "addressing specialists" (p. vii). Another book of the era, *A Guide to Technical Writing* (Rickard, 1908) was aimed at professionals in science and engineering "who wish to write clearly on technical subjects" (p. 3) and focused largely on word-level issues, such as abbreviations, numbers, hyphens, and word choice.

Additional developments in TPC's relationship to workplace practice took place from 1920–1950. In addition to curricular growth and the publication of additional textbooks, practical and philosophical developments occurred in what were in effect TPC curricula (Connors, 1982/2004). The practical development involved textbooks specifically about technical report writing. During the Great Depression, technical writing courses continued to grow, and with them, the perceived importance of serving STEM (science, technology, engineering, math) majors (Connors, 1982/2004).

During the 1950s, technical communication arguably came of age in work-place contexts (Connors, 1982/2004; Durack, 2003). In 1953, the Society of Technical Writers formed, and Rensselaer Polytechnic Institute began offering a master's degree in technical writing (Durack, 2003). In 1954, the first issue of *Technical Writing Review* (the journal that later became *Technical Communication*) was published, and empirical workplace research began appearing (Connors, 1982/2004). When the 1957 launch of Russia's *Sputnik* marked a period of technological rivalry between the United States and the Soviet Union, the emphasis on technological advancement became a boon for technical writing as a field (Connors, 1982/2004). With these developments, technical writers became increasingly commonplace in American workplaces during the second half of the 20th century. Correspondingly, those who taught and researched technical writing began trying to define its purpose and scope (see Britton, 1965; Miller, 1979).

The significant growth in TPC workplace-oriented research that started in the 1980s provides a strong basis for conceptualizing the concept of *workplace* in field-specific terms. Classic TPC workplace studies, such as Dorothy Winsor's (1996) *Writing Like an Engineer: A Rhetorical Education* and Gerald Savage and Dale Sullivan's (2001) *Writing a Professional Life: Stories of Technical Communicators On and Off the Job*, often focused on specific workplaces, such as engineering, healthcare, and technology-centered sites. Since the early 2000s, TPC workplace studies have addressed a larger range of topics, including the role of visual communication in workplace technical writing (Brumberger, 2007), social media communications in distributed work (Pigg, 2014), work-related instant messaging within a virtual team of a global consultancy company (Darics, 2014), and more theoretically-framed arguments about how equality is enacted in non-hierarchical workplaces (Colton et al., 2019). This range can be seen as both a strength and a challenge: a strength because it demonstrates the growing variety of work contexts in which TPC takes place and a challenge because it brings up questions about how those work contexts are characterized and studied. Because of the ubiquity of the concept of *workplace* in TPC over time, it is difficult to capture every nuance of how *workplace* as a concept has evolved. However, the following discussion uses studies focused on TPC to characterize significant trends in that evolution.

■ Method of Analysis: Metasynthesis

The following discussion analyzes the concept of *workplace* in TPC literature using metasynthesis, which, according to Denis Walsh and Soo Downe (2005), is an examination of literature that "attempts to integrate results from a number of different but inter-related qualitative studies" (p. 204) and "[bring] together qualitative studies in a related area [enabling] the nuances, taken-for-granted assumptions, and textured milieu of varying accounts to be exposed, described and explained in ways that bring fresh insights" (p. 205).

Employing a purposeful sampling method (Koerber & McMichael, 2008), the following steps were used in this analysis:

1. Identify studies (articles, books, chapters of edited collections) by keywords (e.g., "technical communication," "workplace") and reference listings.
2. Examine each identified study for conceptualization of workplace, while noting any methodological and theoretical perspectives used.
3. Determine whether each study fits with the inclusion criteria shown in Table 1.1.
4. Determine whether the study should be excluded based on the exclusion criteria shown in Table 1.2.

From an original list of approximately 170 studies, as shown in Table 1.3, 150 were included in the corpus: 94 peer-reviewed articles, 47 book chapters, and 9 full-length books. Data from the review were maintained in Google Sheets.

Table 1.4 shows the breakdown of the 94 included articles by time period and journal. Journal acronyms are as follows: *IEEE* (*IEEE Transactions on Professional Communication*), *JTWC* (*Journal of Technical Writing and Communication*), *JBTC* (*Journal of Business and Technical Communication*), *TC* (*Technical Communication*), *TCQ* (*Technical Communication Quarterly*), *JBC/IJBC* (*Journal of Business Communication/International Journal of Business Communication*).

Table 1.1. Inclusion Criteria for Studies

To be included, a study must meet at least one of the following criteria:
The study uses a work context as a basis for empirical research.
The study makes a significant philosophical or theoretical argument about work contexts in technical and professional communication.
The study incorporates research involving working professionals (such as a survey of people in the workplace).

Table 1.2. Exclusion Criteria for Studies

Remove a study from the corpus if it meets one or more of the following criteria:
The work context is not a significant or integral construct in the research or argument. For example, a study that makes an argument for applying a theory to future workplace research—but does not approach such an argument in detail itself—would not be included.
The study is primarily rooted in a classroom- or pedagogy-based study or argument.
The study is (a) not related to technical and professional communication *and* (b) cannot be related to technical and professional communication in a tangible way that another study *within* the field can achieve.
The study, if included, would provide an oversaturation of specific data points within the corpus (e.g., multiple instances of an author using the same or a similar method and work context without making a substantially new argument).

Table 1.3. Number of Sources by Type, Organized by Decade

Decade	Source type		
	Article	Book chapter	Book
1980s	19	3	0
1990s	22	33	4
2000s	21	8	4
2010s	32	3	1
Total	94	47	9

Table 1.4. Number of Articles by Decade and Journal

Decade	Journal	Number of articles
1980s Total articles: 19	IEEE	3
	JTWC	3
	JBTC	2
	TC	3
	TCQ/Technical Writing Teacher	2
	JBC/IJBC	5
	Other	1
1990s Total articles: 22	IEEE	2
	JTWC	1
	JBTC	4
	TC	2
	TCQ	3
	JBC	6
	Other	4
2000s Total articles: 21	IEEE	2
	JTWC	2
	JBTC	4
	TC	4
	TCQ	4
	JBC/IJBC	2
	Other	3
2010s Total articles: 32	IEEE	2
	JTWC	3
	JBTC	4
	TC	8
	TCQ	9
	JBC/IJBC	4
	Other	2

The following categories of analysis were recorded for each of the studies included in the corpus: citation, publication year, work context(s) studied, method(s), theoretical framework(s), whether an empirical component was included, and additional details about the empirical component if present. An additional category, focus, was included based on the primary intent of the study (see "Foci" section).

Sources from 1980–2019 were included in the initially analyzed corpus. Obviously, these sources were published before the COVID-19 pandemic began in 2020. As we examined additional sources before the publication of this chapter, we noted some workplace-oriented publications that had been published since 2020. These sources included Julia Gerdes' (2023) "Diagnosing Unsettled Stasis in Transnational Communication Design: An Exploration of Public Health Emergency Communication" from *Technical Communication Quarterly*, E. Ashley Rea's (2021) "'Changing the Face of Technology': Storytelling as Intersectional Feminist Practice in Coding Organizations" from *Technical Communication*, Patrick Danner's (2020) "Story/telling with Data as Distributed Activity" from *Technical Communication Quarterly*, and Amy Hodges and Leslie Seawright's (2023) "Transnational Technical Communication: English as a Business Lingua Franca in Engineering Workplaces" from *Business and Professional Communication Quarterly*. In addition, a series of articles, each fewer than 2,000 words, published in a January 2021 special issue of *Journal of Business and Technical Communication* "[blurred] genres that bring together academic analysis and the public scholarship of shorter, more accessible pieces" (Frith, 2021, p. 2) and featured some sources with workplace-relevant connections. For our metasynthesis, we elected to include sources through 2019, as including additional sources would not have altered our metrics significantly and, based on our analysis, would not have changed the definitional argument we make later in this chapter. We do, however, believe subsequent study of these sources would be helpful in mapping the continued evolution of the workplace phenomenon in TPC.

■ Findings and Observations from Metasynthesis

This section summarizes findings based on the primary categories of analysis described earlier and then describes larger trends and developments over time. Many of these points, such as examples of work contexts studied, are taken from specific fields in the corpus spreadsheet, while other points are derived from formulas and calculations within the spreadsheet.

■ Work Contexts Studied

Not surprisingly, many different work contexts have been studied in TPC. Several have been studied empirically and immersively through direct experience, such as via an ethnography of a given workplace setting (e.g., Burnett, 1991; Winsor,

2006). Others have been studied by examining artifacts—usually communications produced by or associated with the organizations or persons in question (e.g., Winsor, 1990b). Still others have been written about in theoretical terms, as when a scholar offers a theoretical basis for future study building upon existing work or theory (e.g., Selzer, 1993; Spinuzzi, 2008). Finally, some studies in TPC consider workplaces broadly, such as in research using surveys of individuals in different workplaces (e.g., Blythe et al., 2014) or treating workplaces in a more generalized way that allows for broad application of a given theoretical framework or concept to multiple workplaces (Spinuzzi, 2013).

Consider this representative range of work contexts discussed in TPC literature:

- County department of social services (Odell et al., 1983)
- R&D group within Exxon's Intermediate Technology Division (Paradis et al., 1985)
- Agricultural and engineering companies (Casari & Povlacs, 1988)
- Medieval workplace and nuclear power plant (Richardson & Liggett, 1993)
- Nursing department in a hospital (Dautermann, 1993)
- Academic department, corporate office, and manufacturing plant (David & Baker, 1994)
- "Moderately sized" government organization (Henderson, 1996)
- Medical writing, freight industry safety, editing, marketing, civil engineering, and R&D (Savage & Sullivan, 2001)
- Traffic work in Iowa (Spinuzzi, 2003)
- Regulated industries, such as coal (Sauer, 2006)
- Medical device manufacturer (Breuch, 2010)
- German multinational technology company (Ehrenreich, 2010)
- Workgroups within a research university (Friess, 2011)
- Israeli high-tech startup (Fraiberg, 2013)
- Coffeehouse (Pigg, 2014)
- Automotive repair shop (Cushman, 2016)
- Generalized work settings or workplaces described not specifically, but *writ large* (Dilger, 2006; Walton & Jones, 2013).

The list is wide-ranging. Examining the work contexts discussed in the corpus, one can see evidence of a gradual expansion in the nature of work contexts studied. For example, in the 1980s and 1990s, much scholarship focused on engineering, medical, and "technology-intensive" workplaces (e.g., Dautermann, 1993; Doheny-Farina, 1992; Paradis et al., 1985; Winsor, 1999)—the kinds of work contexts with which technical communication as a field within industry has historically been associated. While that trend largely continued into the 2000s, nonprofit contexts, such as risk management (Grabill, 2006) and environmental communication (Waddell, 1995), received increasing attention. In the 2010s, work contexts featured in TPC literature expanded even further: e.g., information and communication technology for development (ICTD) projects led by academic or corporate researchers in India (Walton, 2013), an independent coffeehouse using networked communications (Pigg, 2014), Agile Scrum teams in a mid-sized software engineering firm (Friess, 2018), and six "coworking" spaces in the United States, Italy, and Serbia (Spinuzzi et al., 2019).

Throughout 40 years of workplace-oriented TPC scholarship, some work contexts maintained their relevance. For example, there was noticeably strong attention to public and government organizations (e.g., Dayton, 2004; Henderson, 1996), suggesting that these types of organizations have remained an enduring basis for workplace scholarship in TPC. Even as the types of work contexts studied expanded in the 2010s, there was still considerable attention to some of the traditional sites of workplace practice (e.g., Breuch, 2010; Brumberger & Lauer, 2019; Wisniewski, 2018). Therefore, even as times have changed and workplace emphases have evolved, some consistency exists in the sites of TPC workplace research.

▌ Research Methods Used to Study Workplace

Table 1.5 shows the research methods that were noted throughout the corpus. These methods were not mutually exclusive; for example, a study may have included both surveys and interviews (e.g., Brumberger & Lauer, 2019). Within the studies examined, a number of research methods were used in order to empirically obtain data for analysis; the most common methods used in the nonempirical studies were literature review and what was termed "explication"—the advancement of a particular approach to research, practice, or pedagogy (e.g., St.Amant & Melonçon, 2016a; Sullivan & Porter, 1993).

As shown in Table 1.5, other common methods included ethnographies, interview-based studies, and observational studies. Ethnographies involve immersion in a work environment over an extended time period and typically use multiple research methods, including interviews and observations. In-person, phone, or video interview can be used as a method outside of a full ethnography, but can also be used in conjunction with other methods, such as content analysis. Observational studies involve watching and noting work practices and can be used on their own or as part of an extended ethnography.

▌ Theoretical Frameworks

For the purposes of this metasynthesis, a theoretical framework was defined as a theory or concept used to frame an argument or study. Of 150 studies in the corpus, 114 (76.0%) incorporated a theoretical framework of some kind. A wide variety of theoretical frameworks was used. Examples include genre theory (Smart, 1993), cultural studies and critical theory (Scott et al., 2006b), politeness theory

(Darics, 2014; Friess, 2011), and social network analysis (Lauren & Pigg, 2016). Some studies (24.7%) did not use a theoretical framework (e.g., Kleimann, 1993; Lanier, 2018). Notably, several studies that used survey research did not include a theoretical framework (e.g., Blythe et al., 2014; Brumberger, 2007; Fenno, 1987; Sageev & Romanowski, 2001; Whiteside, 2003). Studies that advocated for a specific theory as a corollary of the research were not counted as having a theoretical framework but were instead classified as having a theoretical focus, as discussed in the next section.

Table 1.5. Breakdown of Methods Noted in Study Corpus

Method	Number	Percentage of corpus	Example(s)
Ethnography or autoethnography	29	19.3%	Schreiber, 2017; Winsor, 1989
Case study	35	23.3%	Doheny-Farina, 1992; Gurak, 1999
Interview	57	38.0%	Lauren & Pigg, 2016; Whiteside, 2003
Survey	23	15.3%	Brumberger, 2007
Observation	15	10.0%	Friess, 2011
Content, discourse, or textual analysis	29	19.3%	Brown, 1996; Friess, 2013
Rhetorical analysis	13	8.7%	Bowdon, 2014
Genre analysis	3	2.0%	Wahl, 2003
Historical/archival	10	6.7%	Petersen & Moeller, 2016
Literature review	31	20.7%	Longo, 2006; Spinuzzi, 2007
Explication	41	27.3%	Spinuzzi, 2015
Method not otherwise mentioned	18	12.0%	Leydens, 2008 (phenomenological analysis); Schneider, 2002 (think-aloud protocol); Silker & Gurak, 1996 (focus group); Spinuzzi, 2003, 2008 (genre tracing)

Foci

Table 1.6 shows seven foci, or overarching intents, of research that were identified and coded throughout the analysis:

- **Philosophical:** Advocating a philosophical approach to workplace studies and/or concepts of workplace.
- **Theoretical:** Developing a theoretical framework for workplace research or for thinking of the workplace in practical application—66.7 percent of studies with a theoretical focus were non-empirical.

- **Methodological:** Advocating a new or rethought methodological approach to workplace research—78.9 percent of studies with a methodological focus were also non-empirical.
- **Functional:** Describing, in concrete terms, the functional characteristics of a workplace, including its social dynamics; rhetorical, communicative, or other practices; and/or its relationship to TPC—97.4 percent of studies with a functional focus were empirical.
- **Applied Practice:** Emphasizing implications for practical application —88.0 percent of studies with an applied practice focus were empirical.
- **Analytical/Interpretive:** Analyzing or interpreting a workplace situation, phenomenon, or writing—92.7 percent of studies with an analytical/ interpretive focus were empirical.
- **Programmatic/Pedagogical:** Emphasizing implications for TPC pedagogy and/or programs—66.7 percent of studies with a programmatic/pedagogical focus were empirical. For this metasynthesis, studies with this focus used the work context as the primary emphasis of the research; studies emphasizing the classroom or pedagogy were not included in the corpus.

These research foci, as coded, were not mutually exclusive. Some studies had one focus (e.g., Amidon & Blythe, 2008, coded as analytical/interpretive); some had two (e.g., Lauren & Pigg, 2016, coded as both analytical/interpretive and applied practice); and a few had three or four (e.g., Spinuzzi, 2008, coded as analytical/interpretive, functional, and theoretical).

Table 1.6. Breakdown of Foci Noted in Study Corpus

Focus	Number	Percentage of corpus	Example(s)
Philosophical	3	2.0%	Durack, 1997
Theoretical	30	20.0%	Moses & Katz, 2006
Methodological	19	12.7%	Doheny-Farina, 1993
Functional	38	25.3%	Gonzales & Turner, 2017
Applied Practice	50	33.3%	Fisher & Bennion, 2005
Analytical/Interpretive	110	73.3%	Amidon & Blythe, 2008; Bridgewater & Buzzanell, 2010
Programmatic/Pedagogical	18	12.0%	Haas, 2012

Trends and Developments Noted in Research

Trends and developments noted in the corpus were analyzed by decade. While grouping by decade risks oversimplification, it nonetheless provides a consistent unit of time by which to evaluate and describe important developments. By its nature, a metasynthesis provides a broad qualitative view of how a given phenomenon is conceptualized over time. In this case, that phenomenon is the concept of *workplace* in TPC.

The corpus of 150 studies included 22 from the 1980s, 59 from the 1990s, 33 from the 2000s, and 36 from the 2010s (see Table 1.3). Below are some high-level observations from the data.

Decrease in Time Spent Studying Single Work Contexts

The amount of time that TPC researchers have spent studying a single workplace (e.g., spending time on site, interacting with research participants and/or artifacts) seems to have decreased over time. While this analysis did not attempt to quantify the time spent studying a given work context, it was observed that particularly in the 1990s and early 2000s, many workplace-oriented studies were longitudinal and/or involved detailed empirical study of a specific work context. For example, Dorothy Winsor's work (1996, 1998, 1999, 2000, 2006) was highly ethnographic and longitudinal. Stephen Doheny-Farina (1992) conducted detailed ethnographic case studies of technology transfer in four different organizations. Other research during this time also exhibited that trend (e.g., Dias et al., 1999; Kleimann, 1993; Richardson & Liggett, 1993; Waddell, 1995).

The corpus shows evidence of declining time spent studying a single work context and the reduced longitudinality of the research. Since the mid-2000s, most empirical studies in TPC seem to represent "one-off" studies with little to no future engagement with the work context or studies that call for less time spent directly immersed in the work setting, such as a survey, one set of interviews, or textual analysis, rather than full mixed method ethnographic studies; researchers tend to spend less time in the work settings than did scholars like Winsor, Doheny-Farina, and Patrick Dias and colleagues. Reasons for this trend could include changes in budgets or funding and less ease of access to organizations due to proprietary and/or security concerns. This trend may also be the result of the changing nature of the construct of *workplace* itself.

Alternatives to and Critiques of "Typical" Workplace Structures

In the 1980s and 1990s, much workplace-oriented TPC research focused on work sites typically associated with TPC practice: those involving engineering, manufacturing, health and medicine, and technology-centered work. In contrast, much of the workplace-oriented research published since the early 2000s has increasingly diverged from traditional sites of work in TPC.

Studies that are (a) critical of workplace norms or typifications or that (b) offer alternative models to such norms or typifications, even without direct critique of them, have notably existed for more than 20 years. Over time, at least three trends can be noticed:

1. Studies that take up novel or recontextualized work contexts in TPC have often coincided with scholarly turns in the academic part of the field (see Figure 1.1 in this chapter).
2. The relative volume of such studies seems to have increased over time.
3. The studies are often associated with alternative sites of workplace practice in TPC—those outside the oft-studied work contexts of IT, engineering, and health/medicine that were especially common in the 1980s and 1990s.

Like most of the other observations in this subsection, these trends emerge in academic scholarship yet are not always taken up in industry practice. This phenomenon not only highlights the need for greater connection between academic scholarship and industry practice, but also points to differences in priorities and reward structures in the academy and in the workplace. An academic career path in TPC has generally not tended to provide much reward for direct engagement with the field's practical contexts (Blakeslee & Spilka, 2004), unlike other fields where the academy and the workplace are more easily interconnected, such as medicine.

Informality or Ambiguity in Conceptualizing Workplace

In TPC research, levels of precision can vary in terms of description of research methods (Melonçon & St.Amant, 2019). Some authors describe their methods in significant detail, while others do so more concisely. The same principle applies to descriptions of work contexts. Some studies incorporate detailed descriptions of the work contexts; any of Winsor's work and much of the work by Clay Spinuzzi (particularly the books) provide good examples of that kind of detail. In the corpus, studies that included a *functional* focus (described previously in the "Foci" section) were more likely to include detailed descriptions (e.g., Friess, 2018; Henderson, 1996; Kleimann, 1993), as were studies using ethnographic and/or observational methods (e.g., Walton, 2013). However, such detailed descriptions were not always provided. For example, Vincent Brown's (1996) observation-based piece included a rather light description of the work setting, focusing instead on the kinds of writing and persuasion taking place within that setting. Even though a detailed description of work context may not always be needed, such descriptions can help scholars achieve greater clarity in the collective understanding of *workplace* in TPC.

Importantly, too, even those studies that detail work context most extensively rarely engage directly with *workplace* as a construct within TPC. This observation is extremely important because it further illustrates the relative informality or ambiguity of how *workplace* is defined as a term within TPC. Indeed, some moves have been made toward conceptualizing *workplace,* or toward workplace-inclusive themes such as "workplace writing." For example, Jon Leydens (2008) stated that, in his work, *workplace* referred to "an academic, industrial, or other workplace" and categorized "workplace writing research" as that based on "activities associated with ongoing workplace writing," "workplace texts," "in-depth interviews with workplace practitioners," surveys, and/or examinations of "cultural and/or historical origins of a discipline and/or field" (p. 243). To set up an argument about broadening concepts of *workplace* to better include multinational and cross-cultural considerations, Rebecca Walton (2013) defined "workplace studies of practice" as follows:

> Workplace studies of practice occur at the intersection of academic inquiry and practical challenges regarding "work, interaction and technology in complex organisational environments" (Heath & Luff, 2000, p. 8). Unlike much sociotechnical research, workplace studies of practice do not focus primarily on society-level issues such as power distribution and the influence of technology on democracy. Workplace studies that involve technology instead focus on the practical, day-to-day use of technology and information within organizations and the ways that people use (or do not use) technology to accomplish professional tasks. (p. 411)

Walton (2013) went on to say

> Workplace studies is a productive area of inquiry for technical communication because many technical communicators seek not only to meet immediate workplace needs but also to produce research that can improve work practices (Spilka, 2000). To do so, scholars must uncover and understand current practices. (p. 411)

In their article "Redefining Writing for the Responsive Workplace," Claire Lauer and Eva Brumberger (2019) define the "responsive workplace":

> A "responsive" workplace is one in which writers must adapt to making meaning not just through writing, but across a range of modes, technologies, channels, and constraints. To some extent, writers have always had to be "responsive" to changes in technologies, audiences, and contexts. But what sets the responsive workplace apart at this time is the sheer range of responsive action that is now practiced across a vast landscape of contexts and rhetorical practices, affecting our very notions of what writing is and how it gets done. (pp. 635–636)

While these examples were helpful and valuable, the kind of specificity they provided in conceptualizing *workplace* as a construct of inquiry in TPC was the exception, not the rule. In most sources, the meaning was implied, or it seemed to be presumed that the audience understood the construct experientially or intuitively. This observation has important implications for the definitional approach to *workplace* discussed later in this chapter.

Intrinsic Connection Between Perceptions of Amount of
Workplace Research Over Time and the Conceptualization
of Workplace and Workplace-Oriented Research

Some scholars may conclude that workplace-oriented research has decreased in quantity over time. Whether this is correct depends on how TPC scholars define *workplace* and *workplace-oriented research*. A broad view encompasses a number of different sites or contexts of work. A narrower view is logistically bound to the more specific parameters of what might constitute a *workplace*. Each view has benefits and risks for TPC as both an academic field and a field of practice. A broad view enables TPC to be positioned as applicable to a variety of industries and having growing research potential; however, that broad view also risks diluting the identity of a field that has long struggled with issues of professional identity. In contrast, a narrower view can help pinpoint more precise elements of professional identity yet risks missing legitimate opportunities to expand TPC's practical application and prospects for scholarly research.

All of these observations concerning concepts and definitions of *workplace* and *workplace-oriented research* are important not only in the corpus, but also in developing a consistent notion of *workplace* within TPC—a move that is important for sustaining and building upon workplace-oriented research in the field.

■ Challenges for Conceptualizing *Workplace* in TPC

The observations gleaned from this metasynthesis provide data-driven evidentiary support for many positives in TPC workplace-oriented research. For example, workplace studies continue to be done; journals continue to publish workplace-oriented scholarship; and TPC scholars have, over the time period studied, taken a broad interest in workplace-oriented themes in empirical, theoretical, and methodological terms. Though workplace research may not be the "hottest" trend, the link between workplace and TPC remains present and viable for the foreseeable future.

This metasynthesis also draws attention to challenges for TPC relating to construct conceptualization, research sustainability, professional identity, and the relationship between academic study and professional practice, including the following:

1. There has been no consistent concept of workplace in TPC.
2. In terms of workplace realities in TPC, there are few, if any, metrics or guidelines for determining (a) the extent of engagement between academics and practitioners and (b) the extent to which academic research holds meaning to practitioners and to workplace trends.
3. Greater efforts are needed to engage with practitioners to help conceptualize work contexts in which TPC practice does or can take place.

In point #3, the words *does* and *can* emphasize the idea that the understanding of TPC's potential in varied work settings must be expanded.

While these challenges are not insurmountable, they will need to be addressed over time. And they must be addressed if academics are to contribute more effectively and more consistently through workplace engagement and research that is both sustainable and beneficial to TPC as a field of workplace practice. To help further the efforts to address these challenges, the following definitional approach to *workplace* in TPC is proposed.

■ Toward a Working Definition of Workplace in TPC

The findings of this analysis suggest that how TPC researchers have conceptualized *workplace* has changed; the tendency, as discussed above, has been toward expansion of the *workplace* construct in TPC. This is not an expansion in one direction—toward studies involving nonprofits in major cities, for example. Rather, this is a multidirectional, multifaceted expansion.

Figure 1.1 depicts examples of the growth of the *workplace* construct in common TPC research over 40 years. For reference, we have included points on the bottom line of the figure depicting approximate dates when scholarly "turns" in the field took place: for instance, the humanistic turn (e.g., Miller, 1979), the social turn (e.g., Blyler & Thralls, 1993), the cultural turn (e.g., Longo, 1998), and the social justice turn (e.g., Haas, 2012). Though we are not suggesting that the scholarly turns necessarily compelled the study of particular work contexts with each specific turn, we do find it helpful to map notable growth in the study of such contexts temporally, and the turns provide relatable reference points in the scholarly history of TPC.

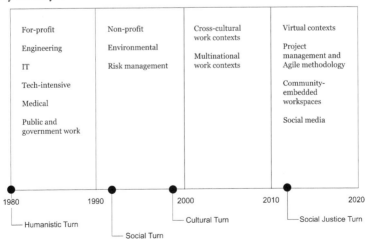

Figure 1.1. Examples of growth in commonly studied work contexts in TPC, 1980–2019.

This evolution is important not only for the value of the observations themselves, but also for the purpose of thinking about where workplace research is likely to go in the future. As a relatable analogy, the scholarly literature has for decades implied or outright argued for variable and at times incongruous concepts of what the field of TPC actually is (see, for example, Allen, 1990; Dobrin, 1983; Henning & Bemer, 2016; Kimball, 2017; Rutter, 1991). In their argument for focusing on collective identity rather than variant definitions for TPC, Lisa Melonçon and Joanna Schreiber (2022) note the "necessity of thinking about the field's present and future in terms of sustainability" (p. 7), tracing that necessity as far back as Robert Johnson's (2004) argument for sustainability in program development in which he stated that sustainability "suggests growth/life but . . . also invokes the inevitable problem of limits" (as cited in Melonçon & Schreiber, 2022, p. 7). The significance of this balance between growth and limits, Melonçon and Schreiber (2022) say, "brings a cautious vitality to merging sustainability with the field's need for a more flexible identity" (p. 7).

Melonçon and Schreiber make good points in arguing for a sustainable identity for the field; they also do justice to this necessity by noting the importance of balancing growth and limits in building such an identity. In arguing for sustainable identity, they resist movements toward definition in the field because, in their view, "definitions in the field have largely been either too broad to offer the field a sense of structure or too narrow to allow for diverse perspectives and emerging practices" (Melonçon & Schreiber, 2022, p. 5). Ironically, for a field so intrinsically tied to workplace practice, concepts of workplace are arguably more tacit and diffuse than concepts of the field of TPC itself (whether those concepts are expressed in terms of a definition or an identity). In terms of *workplace* in TPC, we argue that a mediating concept is needed that will be applicable over time and help bridge the gaps among past, present, and future in TPC workplace research; provide a conceptual basis for a more cohesive understanding of *workplace* in TPC; and relate to both academics and practitioners. And while a definition for a field may be overly limiting, we argue that a flexible definition for a construct such as *workplace*—specifically in TPC—can help achieve those essential goals in productive and sustainable ways. This is the goal we seek to achieve in this section.

■ Applicable Over Time

As Figure 1.1 illustrates, the *workplace* construct in TPC has changed from a fairly focused construct centered in engineering, IT, medicine, and fields where TPC initially found application to one that is increasingly dispersed over a broad spectrum of fields and economic sectors. Over the years, TPC competencies have expanded and evolved, as have the fields in which those competencies have been used (Rosselot-Merritt, 2020). Furthermore, these developments have taken place as part of a field of practice that, in industry, has traditionally been referred to as *technical writing* and, in the academy, as *technical and professional communication*. However it is termed, the field has changed considerably over time. Therefore, the mediating concept of *workplace* must capture the changing nature of workplace as a part of TPC as that construct has evolved into the present; ideally, such a concept will be adaptable to inevitable future changes as well.

▋ Promotes Understanding of TPC

Some of the challenges pertaining to the identity and definition of TPC as a whole relate to the differences in roles that those who practice it perform. The lack of cohesive understanding of TPC's workplace value hinders its effective application in practice and undermines efforts to assert its value among broad groups of stakeholders. For this reason, any mediating concept of workplace in TPC should strive to advance a more cohesive understanding of the field's place within work contexts.

▋ Relates to Both Academics and Practitioners

The gap between academic and practitioner views of TPC is long-standing (Albers, 2016; Andersen & Hackos, 2018; Blakeslee & Spilka, 2004; St.Amant & Melonçon, 2016b). This gap is also readily apparent to anyone who has spent more than a few months in both academia and industry. Therefore, it is important to consider whether any mediating concept of *workplace* developed for use in academic settings can be relatable to practitioners. Following are some ways that scholars can help increase academic-practical relatability:

- Consider practitioner needs in the workplace.
- Involve practitioners in regular conversations about how they use or would like to use research or the types of research they would like to see done.
- Make regular efforts to be immersed in the actual practice of TPC.
- Design future studies with an eye toward practitioner perspectives.

There will indeed be developments in TPC that neither academics nor practitioners can foresee. Yet—by using developments to date as guideposts for formulating a *workplace* concept for TPC and by researching the needs of practitioners—the practitioner perspective can be productively considered in any academic definition.

The following is a working definition of *workplace* in TPC based on the analysis presented in this chapter:

> In technical and professional communication, a workplace is any context in which communicative practices or activities meeting any of the criteria below can and/or do take place. Those practices or activities

Table 1.7. Mapping of "Workplace" to Concepts Represented in TPC Literature

Element of definition	Maps to examples from corpus
In technical and professional communication, a workplace is any context in which communicative practices or activities meeting any of the criteria below can and/or do take place:	
Further a mission or purpose which may be implicit or may be codified in a formal statement (such as a "mission statement")	A sense of organizational purpose can often be interpolated from empirical studies with direct immersion of the researcher. Examples include Breuch (2010) and Hargie et al. (2003). Direct immersion studies made up approximately 65 percent of empirical sources and 49 percent of the total corpus. Studies with a "functional" focus (25% of corpus) often noted the organizational mission or purpose. Examples: Spinuzzi et al. (2019) contains detailed descriptions in the "Findings" section. Doheny-Farina (1992) discusses organizational foci at length.
Involve an exchange of physical materials, virtual quantities of something, and/or ideas	*Physical materials:* e.g., Driskill & Goldstein (1986), manufacturing

Virtual quantities: e.g., Pigg (2014), virtual, networked contexts in which digital contents were shared

Ideas: e.g., Gurak (1999), online fora where ideas are shared, though the organizations studied were not those fora; Waddell (1995), a "broadly defined" environmental community where ideas were shared

Multiple exchange contexts: e.g., Cushman (2016), automotive parts, service documents, ideas in discussions |
Often, but not always, involve material or financial gain on the part of those conducting the communicative practice or activity for the individuals or organization on whose behalf they are acting.	A majority of the persons performing the communicative acts were paid (implying financial gain).
Over time, workplaces relevant to TPC have developed to a point at which work contexts may include any combination of the following:	
For-profit (such as privately owned or publicly traded businesses)	Numerous examples, including Winsor (1990a), engineering firm and Lauren & Pigg (2016), entrepreneurs in consulting and small business
Not-for-profit (such as charities or foundations)	Schneider (2002) and Friess (2011), education
Community-embedded (such as food co-ops or groups of people intrinsically tied to a given locality)	Waddell (1995), environmental community; Colton et al. (2019), co-op

Element of definition	Maps to examples from corpus
Virtual (such as work done "in the cloud" or using networked teams)	Pigg (2014), virtual, networked communication
Decentralized, such as work conducted without specific oversight or without centralized management of resources	Spinuzzi (2015), "adhocracies"

- further a mission or purpose which may be implicit or may be codified in a formal statement (such as a "mission statement");
- involve an exchange of physical materials, virtual quantities of something, and/or ideas; and
- often, but not always, involve material or financial gain on the part of those conducting the communicative practice or activity or the individuals or organization on whose behalf they are acting.

Over time, workplaces relevant to TPC have developed to a point at which work contexts may include any combination of the following:

- for-profit (such as privately owned or publicly traded businesses)
- not-for-profit (such as charities, foundations, or nonprofit educational institutions)
- community-embedded (such as food co-ops, environmental communities, or groups of people intrinsically tied to a given locality)
- virtual (such as work done "in the cloud" or using networked teams)
- decentralized (such as work conducted without specific oversight or without centralized management of resources)

Advancing a definitional approach to *workplace* in TPC is not intended to solve all of the challenges that the field has—and has had for a long time—with conceptualizing work contexts and connecting workplace-oriented scholarship with realities of practice. Doing so is, of course, a gradual process. The intent here is to contribute to an ongoing conversation about workplace research in general and, in TPC, specifically about how *workplace* is not a monolithic concept, but an ideational construct that is inextricably tied to and beneficial to TPC. The definition proposed here is meant to provide a basis both for conceptualizing *workplace* and for advancing studies in TPC in ways that are consistent, sustainable, and necessary.

In this definition, the literature reviewed in the metasynthesis was considered in conjunction with the disciplinary purposes the definition would help achieve. To help illustrate those relationships, Table 1.7 maps the concepts of the definition to concepts in the literature.

Thinking About the Future of Workplace Research in TPC

One of the overarching aims of this work is to advance an important and needed conversation in TPC about concepts of *workplace* that undergird scholarly, pedagogical, and disciplinary approaches in the field. In our analysis of a representative sample of workplace-oriented scholarship in the field, we observed a characteristic implicitness and ambiguity in notions of *workplace* over time. At the same time, we also observed tangible evolutionary features in scholarship that exemplify and, over time, have helped characterize the nature of workplaces in TPC research. Our sampling of the literature does not (and is not meant to) provide blanket generalizations applicable to every workplace-oriented study or argument in TPC scholarship. However, we assert that the methodology behind this metasynthesis has led to worthwhile contributions to this important conversation with simultaneous attention to calls for transparency in methodological explanations with iterative sustainability in research approaches (see, for example, Melançon & St.Amant, 2019).

Part of that sustainability is providing a feasible basis for building upon this work. In the spirit of furthering the goal, we suggest several questions that scholarship in TPC should consider in future research—questions that can help advance not only the larger conversation about *workplace* as a concept, but also findings that can benefit TPC in practical, scholarly, and pedagogical terms:

- To what extent do theoreticians and methodologists in TPC conduct or gain experience in empirical workplace-oriented research?
- Are theoretical and methodological arguments for workplace-oriented research being further examined and taken up in subsequent studies (including empirical work)?
- To what extent do workplace-oriented studies in TPC build upon one another?
- How can the communicative acts taking place in workplaces be effectively studied, particularly as the scope of those acts changes with social and technological evolutions?
- How will the COVID-19 pandemic's effects on how people work (Parker et al., 2020) affect the concept of *workplace* in TPC?

There are also questions that historical developments in TPC's studied work contexts bring up. For example, what developments are associated with philosophical movements or "turns" in TPC—e.g., humanistic (Miller, 1979), social/political (Blyler, 1998; Blyler & Thralls, 1993; Lay, 1991), cultural (Longo, 1998; Scott et al., 2006a), and social justice (Haas, 2012; Walton et al., 2019)? What roles have external influences (such as the ease of access to various sites) played regarding the work contexts studied in technical and professional communication? Though outside the purview of this research, these questions are worth considering in the future.

Another question that could be considered is the extent to which the work contexts studied and written about in TPC scholarship actually reflect the extent to which technical and professional communicators typically work in those contexts—or the extent to which TPC practice actually *takes place* in a given context. There are indeed excellent arguments in academic literature about TPC and how it is incorporated into different work contexts. There are very good arguments, also, about how technical communication takes place in a given setting, even if it is not a technical writer fulfilling all of those communicative practices, such as Jeremy Cushman's (2016) analysis of communicative practices in an automotive repair shop. All of these arguments should be considered in any conceptualization of workplace in TPC, especially as scholars work to expand the viability of TPC in various work contexts.

Yet there has to be a demarcation to this approach and the extent to which scholarship stretches the boundaries; that demarcation should actively consider current workplace realities and contexts that practitioner-engaged research shows as having future potential for practical application. Workplace-oriented research in TPC stems from a common thread in the field—both practical and pedagogical. As this chapter has demonstrated, however, workplace-oriented scholarship nonetheless often reflects different concepts and foci in that space. Navigating such an intriguing dichotomy is an imminent challenge for TPC scholars, but it is a necessary one as scholars seek to keep pace with and engage in the productive study of workplace realities.

■ References

Albers, Michael J. (2016). Improving research communication. *Technical Communication, 63*(4), 293–297.

Allen, Jo. (1990). The case against defining technical writing. *Journal of Business and Technical Communication, 4*(2), 68–77. https://doi.org/10.1177/105065199000400204.

Amidon, Stevens & Blythe, Stuart. (2008). Wrestling with Proteus: Tales of communication managers in a changing economy. *Journal of Business and Technical Communication, 22*(1), 5–37. https://doi.org/10.1177/1050651907307698.

Andersen, Rebekka & Hackos, JoAnn. (2018, August). Increasing the value and accessibility of academic research: Perspectives from industry. In *Proceedings of the 36th ACM International Conference on the Design of Communication* (pp. 1–10). Association for Computing Machinery. https://doi.org/10.1145/3233756.3233959.

Blakeslee, Ann M. & Spilka, Rachel. (2004). The state of research in technical communication. *Technical Communication Quarterly, 13*(1), 73–92. https://doi.org/10.1207/S15427625TCQ1301_8.

Blyler, Nancy. (1998). Taking a political turn: The critical perspective and research in professional communication. *Technical Communication Quarterly, 7*(1), 33–52. https://doi.org/10.1080/10572259809364616.

Blyler, Nancy Roundy & Thralls, Charlotte. (1993). The social perspective and professional communication: Diversity and directions in research. In Nancy Roundy Blyler

& Charlotte Thralls (Eds.), *Professional communication: The social perspective* (pp. 3–34). Sage.

Blythe, Stuart, Lauer, Claire & Curran, Paul G. (2014). Professional and technical communication in a Web 2.0 world. *Technical Communication Quarterly, 23*(4), 265–287. https://doi.org/10.1080/10572252.2014.941766.

Bowdon, Melody A. (2014). Tweeting an ethos: Emergency messaging, social media, and teaching technical communication. *Technical Communication Quarterly, 23*(1), 35–54. https://doi.org/10.1080/10572252.2014.850853.

Breuch, Lee-Ann Kastman. (2010). A work in process: A study of single-source documentation and document review processes of cardiac devices. In James Conklin & George F. Hayhoe (Eds.), *Qualitative research in technical communication* (pp. 177–202). Routledge.

Bridgewater, Melissa J. & Buzzanell, Patrice M. (2010). Caribbean immigrants' discourses: Cultural, moral, and personal stories about workplace communication in the United States. *Journal of Business Communication, 47*(3), 235–265. https://doi.org/10.1177/0021943610369789.

Britton, W. Earl. (1965). What is technical writing? *College Composition and Communication, 16*(2), 113–116. https://doi.org/10.2307/354886.

Brown, Vincent J. (1996). Persuasiveness and audience focus in a nonacademic R&D setting. *Journal of Technical Writing and Communication, 26*(1), 37–55. https://doi.org/10.2190/R60H-A8BY-M8UQ-H08L.

Brumberger, Eva. (2007). Visual communication in the workplace: A survey of practice. *Technical Communication Quarterly, 16*(4), 369–395. https://doi.org/10.1080/10572250701380725.

Brumberger, Eva & Lauer, Claire. (2019). A day in the life: Personas of professional communicators at work. *Journal of Technical Writing and Communication, 50*(3), 308–335. https://doi.org/10.1177/0047281619868723.

Burnett, Rebecca E. (1991). Substantive conflict in a cooperative context: A way to improve the collaborative planning of workplace documents. *Technical Communication*, 532–539. https://www.jstor.org/stable/43095830.

Casari, Laura E. & Povlacs, Joyce T. (1988). Practices in technical writing in agriculture and engineering industries, firms, and agencies. *Journal of Technical Writing and Communication, 18*(2), 143–159. https://doi.org/10.2190/V852-1M21-M5LM-H672.

Colton, Jared S., Edenfield, Avery C. & Holmes, Steve. (2019). Workplace democracy and the problem of equality. *Technical Communication, 66*(1), 53–67. https://www.ingentaconnect.com/content/stc/tc/2019/00000066/00000001/art00005.

Connors, Robert J. (2004). The rise of technical writing instruction in America. In Johndan Johnson-Eilola & Stuart A. Selber (Eds.), *Central works in technical communication* (pp. 3–19). Oxford University Press. (Reprinted from *Journal of Technical Writing and Communication, 12*(4), 329–352,1982).

Cushman, Jeremy. (2016). Distributed labor, writing, and an automotive repair shop. In Patrick Thomas and Pamela Takayoshi (Eds.), *Literacy in practice: Writing in private, public, and working lives* (pp. 217–229). Taylor & Francis; Routledge.

Danner, Patrick. (2020). Story/telling with data as distributed activity. *Technical Communication Quarterly, 29*(2), 174–187. https://doi.org/10.1080/10572252.2019.1660807.

Darics, Erika. (2014). The blurring boundaries between synchronicity and asynchronicity: New communicative situations in work-related instant messaging. *International*

Journal of Business Communication, 51(4), 337–358. https://doi.org/10.1177/23294884 14525440.

Dautermann, Jennie. (1993). Negotiating meaning in a hospital discourse community. In Rachel Spilka (Ed.), *Writing in the workplace: New research perspectives* (pp. 98–110). Southern Illinois University Press.

David, Carol & Baker, Margaret Ann. (1994). Rereading bad news: Compliance-gaining features in management memos. *Journal of Business Communication, 31*(4), 267–290. https://doi.org/10.1177/002194369403100403.

Dayton, David. (2004). Electronic editing in technical communication: The compelling logics of local contexts. *Technical Communication, 51*(1), 86–101.

Dias, Patrick, Freedman, Aviva, Medway, Peter & Paré, Anthony. (1999). *Worlds apart: Acting and writing in academic and workplace contexts.* Lawrence Erlbaum Associates.

Dilger, Bradley. (2006). Extreme usability and technical communication. In J. Blake Scott, Bernadette Longo & Katherine V. Wills (Eds.), *Critical power tools: Technical communication and cultural studies* (pp. 47–70). State University of New York Press.

Dobrin, David N. (1983). What's technical about technical writing? In Paul V. Anderson, R. John Brockmann & Carolyn R. Miller (Eds.), *New essays in technical and scientific communication: Research, theory, practice* (pp. 227–250). Baywood. https://doi .org/10.4324/9781315224060–18.

Doheny-Farina, Stephen. (1992). *Rhetoric, innovation, technology: Case studies of technical communication in technology transfers.* MIT Press.

Doheny-Farina, Stephen. (1993). Research as rhetoric: Confronting the methodological and ethical problems of research on writing in nonacademic settings. In Rachel Spilka (Ed.), *Writing in the workplace: New research perspectives* (pp. 253–267). Southern Illinois University Press.

Driskill, L. P. & Goldstein, Jone Rymer. (1986). Uncertainty: Theory and practice in organizational communication. *Journal of Business Communication, 23*(3), 41–56. https://doi.org/10.1177/002194368602300304.

Durack, Katherine T. (1997). Gender, technology, and the history of technical communication. *Technical Communication Quarterly, 6*(3), 249–260. https://doi.org/10.1207 /s15427625tcq0603_2.

Durack, Katherine T. (2003). From the moon to the microchip: Fifty years of *Technical Communication. Technical Communication, 50*(4), 571–584. https://www.jstor.org/stable /43095603.

Earle, Samuel Chandler. (1911). *The theory and practice of technical writing.* Macmillan.

Ehrenreich, Susanne. (2010). English as a business lingua franca in a German multinational corporation: Meeting the challenge. *Journal of Business Communication, 47*(4), 408–431. https://doi.org/10.1177/0021943610377303.

Fenno, Charles R. (1987). "But what if the shoe doesn't fit?": User comfort in the electronic office. *Technical Communication, 34*(3), 146–149.

Fisher, Lori & Bennion, Lindsay. (2005). Organizational implications of the future development of technical communication: Fostering communities of practice in the workplace. *Technical Communication, 52*(3), 277–288. https://www.jstor.org/stable /43089274.

Fraiberg, Steven. (2013). Reassembling technical communication: A framework for studying multilingual and multimodal practices in global contexts. *Technical Communication Quarterly, 22*(1), 10–27. https://doi.org/10.1080/10572252.2013.735635.

Friess, Erin. (2011). Politeness, time constraints, and collaboration in decision-making meetings: A case study. *Technical Communication Quarterly, 20*(2), 114–138. https://doi.org/10.1080/10572252.2011.551507.

Friess, Erin. (2013). Rhetorical appeals of professional designers in decision-making sessions. *IEEE Transactions on Professional Communication, 56*(4), 313–331. https://doi.org/10.1109/TPC.2013.2286224.

Friess, Erin. (2018). "Filling to capacity": An exploratory study of project management language in Agile Scrum teams. *Technical Communication, 65*(2), 169–180. https://www.ingentaconnect.com/contentone/stc/tc/2018/00000065/00000002/art00006.

Frith, Jordan. (2021). Introduction to business and technical communication and COVID-19: Communicating in times of crisis. *Journal of Business and Technical Communication, 35*(1), 1–6. https://doi.org/10.1177/1050651920959208.

Gerdes, Julia. (2023). Diagnosing unsettled stasis in transnational communication design: An exploration of public health emergency communication. *Technical Communication Quarterly, 32*(1), 17–32. https://doi.org/10.1080/10572252.2022.2069286.

Gonzales, Laura & Turner, Heather Noel. (2017). Converging fields, expanding outcomes: Technical communication, translation, and design at a non-profit organization. *Technical Communication, 64*(2), 126–140. https://www.ingentaconnect.com/content/stc/tc/2017/00000064/00000002/art00005.

Grabill, Jeffrey T. (2006). The study of writing in the social factory: Methodology and social agency. In J. Blake Scott, Bernadette Longo & Katherine V. Wills (Eds.), *Critical power tools: Technical communication and cultural studies* (pp. 151–170). State University of New York Press.

Gurak, Laura J. (1999). *Persuasion and privacy in cyberspace: The online protests over Lotus Marketplace and the Clipper Chip.* Yale University Press.

Haas, Angela M. (2012). Race, rhetoric, and technology: A case study of decolonial technical communication theory, methodology, and pedagogy. *Journal of Business and Technical Communication, 26*(3), 277–310. https://doi.org/10.1177/1050651912439539.

Hargie, Owen, Dickson, David & Nelson, Seanenne. (2003). Working together in a divided society: A study of intergroup communication in the Northern Ireland workplace. *Journal of Business and Technical Communication, 17*(3), 285–318. https://doi.org/10.1177/1050651903017003002.

Heath, Christian & Luff, Paul. (2000). *Technology in action.* Cambridge University Press.

Henderson, Powell G. (1996). Writing technologies at White Sands. In Patricia Sullivan & Jennie Dautermann (Eds.), *Electronic literacies in the workplace: Technologies of writing* (pp. 65–88). National Council of Teachers of English.

Henning, Teresa & Bemer, Amanda. (2016). Reconsidering power and legitimacy in technical communication: A case for enlarging the definition of technical communicator. *Journal of Technical Writing and Communication, 46*(3), 311–341. https://doi.org/10.1177/0047281616639484.

Hodges, Amy & Seawright, Leslie. (2023). Transnational technical communication: English as a business lingua franca in engineering workplaces. *Business and Professional Communication Quarterly.* https://doi.org/10.1177/23294906231154860.

Johnson, Robert. (2004). (Deeply) sustainable programs, sustainable cultures, sustainable selves: Essaying growth in technical communication. In Teresa Kynell-Hunt & Gerald J. Savage (Eds.), *Power and legitimacy in technical communication, Volume II: Strategies for professional status* (pp. 101–119). Baywood.

Kimball, Miles A. (2017). The golden age of technical communication. *Journal of Technical Writing and Communication, 47*(3), 330–358. https://doi.org/10.1177/0047281616641927.

Kleimann, Susan. (1993). The reciprocal relationship of workplace culture and review. In Rachel Spilka (Ed.), *Writing in the workplace: New research perspectives* (pp. 56–70). Southern Illinois University Press.

Koerber, Amy & McMichael, Lonie (2008). Qualitative sampling methods: A primer for technical communicators. *Journal of Business and Technical Communication, 22*(4), 454–473. https://doi.org/10.1177/1050651908320362.

Lanier, Clinton R. (2018). Toward understanding important workplace issues for technical communicators. *Technical Communication, 65*(1), 66–84. https://tinyurl.com/5d67mnub.

Lauer, Claire & Brumberger, Eva. (2019). Redefining writing for the responsive workplace. *College Composition and Communication, 70*(4), 634–663.

Lauren, Benjamin & Pigg, Stacey. (2016). Networking in a field of introverts: The egonets, networking practices, and networking technologies of technical communication entrepreneurs. *IEEE Transactions on Professional Communication, 59*(4), 342–362. http://doi.org/10.1109/TPC.2016.2614744.

Lay, Mary M. (1991). Feminist theory and the redefinition of technical communication. *Journal of Business and Technical Communication, 5*(4), 348–370. https://doi.org/10.1177/1050651991005004002.

Leydens, Jon A. (2008). Novice and insider perspectives on academic and workplace writing: Toward a continuum of rhetorical awareness. *IEEE Transactions on Professional Communication, 51*(3), 242–263. https://doi.org/10.1109/TPC.2008.2001249.

Longo, Bernadette. (1998). An approach for applying cultural study theory to technical writing research. *Technical Communication Quarterly, 7*(1), 53–73. https://doi.org/10.1080/10572259809364617.

Longo, Bernadette. (2006). An approach for applying cultural study theory to technical writing research. In J. Blake Scott, Bernadette Longo & Katherine V. Wills (Eds.), *Critical power tools: Technical communication and cultural studies* (pp. 111–132). State University of New York Press.

Melonçon, Lisa & Schreiber, Joanna. (2022). Introduction: Promoting a sustainable collective identity for technical and professional communication. In Joanna Schreiber & Lisa Melonçon (Eds.), *Assembling critical components: A framework for sustaining technical and professional communication* (pp. 3–16). The WAC Clearinghouse; University Press of Colorado. https://doi.org/10.37514/TPC-B.2022.1381.

Melonçon, Lisa & St.Amant, Kirk. (2019). Empirical research in technical and professional communication: A 5-year examination of research methods and a call for research sustainability. *Journal of Technical Writing and Communication, 49*(2), 128–155. https://doi.org/10.1177/0047281618764611.

Miller, Carolyn R. (1979). A humanistic rationale for technical writing. *College English, 40*(6), 610–617. https://doi.org/10.2307/375964.

Moses, Myra G. & Katz, Steven B. (2006). The phantom machine: The invisible ideology of email (a cultural critique). In J. Blake Scott, Bernadette Longo & Katherine V. Wills (Eds.), *Critical power tools: Technical communication and cultural studies* (pp. 71–110). State University of New York Press.

Odell, Lee, Goswami, Dixie, Herrington, Anne & Quick, Doris. (1983). Studying writing in non-academic settings. In Paul V. Anderson, R. John Brockmann & Carolyn

R. Miller (Eds.), *New essays in technical and scientific communication: Research, theory, practice* (pp. 17–40). Baywood.

Paradis, James, Dobrin, David & Miller, Richard. (1985). Writing at Exxon ITD: Notes on the writing environment of an R&D organization. In Lee Odell & Dixie Goswami (Eds.), *Writing in nonacademic settings* (pp. 281–307). Routledge.

Parker, Kim, Horowitz, Juliana Menasce & Minkin, Rachel. (2020). *How the coronavirus outbreak has—and hasn't—changed the way Americans work*. Pew Research Center. https://www.pewsocialtrends.org/2020/12/09/how-the-coronavirus-outbreak-has-and-hasnt-changed-the-way-americans-work/.

Petersen, Emily January & Moeller, Ryan M. (2016). Using antenarrative to uncover systems of power in mid-20th century policies on marriage and maternity at IBM. *Journal of Technical Writing and Communication, 46*(3), 362–386. https://doi.org/10.1177/0047281616639473 .

Pigg, Stacey. (2014). Coordinating constant invention: Social media's role in distributed work. *Technical Communication Quarterly, 23*(2), 69–87. https://doi.org/10.1080/10572252.2013.796545.

Rea, E. Ashley. (2021). "Changing the face of technology": Storytelling as intersectional feminist practice in coding organizations. *Technical Communication, 68*(4), 26–39. https://tinyurl.com/nmm3ezae.

Richardson, Malcolm & Liggett, Sarah. (1993). Power relations, technical writing theory, and workplace writing. *Journal of Business and Technical Communication, 7*(1), 112–137. https://doi.org/10.1177/1050651993007001006.

Rickard, Thomas Arthur. (1908). *A guide to technical writing*. Mining and Scientific Press.

Rosselot-Merritt, Jeremy. (2020). Fertile grounds: What interviews of working professionals can tell us about perceptions of technical communication and the viability of technical communication as a field. *Technical Communication, 67*(1), 38–62.

Rutter, Russell. (1991). History, rhetoric, and humanism: Toward a more comprehensive definition of technical communication. *Journal of Technical Writing and Communication, 21*(2), 133–153. https://doi.org/10.2190/7BBK-BJYK-AQGB-28GP.

Sageev, Pneena & Romanowski, Carol J. (2001). A message from recent engineering graduates in the workplace: Results of a survey on technical communication skills. *Journal of Engineering Education, 90*(4), 685–693. https://doi.org/10.1002/j.2168-9830.2001.tb00660.x.

Sauer, Beverly. (2006). Living documents: Liability versus the need to archive, or, why (sometimes) history should be expunged. In J. Blake Scott, Bernadette Longo & Katherine V. Wills (Eds.), *Critical power tools: Technical communication and cultural studies* (pp. 171–198). State University of New York Press.

Savage, Gerald J. & Sullivan, Dale L. (Eds.). (2001). *Writing a professional life: Stories of technical communicators on and off the job*. Longman.

Schneider, Barbara. (2002). Theorizing structure and agency in workplace writing: An ethnomethodological approach. *Journal of Business and Technical Communication, 16*(2), 170–195. https://doi.org/10.1177/1050651902016002002.

Schreiber, Joanna. (2017). Toward a critical alignment with efficiency philosophies. *Technical Communication, 64*(1), 27–37. https://www.ingentaconnect.com/contentone/stc/tc/2017/00000064/00000001/art00004.

Scott, J. Blake, Longo, Bernadette & Wills, Katherine V. (Eds.). (2006a). *Critical power tools: Technical communication and cultural studies*. State University of New York Press.

Scott, J. Blake, Longo, Bernadette & Wills, Katherine V. (2006b). Introduction: Why cultural studies? Expanding technical communication's critical toolbox. In J. Blake Scott, Bernadette Longo & Katherine V. Wills (Eds.), *Critical power tools: Technical communication and cultural studies* (pp. 1–24). State University of New York Press.

Selzer, Jack. (1993). Intertextuality and the writing process: An overview. In Rachel Spilka (Ed.), *Writing in the workplace: New research perspectives* (pp. 171–180). Southern Illinois University Press.

Silker, Christine M. & Gurak, Laura J. (1996). Technical communication in cyberspace: Report of a qualitative study. *Technical Communication, 43*(4), 357–368. https://www.jstor.org/stable/43088097.

Smart, Graham. (1993). Genre as community invention: A central bank's response to its executives' expectations as readers. In Rachel Spilka (Ed.), *Writing in the workplace: New research perspectives* (pp. 124–140). Southern Illinois University Press.

Spilka, Rachel. (2000). The issue of quality in professional documentation: How can academia make more of a difference? *Technical Communication Quarterly, 9*(2), 207–221. https://doi.org/10.1080/10572250009364694.

Spinuzzi, Clay. (2003). *Tracing genres through organizations: A sociocultural approach to information design* (Vol. 1). MIT Press.

Spinuzzi, Clay. (2007). Guest editor's introduction: Technical communication in the age of distributed work. *Technical Communication Quarterly, 16*(3), 265–277. https://doi.org/10.1080/10572250701290998.

Spinuzzi, Clay. (2008). *Network: Theorizing knowledge work in telecommunications.* Cambridge University Press.

Spinuzzi, Clay. (2013). How can technical communicators study work contexts? In Johndan Johnson-Eilola & Stuart A. Selber. (Eds.), *Solving problems in technical communication* (pp. 262–284). University of Chicago Press.

Spinuzzi, Clay. (2015). *All edge: Inside the new workplace networks.* University of Chicago Press.

Spinuzzi, Clay, Bodrožić, Zlatko, Scaratti, Giuseppe & Ivaldi, Silvia. (2019). "Coworking is about community": But what is "community" in coworking? *Journal of Business and Technical Communication, 33*(2), 112–140. https://doi.org/10.1177/1050651918816357.

St.Amant, Kirk & Melonçon, Lisa. (2016a). Addressing the incommensurable: A research-based perspective for considering issues of power and legitimacy in the field. *Journal of Technical Writing and Communication, 46*(3), 267–283. https://doi.org/10.1177/0047281616639476.

St.Amant, Kirk & Melonçon, Lisa. (2016b). Reflections on research: Examining practitioner perspectives on the state of research in technical communication. *Technical Communication, 63*(4), 346–364. https://www.ingentaconnect.com/content/stc/tc/2016/00000063/00000004/art00006.

Sullivan, Patricia & Porter, James E. (1993). On theory, practice, and method: Toward a heuristic research methodology for professional writing. In Rachel Spilka (Ed.), *Writing in the workplace: New research perspectives* (pp. 220–237). Southern Illinois University Press.

Waddell, Craig. (1995). Defining sustainable development: A case study in environmental communication. *Technical Communication Quarterly, 4*(2), 201–216. https://doi.org/10.1080/10572259509364597.

Wahl, Scott. (2003). Learning at work: The role of technical communication in organizational learning. *Technical Communication, 50*(2), 247–258.

Walsh, Denis & Downe, Soo. (2005). Meta-synthesis method for qualitative research: A literature review. *Journal of Advanced Nursing, 50*(2), 204–211. https://doi.org/10.1111/j.1365-2648.2005.03380.x.

Walton, Rebecca. (2013). Stakeholder flux: Participation in technology-based international development projects. *Journal of Business and Technical Communication, 27*(4), 409–435. https://doi.org/10.1177/1050651913490940.

Walton, Rebecca & Jones, Natasha N. (2013). Navigating increasingly cross-cultural, cross-disciplinary, and cross-organizational contexts to support social justice. *Communication Design Quarterly Review, 1*(4), 31–35. https://doi.org/10.1145/2524248.2524257.

Walton, Rebecca, Moore, Kristen R. & Jones, Natasha N. (2019). *Technical communication after the social justice turn: Building coalitions for action.* Routledge.

Whiteside, Aimee L. (2003). The skills that technical communicators need: An investigation of technical communication graduates, managers, and curricula. *Journal of Technical Writing and Communication, 33*(4), 303–318. https://doi.org/10.2190/3164-E4V0-BF7D-TDVA.

Winsor, Dorothy A. (1989). An engineer's writing and the corporate construction of knowledge. *Written Communication, 6*(3), 270–285. https://doi.org/10.1177/0741088389006003002.

Winsor, Dorothy A. (1990a). Engineering writing/writing engineering. *College Composition and Communication, 41*(1), 58–70. https://doi.org/10.2307/357883.

Winsor, Dorothy A. (1990b). The construction of knowledge in organizations: Asking the right questions about the Challenger. *Journal of Business and Technical Communication, 4*(2), 7–20. https://doi.org/10.1177/1050651990000400201.

Winsor, Dorothy A. (1996). *Writing like an engineer: A rhetorical education.* Routledge.

Winsor, Dorothy A. (1998). Rhetorical practices in technical work. *Journal of Business and Technical Communication, 12*(3), 343–370. https://doi.org/10.1177/105065199801200 3004.

Winsor, Dorothy A. (1999). Genre and activity systems: The role of documentation in maintaining and changing engineering activity systems. *Written Communication, 16*(2), 200–224. https://doi.org/10.1177/0741088399016002003.

Winsor, Dorothy A. (2000). Ordering work: Blue-collar literacy and the political nature of genre. *Written Communication, 17*(2), 155–184. https://doi.org/10.1177/07410883000017002001.

Winsor, Dorothy. (2006). Using writing to structure agency: An examination of engineers' practice. *Technical Communication Quarterly, 15*(4), 411–430. https://doi.org/10.1207/s15427625tcq1504_1.

Wisniewski, Elaine C. (2018). Novice engineers and project management communication in the workplace. *Technical Communication, 65*(2), 153–168.

2. Emphasizing Place in Workplace Research

Lisa Melonçon
UNIVERSITY OF SOUTH FLORIDA

Abstract

This chapter seeks to understand workplace writing contexts by addressing the following questions: What happens when technical and professional communication (TPC) considers the material dimensions of context more deliberately and more specifically? Often scholarship wants to focus on the how and why, but what do we learn if we emphasize the *where?* Drawing on scholarship in TPC and geography and a two-year ethnographic study as a practical example, I inductively build the theory of *micro-contexts*— highly localized places where communication can be created and/or be used. Emphasizing the *where* of workplace writing provides TPC (and workplace communication practices) both a history and a geography and offers a much needed theoretical and practical expansion of contexts and approaching writing in place. By paying close attention to the geographic aspects of discourse production and circulation, this chapter shows the intimate connections between physical locations and the discourses produced, and in doing so, it illustrates how each place is a distinct area of knowledge making.

Keywords

contexts, micro-contexts, theory building, place

> Being informed by place involves far more than simply
> writing about this place or that place.
> It involves thinking about the implications
> of the idea of place for whatever is being researched.
>
> – *Cresswell, 2004, p. 122*

It's snowing. I grumble as I get out of my car because the Southerner in me still hates the winter, but for the last two years, I've come to this workplace often through all four seasons. At the sound of the welcome beep that greets everyone when the front door opens, the receptionist looks up. The entryway is small, with room enough for a single chair and the receptionist desk.

She smiles big, and says, "Hey, Lisa, who you need to talk to today?"

"I need to see Joe (pseudonym). He's expecting me. You want me to just go on back?" I ask as I point at the door to the right that always remains locked. Guests are usually escorted through the building.

DOI: https://doi.org/10.37514/TPC-B.2023.2128.2.02

"Yeah, if you don't mind cause I gotta get this done." She motions to her computer and some papers she picks up. "I just buzzed you in. Come back out this way, though, so you can sign in and out!"

I smile and nod my acknowledgement of the procedures since I know they reconcile the sign-in sheet with the security camera tapes. I wave to her as I make it to the door within the short window of time so she'd doesn't have to reprogram the entry lock system.

I wind my way through the building. I know it well at this point; I've been welcomed in because everyone understands my role in trying to improve several work processes related to communication within the organization. I pass the "cube area" that consists of roughly 10–12 cubicles, although the range depends on the number of interns on site and what the tasks of those interns are. Sometimes two cube areas are collapsed into one where several folks can collaborate easier, but still not as comfortable a collaboration space as the conference room, which is the next area I pass through on the way to my destination. Once through the conference room, I'm in a kitchen. The only way to get to my destination is to go through the kitchen. At the back of the kitchen is a door that puts me down a short hallway, another turn, another door. Here I knock as I open the door, because on the other side of the door, without any notice, is a makeshift office. Joe, who is my interview for that day, is sitting at his desk. He stands up to hug me. Simultaneously, we talk over each other, saying "hello" and "how are you?" Mid-hug, his door swings open, causing us to release and step back quickly so the door doesn't hit us. Another person walks on through with a quick hello.

We look at each other and laugh. He sits down at his desk. I drag a box over next to him and take a seat. For the next hour, we talk. I lost count of the number of times the door opened and hit the corner of his desk, and someone just walked through. Because that interruption is so normal, my interviewee never blinked or even acknowledged that anything happened. It took me until the third or fourth person for my embodied memory to kick in and just block out (for the most part) the sound of the door hitting the desk and the oddity of someone walking through as we just talked as if nothing out of the ordinary was happening.

I have been unable to escape the memory of that conversation in that makeshift office and how it impacted the way I consider the role of place on the work that technical and professional communicators do. Without doubt, the vignette described above is an extreme example; however, the example re-emphasizes the impact of material locations of place on writing and communication. My interviewee from the vignette did much of his internal communication and report writing in the morning or late in the afternoon. He scheduled the rest of his day around that time so that he would be interrupted less when the office was less busy. In technical and professional communication (TPC), the idea of the rhetorical situation or that writing is situated within a context is so commonplace as to be nearly forgotten. In this chapter, I want to highlight *context* to better understand one of its constituent parts, *place*. I started with two guiding questions:

What happens when TPC considers the material dimensions of context more deliberately and more specifically? Often scholarship wants to focus on the how and why, but what do we learn if we examine the *where?*

I work through tentative answers to these questions by drawing on a two-year ethnographic study as a practical example. I begin with an introduction to the ethnographic case study that expands on examples of the importance of *where's* impact on communication practices. From the ethnographic case and from existing literature in geography, rhetoric, and TPC, I move to inductively build the theory of *micro-contexts*, which are highly localized places where communication can be created and/or be used. I end with implications of this theory for TPC.

Emphasizing the *where* of workplace writing provides TPC (and workplace communication practices) both a history and a geography and offers a much needed theoretical and practical expansion of contexts. By paying close attention to the geographic aspects of discourse production and circulation, I want to show the intimate connections between physical locations and the discourses they produce, and in doing so, to illustrate how each place is a distinct area of knowledge making.

■ Ethnographic Case Study

Good Works Store (pseudonym) is a nonprofit with around 110 employees. Over the two years prior to my arrival, Good Works Store had doubled in size in resources, transactions, and employees. C-Suite executives and middle managers had been undergoing different types of business administration training (such as Lean and Six Sigma), and several senior managers recognized the need to start documenting internal processes. I was invited to consult on the documentation project. In our initial discussion of what information was presently documented and potential strategies to address the documentation needs of the organization, it became clear that the bigger concern, one where internal documentation of processes could reside, was to capture and find a way to manage the knowledge work of the organization. So, what initially started as a documentation project morphed into a two-year ethnographic study of knowledge management practices.[1]

When the organization grew so quickly, it expanded from a single location to three locations that I refer to as the executive building, the warehouse, and the client center. The three locations are radically different in size, purpose, and culture. All three locations are within five miles of each other. In thinking through the *where* of work*places*, one should consider the material dimensions of the places where work occurs.

The executive building housed the C-Suite, a number of middle managers, the technical staff (e.g., application developers and web designer), support staff

---

1.   As a singular case study, this project was not considered "human subjects research" and was exempted from institutional review.

(e.g., administrative assistants) and the entire financial division. The opening scene of this chapter was at the executive building. A feature not described previously is that there are closed-door offices around the perimeter of the building to the cubicle area, and collaboration areas are in the middle of the space. This setup is not unfamiliar and aligns with terms in popular workplace discourse such as "cube farm" and "corner office." The setup of the executive building was meant to provide a "look and feel" of a "corporate entity" because, as the chief operating officer told me, Good Works Store needed to be seen differently, more professional, by stakeholders in the region. Employees from the other two locations often came to the executive office building for meetings, while those in the executive office building rarely went to the other locations. Thinking of the cubicle or the office or the conference room as a component part—a material component part—of a "workplace" emphasizes how the different locations produce the work of technical and professional communication.

The client center was a public-facing location that looked like many organizations that have public-facing areas. The main lobby had a receptionist and many chairs. On the left side of the area, there were closed-door offices, and additional offices were on two floors above the public reception area. The client center was a high-volume center that usually recorded over 100 people checking in and out in a day. Once people checked in, they went to one of the office areas for additional assistance. This was the main location for initial client interactions.

The warehouse was a reclaimed building that had a part-time administrator in the lobby area and then a group of ten employees in a cavernous warehouse area, which was likely some 8,000 square feet. The size was necessary because at times this space was also home to hundreds of volunteers. As the name implies, this building was used to store a lot of stock that had multiple daily deliveries both coming into the warehouse and leaving the warehouse. At times, the warehouse could barely hold all the materials. At other times, it stood almost empty. One of the first things I noticed when I went to the warehouse the first time was the contrast of silence when walking into the lobby area versus the noisy din in the storage area. There was a breakroom with a table and a few chairs where employees (and volunteers) could gather. Of the three locations, the warehouse had had few updates and looked worn and out of date, but unlike the other two locations, no one but employees or volunteers would ever be in this location.

This multiplicity of sites immediately became a key consideration because this material, location-based expansion directly impacted communication processes in both positive and negative ways. More so, it was difficult for employees at all levels to articulate or to even recognize how this shifting of place made such a big impact. As an outsider without prior knowledge, it took only a couple of weeks for me to identify some immediate things to improve, and by the time the larger project ended, the organization had developed a better sense of itself as a multisite organization, as well as the impact of the multiple places on how they interacted and communicated. In some ways, the descriptions of the different locations embedded within this one ethnographic case study are not surprising. It's almost a moment of "of course!" But, TPC scholarship has not codified some of the ideas that are taking place in practice; thus, the field lacks a vocabulary and appropriate theories to make sense of place and its impact on communication.

The research category that I deployed for this study was ethnographic research. As an ethnography, it was an observational study with related interviews. It follows Yin's (2003) definition of a case study that includes a study conducted in a real-life context where multiple forms of evidence are used (pp.13–14). I expanded Yin to include a distinct starting and stopping point and full description of materials included in the research (Melonçon & St.Amant, 2019, p.138). The messiness of research, particularly a research study that was done at times in tandem with a larger consulting project, made it difficult to separate information. The observational method of watching and learning an organization was often one of the first steps of any consulting project that I took on because it gave me time to watch everyday practices. The silent observations uncovered how the organization worked, what different divisions did, and how they communicated with each other. Following are the characteristics of the case study, methods used, and amount of material for this part of the research study:

- 18 one-hour interviews with key stakeholders
- 3 hours on average of time observing before and after the interviews
- observations at all three locations of the organization
- 6-month timeframe for this aspect of the study
- field notes and diagrams, as well as some insights from the interviewees

What I discuss here is a small slice of the larger research study, and the discussions of place are at times an experiential composite. I use this term in the same way as composite narratives, which use data from several interviews to provide evidence or support around a common issue or theme. (Refer to Willis, 2019 for more information.) An experiential composite combines experiences from the field, which allows for the composition of observational studies, community projects, and other types of research that may bring together experiences based on observation rather than those drawn from interviews. The experiential composite illustrates a broader importance of bringing place to the forefront in discussions of communication and writing in the workplace. Later in the chapter when I provide examples, those examples appear to be a singular, but rather, they bring together characteristics and multiple experiential moments. The examples here from one organization led to me rethinking other research that I have conducted at numerous other sites. In that rethinking, I came to the realization that technical and professional communication needs a different way to describe the impact of *where*. This case study helps with theory building specific to theorizing the place of place within the work of TPC.

■ Entering Existing Scholarly Conversations

Due to the constraints of the length of a book chapter, I confine my discussion of existing conversations in the scholarship to brief overviews of place from a geographic perspective and geography scholars; to perspectives of place in broader rhetorical studies; and finally, to TPC scholarship that in some capacity directly discusses issues of material places as they relate to communication creation and circulation.

▌ Place in Geography

A well-used difference between space and place comes from geographer (and philosopher) Yi-Fu Tuan (1977): "If we think of space as that which allows movement, then place is a pause" (p. 6). Tuan argues that place is defined by a person's experience with the world. I take Tuan's approach as a key component to how I am using place. It is not only keyed to a person's experience in the world, but that experience is connected to a physical, material location.

Place as a theoretical concept has long been examined as primary tenet in geographic scholarship,[2] particularly in human geography, which, as its names implies, studies the interactions of people with the environment to include social, political, economic, and cultural aspects of that interaction.

A key concern for a human geographer is to gain deeper understandings in how a person's interactions with their surroundings (natural and built) shape those surroundings and in turn, how the surroundings reshape the person. For example, a human geographer might study how urban sprawl affects quality of life for those who live in the heart of the city as well as those who live in the suburbs. As Arturo Escobar (2008) argues forcefully, "place continues to be an important source of culture and identity" (p. 7), which would occur even in workplaces. For example, the geographic location was an important part of Good Works Store's organizational ethos. It was committed to its mission of providing a public and social good for people who resided in the region. In addition, the people who worked there were not only proud of that mission and its local impact, but they highlighted how much their own cultural differences (e.g., urban versus rural Appalachian identities) were respected and contributed to the organization's overall culture.

Moving to place as context also means incorporating the interactions of other actors, and things such as technology. Moreover, "to travel between places is to move between collections of trajectories and to reinsert yourself in the ones

---

2. I make a distinction between place and space which is fully explained in geographic literature, and space constraints do not allow a full examination and explanation in this chapter. I follow the differences set forth by scholars such as Paul Adams (2017) and Doreen Massey (2005) in geography and Edward Casey (2009) in philosophy.

to which you relate" (Massey, 2005, p. 130). There is a need for a corrective theory that neutralizes this erasure of place, the asymmetry that arises from giving far too much importance to "the global" and far too little value to "place." (Escobar, 2008, p. 7). Place as context also must be critically approached in research. If scholars are ever to fully understand how technical communication reinforces, creates, or dismantles inequitable systems, then we must take seriously geographer John Agnew's (2007) argument that to understand knowledge and power, scholars need to situate institutions and their knowledge in the place-specific contexts.

To get at the idea of situatedness, the specific context and relationship between reader and text, is to necessitate bringing place to the forefront of discussions of audience. Using place as a theoretical, metaphorical, and material lens requires that we expand our existing understanding of audience and consider head on as one of the most important aspects of audience analysis the impact place has on the effectiveness of discourse; thus, the need to consider place from a rhetorical perspective.

▮ Place in Rhetorical Studies Broadly

In rhetorical scholarship, scholars can look to the work of Jenny Edbauer (2005) as a distinct moment of invoking place more materially. Edbauer (2005) brought place into the rhetorical conversation through "rhetorical ecology." In doing so, she "destabilize[d] the discrete borders of a rhetorical situation" and expanded those borders to "a network of lived practical consciousness or structures of feeling" (Edbauer, 2005, p. 5). Edbauer's theoretical expansion of the rhetorical situation emphasized the complexities of context, of place, by arguing the "rhetorical situation" was in constant flux and not self-contained as a bounded "situation." Her ecological metaphor drew attention to the relationality between the parts such as between texts, people, events, places, and contexts of use in an expansive system.

Many have taken up Edbauer's ecologies. In an overview of ecological turn in rhetorical studies, Madison Jones (2021) reviewed work specific to environmental communication (Druschke, 2019), literacies (Grant, 2009; Rìos, 2015), pedagogy (Inoue, 2015; Rivers & Weber, 2011), and ontologies (Ehrenfeld, 2020; Stormer & McGreavy, 2017). This list is by no means exhaustive, but it underscores that rhetorical studies, broadly construed, continues to situate the work of rhetoric through an ecological metaphor. Further, taking Jenny Rice's (2012) work as an inspiration or a starting place, other rhetorical scholars have tended to emphasize the vastness of the situation or context by building on the ecological model (e.g., Jensen, 2015); discussing context as network (e.g., Dingo, 2012; Rice, 2012); or examining assemblages of places, people, and things (e.g., Wingard, 2013). In trying to make more parts of the larger network (or of space) visible, researchers may lose sight of the dynamics that push and pull on those larger structures. For my own thinking, trying to make the context of the situation or context larger makes models and theories more difficult to use, particularly something so localized as a workplace setting.

One way to adequately address situated rhetoric is to find ways to physically ground theoretical concepts in the practice of workplace writing and communication, much like John Muckelbauer's (2008) offering a different type of invention, one where instead of "teaching students how to know a situation, a situated rhetoric attempts to provoke the ability to respond to the situatedness itself" (p. 121). Muckelbauer's insistence on the situatedness itself is a nice bridge between rhetorical studies and TPC since much workplace research is indeed centered on understanding the situatedness of the communication practices.

▌ Place in TPC

While other fields have taken a "spatial turn," TPC has not yet fully engaged theoretically or practically with place as a means to understand the interrelated nature of writing and communication and the places that produce and/or impact that same work.[3] Much more is needed to bring Doreen Massey's (2005) concept that places have roles to play in the work that we do, but recent studies in TPC have begun to be more explicit in examining the role of place as a material part of writing and communication. For example, one of the best articulations is from Elizabeth Angeli (2019), who uses emergency medical services (EMS) and ride-alongs to clearly situate the communication practices of EMS technicians within specific locations of work. Meanwhile, Stacey Pigg (2020) looked to the same location, a coffee shop, to begin to understand the writing and communication practices of those who choose to work in this location. Another work related to place is from Derek Ross and his collaborators (2019), who argued for a place-based ethic that "actively acknowledge[s] the environment."

Some scholarship in user experience research has focused more explicitly on place to situate users within their locations. For example, Dan Richards and Sonia Stephens (2022) asked community members for their reactions to a video that discussed environmental risks to their community. They were seeking information on their comprehension and emotional reactions. Richards and Stephens' focus group research aligns—in some ways—to what I am trying to do with considering a theory that focuses on smaller, localized contexts. Even though Richards and Stephens did not frame their work specific to context (since their study was focused on users' reaction to information), the impact of a context on those

---

3.   The extensive work on methodologies of research that are tied to place through community-based or participatory action research are not discussed here. There is definitely a connection to place in this work, but the goal of that research is about the research enterprise rather than writing and communicating in workplaces. It also gave me a boundary limit for the length of this chapter.

same users deserves increased attention. Similarly, Emma Rose's (2016) investigation of homeless bus riders focused on the design of information and communication technologies, but also points to the necessity of where users would access and/or use the information.

Moving closer to an explicit connection to place, Catherine Gouge (2017) looked at patient discharge instructions and concluded that new information design approaches are necessary because current approaches need to "[let] go of the hyperstandardization as an abstract ideal" because "we need to consider approaches that can recognize and work with the improvisational aspects of transitional care communication events" (p. 17). Gouge's finding that patients and caregivers are often having to improvise and adapt information to different care events underscores the need for more attention to place. While Gouge did not tie her work explicitly to context or place, I found her work compelling because it highlights what goes wrong when information design does not fully consider place. Gouge's discussion of patient discharge instructions highlighted for me the necessity that instructions for "transitional care" will take place in different locations. Thus, when Gouge encourages technical communication to let go of a hyperstandardization, she is pointing to the need to consider the effect of place more fully on contexts of use.

Finally, when looking at the TPC literature, I found a number of works that started to engage with place—the effect of *where* on the design and the use of information—but I was still left wanting. From geography, I want to bring forward that places are bounded and experienced, while research in rhetorical studies shows that expanding the rhetorical situation has brought important critical insights but leaves unexplored what happens when rhetorical situations are reduced. So I moved to a more specific question: How can TPC better account for the effect of *where* when also considering the contexts of the rhetorical situation and the material dimensions of place? In the next section, I illustrate a tentative answer to this question by offering a theory of *micro-contexts*.

■ Inducing a Theory of Micro-Contexts

Based on the existing scholarship within rhetorical studies and TPC, current theoretical models of context and place are insufficient, particularly as they relate to TPC and more localized needs of communication. Thus, TPC could use attention to theory building because it "should be recognized as an important methodological goal and practice" (Scott & Melonçon, 2018, p.11). Theory building should not be considered in contrast to the TPC's attention to applied research practices. Rather, theory building should be part of the invention process in research, in practice, and in teaching. Considering theory building as inventive (Scott & Melonçon, 2018, p. 12; Scott & Gouge, 2019) allows TPC to pose better questions, to allow different ways of knowing, and to expose new insights that may otherwise not be seen. And as I noted with J. Blake Scott (2018), "theory building can also be seen as a framework for imagining a better world" (p. 12). Even though imagining and changing a world takes time, good theories can help scholars and practitioners begin this arduous work. "Theory building" develops "the tools and approaches for *how* to do such work"(Scott & Gouge, 2019, p. 181). The first step to theory building is to make sure there is a shared understanding of what theory is. Here, I take theory to mean a system of ideas intended to better understand a specific phenomenon. Using this definition allows TPC to move toward a more enhanced understanding of the general principles of context by adding a material place dimension that is currently not directly explicitly in the scholarship. If TPC wants to take seriously the importance of context, then *where* needs to be theorized to broaden and deepen our understanding of rhetorical situations and the impact of place on the work TPC does.

Both Kirk St.Amant (2018) and I (2017) discussed expanding purpose to include a greater emphasis on place in specific contexts of use. St.Amant (2018) explained that prototypes of place, or the "expectations associated with a space," (p. 48) include object-, individual-, and access-related items. These items are then used to "provide UXD [user experience design] professionals with a method for identifying core variables affecting dynamics of usability and space in relation to culture and accessibility" (St.Amant, 2018, p. 51). Overall, the goal of St.Amant's article was to focus on how prototypes of place can be used to "study the expectations users associate with performing an activity in a particular setting" (p. 51). While St.Amant gets TPC started with his emphasis on the cognition and prototypes from an audience perspective, he does not fully account for changing the particular setting. This is where my own work (2017) that emphasizes smaller scales comes into play. In my initial thinking about how patients and others interact with health information, I considered the cognitive components discussed by St.Amant, while also wanting to gain a better understanding of the particular—a smaller—context. I started thinking of this smaller, localized context as a *micro-context*.

Thinking in terms of "micro" means to make smaller, to shrink the scale. When the scale shrinks, analysis of that context can be deeper to shed light on what parts of the larger systems may have more force and function. Using micro-contexts as a unit of analysis also allows for a bounded and limited object to examine. In something of a complementary move, Ashley Clayson (2018) argued for an analytic frame she called microanalysis because it is useful for when "researchers are seeking to understand deep interactions among tools, artifacts, and bodies" (p. 221). While Clayson was interested in distributed writing, she complements micro-contexts since she too wanted to examine a more particular, a smaller, context of use. In another example, Kathleen Connellan and her collaborators (2015) asked the provocative question of whether glass can speak. Their study analyzed windows in a mental health facility, and it prompted "(re)considerations of the materiality of the spaces and the impact those spaces have on the communication design of discourses" (Melançon & Frost, 2015, p. 10). Similar to my own ethnographic case study, Connellan and colleagues (2015) wanted to consider the material effects of the building. While Connellan and her collaborators looked to glass in a place, I looked to the places themselves—the physical features of the three locations of Good Works Store—and how they effected communication practices.

Current challenges related to rhetorical situations or context were questions of scale While much of the scholarship discussed above has considered the scale of context as bigger and more complex, I want to go in the opposite direction—to scale back, to reduce to specific, localized contexts of use. The overemphasis on the vastness of context has left scholarship in TPC devoid of its inductive history that can offer valuable insights into communication practices. Thus, I follow Massey (2005), who did not want to use *place* as a stand-in for *here* (pp.138–9) by splitting apart larger contexts, to reduce them, to make them more manageable. In turn, I am using place to prioritize *where* because

> current scholarship that insists on larger and more complex con-
> texts suggests that everything in an ecology (or network, etc.)
> reverberates equally from everything else. But it does not. There are
> parts of the ecology that have more force and function in effecting
> outcomes than other parts. (Melançon, 2017, p. 22)

Shrinking of scale enables TPC to think of micro-contexts when practi-
tioners *create* communication and information *and* to consider micro-contexts (which are likely different) for when that same communication is used. Thus, the *here* of place shifts and moves, which doesn't make a singular consideration of context—place—helpful. TPC "must be aware of and sensitive to whatever it is that writing *does* in the workplace" (Paré, 2002, p.70). Anthony Paré's (2002) assertion of action—doing—in the workplace is tied to the location, the *where*. Thinking of the impact of *where* through the theoretical lens of a micro-context enables TPC scholars and practitioners to reconsider both audience and purpose.

A micro-context can be defined as a localized and bounded context to make manageable the rhetorical situation of purpose, audience, location, delivery, and use. Limiting the rhetorical situation offers practitioners the opportunity to gain deeper insights into where the information will be produced and where it will be used. As Massey (2005) explained,

> what is special about place is precisely that throwntogetherness,
> the unavoidable challenges of negotiating a here-and-now (itself
> drawing on a history and a geography of thens and theres); and
> a negotiation which must take place within and between both
> human and nonhuman. (p. 140)

Massey's insistence that throwntogetherness and negotiation are what make a place a place lays the foundation for emphasizing place more deliberately when faced with information design and its subsequent use. What is thrown together in a particular place at a particular time impacts communication and forces a negotiation between user and information that is dependent on the influence of the micro-contexts. The negotiation of multiplicity exists as information moves or is used in multiple micro-contexts. Negotiation also makes available a variety of interpretations and uses of the communication. No matter the original intention, when others interact with communication in different micro-contexts, there is an unknown range of means of use and interpretation. This aspect of negotiation is keyed directly to the idea of micro-contexts because it is the places, the locations, that often shift the original meaning to a new negotiated one.

The challenge of differences found in micro-contexts illustrates the need for an expansion between a limited, one-dimensional view of context. Micro-contexts move TPC toward a multi-dimensional understanding of micro-contexts that account for the challenge and the negotiation that communication brings with it as that communication is created and moves into being used. The examples in the next section help to show how this happens.

▌ Examples of Micro-Contexts in Action

The ethnographic study offers insights into the question of what happens when the *where* moves. While technical and professional communicators cannot control where information may be used, academics and practitioners alike need to consider the impact of place more fully than the field has done so in the past. Micro-contexts allow for movement when the *where* shifts not only in the creation, but as importantly, in its use. Let me try to operationalize this idea of micro-contexts by returning to Good Works Store and providing three specific communication problems that simultaneously show the power of micro-context in action, and the importance of thinking in terms of micro-contexts.

The first example focuses on a fund raising event. Each year, Good Works Store sponsored a large fund-raising event, the Hot Wheel race. This was a cornerstone of its ethos as an organization, as well as a large percentage of the annual operating revenue. The Hot Wheel race allowed people to buy a toy car for the race. All the toy cars were raced down a hill, and the cars that crossed the finish line first were awarded a prize, but the bulk of the proceeds from the toy car sales went back to Good Works Store and its partners. Toy car sales started months in advance of the early fall event, and the cars were sold online, at in-person events, and by partner organizations (usually student groups). Sales at in-person events and partner organizations were all manually completed so that these sales had to be combined with online sales for an accurate and complete list. The main sales list was key to coordination of race day because each car had a unique number associated with the person who bought it, which allowed for identifying the winners.

Looking at the Hot Wheel race fundraising event from a network view, such as Clay Spinuzzi's (2003) tracing genres, it would appear the event was a strength of the organization. However, micro-contexts exposed several problems, and highlighted "what part of the context has more force and function" (Melonçon, 2017, p. 22) on the larger system. First, rather than leveraging technology available and on hand to keep track of the sales, the person who had long been in charge of the toy car sales insisted on keeping manually generated paper lists of all sales, which made double-checking information or locating information if questions came up a time-consuming process. In other words, she printed out the online sales information and then added by hand the other sales information. She never went back to the technological system and updated those records with other sales. It also exposed that there was a single person who understood all the details of the system. Members of the C-Suite did not realize there were any problems in compiling or exchanging information since they only ever received updates from her at the weekly team meetings. The process of updating team members looks like a positive event of transparent communication, but in fact, it obscured the problems of information gathering and distribution. Finally, it took weeks to reconcile the accounts from the fundraising event the year I was conducting the majority of the interviews (for this and the larger project) because most of the executives assumed the information was in their accounting system when in fact it was not. For reconciliation, the manual lists created by the toy car sales coordinator were handed over to finance to then enter into the accounting and sales system. Thus, there were always unnecessary delays in paying expenses and providing revenue to partner organizations. The changes within the organization from one year to the next and the material locations of the key people for the annual Hot Wheel race had major ramifications for the event. While the problems would have been exposed eventually, I am still surprised years later that a different orientation to the change in communication practices—such as micro-contexts—may have solved the problem sooner and with less stress.

Another example shows how the micro-context and the small pressure points in the organization can have adverse, rippling effects. When the Good Works Store warehouse was purchased, it became the location for what used to be two separate and distinct divisions handled by sub-contractors. On the surface, the manager of the warehouse could see how consolidating the two divisions would ultimately save time and money, but in the short term, there was a lot of confusion about roles and responsibilities and communication processes, such as direct reporting and accountability. As the CEO reported to me, Good Works Store had increased distributions by 57 percent over the prior year, but this seemingly positive effect was, in fact, highly resented by the majority (15 of 18) of those I interviewed. Those who expressed concerns over the increased productivity reported that the productivity was accomplished at the cost of increased tension and collapsed communication and collaboration. The "family spirit" of the nonprofit had been eroded to one of "continuous improvement" and "increased productivity." The expansion to three locations intensified communication problems because of the literal move to three physical places, but it also simultaneously meant, in the words of a longtime employee, "we were just thrown together differently and it seemed like no one understood what their roles were anymore." Shrinking the context of some of the communication problems to this example from the warehouse exposed competing goals and demands and the necessity of improving communication channels at each location and across the three locations.

Without doubt, TPC has always considered issues of purpose and the desired result, but the ethnographic case study pointed to problems of information design and transmission. For example, the growth in the organization meant that it could no longer handle payroll using the paper system it had in the past. The organization needed to move to an automated system. This new system meant that all full-time and part-time employees—both hourly and salary—needed to enter their work hours into a computerized system to generate paychecks (direct deposits and actual checks). The director of HR and part of his team took the time to write instructions for the new system and distributed those instructions along with a rationale for this change to all employees. The information was posted in the internal system as an announcement only. However, it became clear early in this transition period that few people had actually read the documentation (which likely surprises few readers of this chapter). In talking with employees during this rollout, I learned that the biggest problem was in how the information was distributed. The warehouse employees were overwhelmed since many of them had never used a computer system before and hands-on training was not provided. Those working in client services were resentful because no one explained why the system they preferred was being changed, and they had trouble finding a specific place for the computer system they would all need to use. Even those in the executive building expressed frustration because they didn't realize the information applied to them as well. The three locations compounded a complex communication issue because no one considered the impact the different locations would have on how the information was received.

Prior to the move to three locations, the distribution of information about changes was easily handled because everyone was in the same location and received information in similar ways. Not only was the payroll system update a major change in functionality, but sending out information in the same way as before simply could not work because of the expansion across locations and the increase in the number of employees. The assumption that communication practices would work like they had in the past didn't come to the fore until I was able to describe to the key stakeholders not only what happened but the negative feelings that were also compounding the original problem.

Micro-contexts show technical and professional communicators how material place affects the creation and reception of information, particularly when it comes to technology. During the changes that were occurring, Good Works Store was moving a large amount of information on processes, including all the information for the large cadre of volunteers, online. Instead of going to the filing cabinet and handing new volunteers the series of forms they needed, the new process involved them logging on to the intranet and completing those same forms. The new volunteer forms had to be completed before training could take place. Two things happened, however, with this move of documentation to a different place. No one could find information because no training was given on where it was stored electronically, and while much of this occurred at the client services location, no one in that location had access to the intranet. The latter was something no one in the executive office realized until a large volunteer training event turned chaotic. In the past, these sorts of events were in a single location where all the documentation was stored. Splitting apart to different locations *and* moving information to an online place proved to be a challenge no one had fully anticipated. This challenge aligns with complementary issues of place as seen in recent research work about hybrid workplaces (e.g., Suri et al., 2022).

As described in the literature review, scholars have intermittently and recently taken up issues of material places, and micro-contexts provide a way to expand on this existing scholarship in new ways. For example, the ethnographic study described highlighted several ways the place(s) of the organization impacted the communication strategy and effectives of communication within the organization in both positive and negative ways. The actual distance between the three locations expanded and compounded already unstable communication practices. As these examples show, the physical spaces of the three different "offices" directly impacted the way communication was considered and done. Without thinking through the *where*, much of the work we did would not have been as successful because of the impact the material places had on work. This brief summary of the case should shed light on some of the background as to why material places—the *where*—consistently came to the forefront of my work with this organization.

Micro-contexts take into consideration that TPC work often occurs outside of ideal scenarios. Thus, a consideration of the expected versus the actual is often quite different. In the ethnographic case study, there were moments that illustrates the necessity of the *where* and how the actual material work conditions, the actual places, make the work of communication often more challenging than the ideal scenarios considered by academic TPC. "Thus, shifting our contextual scale and rhetorical reasoning approach enables scholars to begin to form theories and generalize knowledge on a series of 'n=1' cases" (Melonçon, 2017, p. 23). Taking my own claim a step further, what qualitative work does well is to move toward a generalization of processes or practices. The case study's three locations expose in explicit ways how and why context matters, and often small contexts, in the creation and dissemination of information. If TPC is to realize its full theoretical potential, the field should move toward testing theories as well as generating them. An area that comes immediately to mind for next steps in research is the relationship between place and power.

We cannot begin to unseat power structures and change systemic issues without a greater understanding of the relationship between power and place—the materiality of where information is created. As Tim Cresswell (2019) argued, power is "the outcome of relations between people, things, and places. . . . Power exists in and through place" (p. 198). The physical structures of workplaces offer yet another layer of the communication practice, and without understanding the impacts of place on decisions and communication, change is likely to be incomplete or unsuccessful. Raka Shome (2003), one of the leading scholars of the spatial turn in communication studies, argued that "our approaches to power may benefit from a contextual and spatial focus where contexts are understood not as static backgrounds but as dynamic relations of force" (p. 54). In the examples from the case study, there were clear moments of power dynamics between the locations and the people within them. While my study did not focus on power dynamics, I can in hindsight see how micro-contexts can illuminate power in ways that may be missed with other theoretical approaches.

The study of workplaces should not be devoid of how power works within organizational settings. My hope is that by understanding the features of places through micro-contexts, we can better identify larger structural problems kept in place through technical communication policies and procedures. Often by focusing on specific smaller situations, systemic problems can be tackled systematically and strategically. By shifting the scale smaller, via micro-context, the identification of those things that reinforce social differences and perpetuate exclusions can be more readily addressed by finding ways to implement incremental and powerful change. Technical and professional communicators need a toolkit to adapt to each situation so that they can continue to "read" places and understand the "politics" of those places.

A collection of micro-contexts can come back together to form the larger ecologies, networks, systems, or assemblages. But micro-contexts offer an alternative way to analyze the physical, material locations of bounded places that more intimately impact information design's creation and use. In consideration of user experience design, which is associated with more of a workplace methodology meant to incorporate the experience of users more directly, micro-contexts as a theory fits into those frameworks as a means to foreground even more directly the experience of the users within their own micro-contexts of use. In other words, a single user experience can be considered a micro-context since it examines in depth and in detail the experiences of a single user's interaction with information. For user experience research and technical communication, micro-contexts offers a designated way to emphasize the need to go further along the continuum of context to smaller rather than larger. Writing and communication tasks are made more manageable by the reduction of the context, by making the situation smaller and bringing it into a more exacting focus.

Micro-contexts have assuredly impacted the way I have approached recent research on information design and patient education materials. As a result, I have added to my repertoire the need to ask more specific questions during the audience analysis stage of the project as well as the need to ask questions during testing and discussions about where the information may be used. Without my being on location and walking through certain processes or sitting listening to the door hit the desk as described in the opening vignette, I would have never fully understood the impact of place on writing and communication. Theorizing place through micro-contexts became visible when I was on site to observe the physical negotiations that occurred during the creation of information and in the use of it. Micro-contexts open up the potential for TPC scholars and practitioners to more seriously consider what happens when the *where* moves.

■ Conclusion

Moving TPC to specific geographic study as a placed-based knowledge enterprise (as of its iterations) means that it brings places together to create an understanding of the micro-contexts within and beyond the "rhetorical situation." Micro-contexts encourage technical and professional communicators to incorporate a direct connect to the place in considerations of purpose, audience, design, and delivery. Considering spatial dimensions and material places when we think of writing and communication encourages different kinds of questions. For instance, why do things happen where they do, and what are the connections between these things? These spatially induced questions bring context into stark view and ensure technical and professional communicators do not lose focus on how the *where* of production is as important as the production itself.

To re-emphasize material place as a key to understanding communication through the rhetorical situation, I did this work through theory building and micro-contexts, which reduces the context to specific and identified places. Given TPC's acceptance that context matters, the field should consider parsing out and examining the material places, the micro-contexts, where writing and communication occur. Focusing on the micro-context allows scholars and practitioners the opportunity to move beyond ideal contexts and situations and instead provide more realistic, valuable, and usable information for audiences and purposes.

As the other chapters in this volume show, writing and work are no longer fixed. They occur in a variety of places, and scholars and practitioners in TPC should pay closer attention to the material dimensions of those *places* and the impact they make on writing and communication practices. Shifting to theorizing about micro-contexts brings to the forefront the need to take seriously the *where* of technical and professional communication and, more importantly, the impact of the where-ness, or place, on writing and communication produced.

In our position as teachers and researchers of technical and professional communication, emphasizing place in workplace writing and communication turns the field's attention back to important locations of work. Like Cresswell reminds us in the opening epigram, the place in workplaces encourages TPC scholars to consider what place can tell us about communication. Unless we take the necessary steps to know our *place,* it will be impossible for others to recognize the importance of technical communication within their own locations.

■ References

Adams, Paul C. (2017). Geographies of media and communication II: Arcs of communication. *Progress in Human Geography, 42*(4), 590–599. https://doi.org/10.1177/03091325 17702992.

Agnew, John. (2007). Know-where: Geographies of knowledge of world politics. *International Political Sociology, 1*(2), 138–148. https://doi.org/10.1111/j.1749-5687.2007 .00009.x.

Angeli, Elizabeth L. (2019). *Rhetorical work in emergency medical services: Communicating in the unpredictable workplace.* Routledge.

Casey, Edward S. (2009). *Getting back into place: Toward a renewed understanding of the place-world* (2nd ed.). Indiana University Press.

Clayson, Ashley. (2018). Distributed writing as a lens for examining writing as embodied practice. *Technical Communication Quarterly, 27*(3), 217–226. https://doi.org/10.1080/10 572252.2018.1479607.

Connellan, Kathleen, Riggs, Damien W. & Due, Clemence. (2015). Light lies: How glass speaks. *Communication Design Quarterly, 3*(4), 15–24. https://doi.org/10.1145/2826972 .2826974.

Cresswell, Tim. (2004). *Place: A short introduction.* Blackwell Publishing.

Cresswell, Tim. (2019). *Maxwell Street: Writing and thinking place.* University of Chicago Press.

Dingo, Rebecca. (2012). *Networking arguments: Rhetoric, transnational feminism, and public policy writing.* University of Pittsburgh Press.

Edbauer, Jenny. (2005). Unframing models of public distribution: From rhetorical situation to rhetorical ecologies. *Rhetoric Society Quarterly, 35*(4), 5–24. https://www.jstor. org/stable/40232607.

Ehrenfeld, Dan. (2020). "Sharing a world with others": Rhetoric's ecological turn and the transformation of the networked public sphere. *Rhetoric Society Quarterly, 50*(5), 305–320. https://doi.org/10.1080/02773945.2020.1813321.

Escobar, Arturo. (2008). *Territories of difference: Place, movements, life, redes.* Duke University Press.

Gottschalk, Druschke, C. (2019). A trophic future for rhetorical ecologies. *Enculturation, 28.*

Gouge, Catherine C. (2017). Improving patient discharge communication. *Journal of Technical Writing and Communication, 47*(4), 419–439. https://doi.org/10.1177/004728 1616646749.

Grant, David M. (2009). Toward sustainable literacies: From representational to recreational rhetorics. In Peter N. Goggin (Ed.), *Rhetorics, literacies, and narratives of sustainability* (pp. 202–216). Routledge.

Inoue, Asao B. (2015). *Antiracist writing assessment ecologies: Teaching and assessing writing for a socially just future.* The WAC Clearinghouse; Parlor Press. https://doi.org/10 .37514/PER-B.2015.0698.

Jensen, Robin E. (2015). An ecological turn in rhetoric of health scholarship: Attending to the historical flow and percolation of ideas, assumptions, and arguments. *Communication Quarterly, 63*(5), 522–526. https://doi.org/10.1080/01463373.2015.1103600.

Jones, Madison. (2021). A Counterhistory of rhetorical ecologies. *Rhetoric Society Quarterly, 51*(4), 336–352. https://doi.org/10.1080/02773945.2021.1947517.

Massey, Doreen. (2005). *For space.* Sage.

Melonçon, Lisa. (2017). Patient experience design: Expanding usability methodologies for healthcare. *Communication Design Quarterly, 5*(2), 19–28. https://doi.org/10.1145/3131201.3131203.

Melonçon, Lisa & Frost, Erin A. (2015). Charting an emerging field: The rhetorics of health and medicine and its importance in communication design. *Communication Design Quarterly, 3*(4), 7–14. https://doi.org/10.1145/2826972.2826973.

Melonçon, Lisa & St.Amant, Kirk. (2019). Empirical research in technical and professional communication: A five-year examination of research methods and a call for research sustainability. *Journal of Technical Writing and Communication, 49*(2), 128–155. https://doi.org/10.1177/0047281618764611.

Muckelbauer, John. (2008). *The future of invention: Rhetoric, postmodernism, and the problem of change.* SUNY Press.

Paré, Anthony. (2002). Keeping writing in its place: A participatory action approach to workplace communication. In Barbara Mirel & Rachel Spilka (Eds.), *Reshaping technical communication: New directions and challenges for the 21st century* (pp. 57–73). Lawrence Erlbaum Associates.

Pigg, Stacey. (2020). *Transient literacies in action: Composing with the mobile surround.* The WAC Clearinghouse; University Press of Colorado. https://doi.org/10.37514/WRI-B.2020.1015.

Rice, Jenny. (2012). The ecology of the question: Reading Austin's public housing debates, 1937–1938. In Sidney Dobrin (Ed.), *Ecology, writing theory, and new media: Writing ecology* (pp. 180–194). Routledge.

Richards, Daniel P. & Stephens, Sonia H. (2022). Do voices really make a difference? Investigating the value of local video narratives in risk perceptions and attitudes towards sea-level rise. *Technical Communication, 69*(4), 79–96. https://doi.org/10.55177/tc105639.

Rios, Gabriela. (2015). Cultivating land-based literacies and rhetorics. *Literacy in Composition Studies, 3*(1), 60–70. https://doi.org/10.21623/1.3.1.4.

Rivers, Nathaniel & Weber, Ryan P. (2011). Ecological, pedagogical, public rhetoric. *College Composition and Communication, 63*(2), 187–218. https://www.jstor.org/stable/23131582.

Rose, Emma J. (2016). Design as advocacy: Using a human-centered approach to investigate the needs of vulnerable populations. *Journal of Technical Writing and Communication, 46*(4), 427–445. https://doi.org/10.1177/0047281616653494.

Ross, Derek G., Oppegaard, Bea & Willerton, Russell. (2019). Principles of place: Developing a place-based ethic for discussing, debating, and anticipating technical communication concerns. *IEEE Transactions on Professional Communication, 62*(1), 4–26. https://doi.org/10.1109/TPC.2018.2867179.

Scott, J. Blake & Gouge, Catherine. (2019). Theory building in the rhetoric of health & medicine. In Andrea Aldren, Kendall Gerdes, Judy Holiday & Ryan Skinnell (Eds.), *Reinventing (with) theory in rhetoric and writing studies: Essays in honor of Sharon Crowley* (pp. 181–195). Utah State University Press.

Scott, J. Blake & Melonçon, Lisa. (2018). Manifesting methodologies for the rhetoric of health and medicine. In Lisa Melonçon & J. Blake Scott (Eds.), *Methodologies for the rhetoric of health and medicine* (pp. 1–23). Routledge.

Shome, Raka. (2003). Space matters: The power and practice of space. *Communication Theory, 13*(1), 39–56. https://doi.org/10.1111/j.1468-2885.2003.tb00281.x.

Spinuzzi, Clay. (2003). *Tracing genres through organizations: A sociocultural approach to information design (acting with technology)*. MIT Press.

St.Amant, Kirk. (2018). Reflexes, reactions, and usability: Examining how prototypes of place can enhance UXD practices. *Communication Design Quarterly*, *6*(1), 45–63. https://doi.org/10.1145/3230970.3230976.

Stormer, Nathan & McGreavy, Bridie. (2017). Thinking ecologically about rhetoric's ontology: Capacity, vulnerability, and resilience. *Philosophy & Rhetoric*, *50*(1), 1–25. https://doi.org/10.5325/philrhet.50.1.0001.

Suri, Siddharth, Counts, Scott & Bruch, Mia. (2022). Society. In Jamie Teevan, Nancy Bayum, Jenna Butler, Brent Hecht, Sonia Jaffe, Kate Nowak, Abigail Sellen & Longqi Yang. (Eds.), *Microsoft new future of work report 2022* (MSR-TR-2022-3). Microsoft. https://aka.ms/nfw2022.

Tuan, Yi-Fu. (1977). *Space and place: The perspective of experience*. University of Minnesota Press.

Willis, Rebecca. (2019). The use of composite narratives to present interview findings. *Qualitative Research*, *19*(4), 471–480. https://doi.org/10.1177/1468794118787711.

Wingard, Jennifer. (2013). *Branded bodies, rhetoric, and the neoliberal nation-state*. Lexington Books.

Yin, Robert. (2003). *Case study research: Design and methods* (3rd ed.). Sage.

3. Understanding 21st-Century Workplace Writing Communities: An Ethnomethodological Study of Phatic Communication in Large Corporations

Lance Cummings
UNIVERSITY OF NORTH CAROLINA WILMINGTON

Abstract

This chapter examines how phatic communication is used to build community in large multinational corporations (MNCs). Drawing on ethnomethodological research and interviews with employees at nCino, a global software company, the author shows how phatic communication helps writers build networks through goodwill to support and manage complex writing projects. As companies adopt more agile and distributed organizational models, employees must cultivate networks of relationships to work together effectively. This chapter explores how employees deploy interactive technologies like Slack, Jira, and whiteboards to build community for both work- and non-work-related purposes. The ability to build community through phatic communication is an important soft skill for the 21st-century workplace. This research provides insights into how we might prepare students to navigate the social complexities of modern work environments.

Keywords

phatic communication, ethnomethodology, multinational corporations (MNCs), agile organizational models, soft skills, networks

As companies continue to navigate the complex terrain of distributed workflows, writers and employees must work together to establish stronger networks of collaboration through phatic communication—the type of communication that builds connections through goodwill, identification, and playful fun. Drawing on examples from multinational corporations (MNCs), I will analyze how phatic discourse is used to create community and reshape workplace dynamics. We can use this understanding to build strong writing cultures in the classroom and prepare students for writing in these networked environments.

In the college classroom, students create a social environment mostly through in-class activities and learning management systems (LMSs) like Canvas that do not accurately represent the way that professionals collaborate in most workplaces today. By becoming familiar with distributed writing environments like Slack and Microsoft Teams, students will be better prepared to foster relationships in

DOI: https://doi.org/10.37514/TPC-B.2023.2128.2.03

the workplace by adapting to new and emerging collaborative tools. To prepare my own students, I take many classes on visits to actual workplaces and introduce them to the programs and software that they will likely be using after they graduate. This gives students opportunities to see how writers create culture and collaborate through writing in these distributed environments.

In fall 2019, students from my honors class Writing and the Art of Problem-Solving visited a multinational software company called nCino, headquartered in Wilmington, North Carolina. Our main goal was to explore different ways employees solved problems through writing, but we also discussed how institutional contexts influenced collaboration and the writing process. As I expected, many students were impressed by what they saw and how it contrasted with their imagined versions of corporate life. Yes, there were lots of cubicles. But there were also free beverages and snacks, a game room, ping pong tables, comfortable chairs, and even surfboards to borrow (see Figure 3.1).

These observations seemed irrelevant to the work nCino does with cloud banking—possibly even counterproductive. Several students discussed in class how skeptical they were of this ethos . . . was nCino trying too hard to have fun? But as we became acquainted with nCino and its employees, "having fun," one of nCino's six core values, appeared to be crucial to productivity. As shown in Figure 3.2, nCino's web page on workplace culture lists six items:

1. Bring Your A-game
2. Do the Right Thing
3. Respect Each Other
4. Make Someone's Day
5. Have Fun
6. Be a Winner (nCino, 2020).

Figure 3.1. Surfboards to borrow at nCino. Author's photo.

Figure 3.2. Six core values from nCino's web page on workplace culture. (nCino, 2020). Used with permission.

Only two of these can arguably be oriented towards productivity and achievement: "Bring your A-Game" and "Be a Winner." The rest of these are about how employees connect and treat each other, which plays out through all kinds of phatic discourse, but especially in environments like Slack.

nCino works hard to cultivate networked and multi-directional relationships — horizontally, vertically, and diagonally. For students functioning mostly in a hierarchical (and vertical) structure like a university, this seems strange and unfamiliar—suspect even. I imagine new employees may have similar reactions, though mixed with the anxiety of needing to fit into this new job and its communities. Without context, these values seem vague and meaningless. But for nCino employees, these slogans carry deep meaning because of the daily interactions they produce around these values. To fully understand these cultural values, one has to participate in their making. The leadership team may have come up with these phrases, but it is the workplace writers that build their meaning every day. Interviews with employees repeatedly reinforced these values, as many of them could recall them from memory and connect them to interactions in their community both online and in person.

Anyone outside the community may indeed be skeptical, especially when focusing on positive and successful examples. I will not be arguing that these workplace communities are flawless. Communities of goodwill and communication channels break down every day, which only underlines the importance of examining successful moments where students can see phatic discourse at work. While this workplace culture works well in one organization, it may not be applicable in others. These cultures are something that any workplace must actively cultivate and maintain within its own context. But by studying and analyzing successful examples, like nCino, we can learn how phatic discourse can be used to create communities of goodwill, not as a model to emulate, but as an example for reflection.

To understand how these communities work, we also must consider how the workplace has become more distributed, undergoing several hierarchical shifts to accommodate work that is fast-paced and constantly in flux, especially in multinational corporations (MNCs) and companies in the tech industry. These workplaces continue to deploy more horizontal project management systems like Agile, Scrum, and Kanban to stoke creativity and increase adaptability for handling timely and unexpected troubleshooting with software and equipment. A more collaborative atmosphere is essential for these businesses to succeed, requiring workplace writers to create and maintain a community of goodwill.

Scholars in technical and professional communication have tangentially explored these project management systems to prepare students for deeper forms of collaboration in the workplace (Pope-Ruark, 2014; Ranade & Swarts, 2019; Rooksby & Ikeya, 2102). Though understanding how these new collaborative processes and technologies influence the writing process and productivity is important, this shift also requires new kinds of communication around writing focused on creating and maintaining relationships—not necessarily on getting work done.

Many of these systems create deeper writing communities and networks that go beyond project management. They also require a new set of phatic communication skills for employees who work in these contexts. How writers create and maintain networks is crucial to our understanding of 21st-century workplace writing and how to prepare students for the human side of technical communication.

■ Phatic Communication in the Workplace

In "Professional Communication as Phatic: From Classical *Eunoia* to Personal Artificial Intelligence," James Porter (2017) re-orients professional communication theory around phatic functions that open channels of communication and cultivate ongoing relationships within collaborative networks (p. 174). Scholars in linguistics have spent the most time developing theories around phatic communication, mostly looking at conversational interactions that establish personal bonds instead of conveying actual meaning (Malinowski, 1923). Though definitions of communication vary greatly, we most often see the workplaces through a transmission lens first articulated by Claude Shannon and Warren Weaver (1948), based on their work at Bell Telephone Labs. The transmission model often overlooks phatic communication, de-emphasizing many seemingly unimportant communicative events, like "water cooler conversations." Any action that does not convey information is insignificant. According to Porter, though, phatic communication derives its purpose from *ethos* rather than *logos*. These types of interactions are required to "create goodwill, trust, cooperation, partnership, harmony" (Porter, 2017, p. 175). When looking at how people collaborate in the workplace, understanding these phatic forms of communication is key. Telephone metaphors no longer provide a complete picture of the communicative work writers are doing in networked environments.

The ability to deploy phatic discourse in the workplace is a "soft skill" that is not always highlighted in our writing research, but is necessary for understanding modern workplace writing, where work and writing is more distributed across networks. The U.S. Army first used the term *soft skills* to describe any skill not related to the use of mechanics or technology (Silber & Foshay, 2009). More recently, workplace managers define soft skills in terms of interpersonal and organizational skills that transcend specific roles or professions. Hard skills in writing refer to the use of specific software like Microsoft Office and Adobe Creative Cloud, usually focusing on a writer's ability to develop effective content for specific digital or print environments. For a workplace writer, soft skills refer to their ability to collaborate, manage complex projects, and solve complicated problems. Being able to develop and maintain networks of goodwill with other writers and stakeholders is an important soft skill in the MNC workplace, especially when the organization tends towards a more distributed workflow where projects and tasks are spread out more horizontally across networks. Charles Darah (1994), one of the first scholars to observe a more distributed organizational structure, describes this workplace as a "heterogeneous workplace held together by networks of assistance with expertise distributed throughout" (p. 80). We cannot assume that all workers require the same skills in the same way, but distributed expertise requires social skills and the ability to adapt to new organizational structures.

Navigating formal and informal forms of writing in the workplace has become a key soft skill in any workplace where genres or communication tools can be used across a spectrum of formality registers. For example, email was one of the first forms of writing to introduce more informal modes of writing to the workplace. Early research into email focused on the hybridity between written and oral discourse, and the potential for communication breakdown resulting from the lack of contextual cues. At the same time, the informal nature of email made room for innovation by allowing ideas to flow more easily in ways accessible to more people across hierarchies, gender, and race (Sims, 1996). Even in its earliest forms, email performed many of the phatic functions that messaging apps use today. For example, a 1996 study of two corporate contexts found that many writers would decorate their emails with images, emoticons, and unconventional spelling/punctuation (Sims, 1996). All these elements are seemingly irrelevant to the transmission of information or project development, but they play a key role as workplaces develop more flattened hierarchies that rely more deeply on collaboration.

In work environments that depend on distributed forms of writing, theories of phatic communication must be re-articulated as the focus of workplace writing (rather than just tertiary). Though Porter focuses on virtual teams, intercultural communication, and user help forums, all forms of phatic communication are important in MNC cultures that encourage flattened hierarchies and a more distributed work process. If we take a second look at nCino's cultural values page, we can line the values up with each critical element of ethos (Table 3.1), as described by Aristotle (as cited in Porter, 2017, p. 177).

Table 3.1. Elements of Ethos in nCino Values

Element of ethos	nCino values
Eunoia (goodwill)	Make someone's day; Respect each other
Phronesis (practical judgement)	Bring your A-game; Have fun
Arête (virtue)	Do the right thing; Be a winner

To encourage more efficient distributed workflows, MNCs work hard to develop an ethos-driven community that creates goodwill between employees and keeps channels of communication and collaboration open. For nCino, this means having game rooms, snacks, comfortable chairs, and good-humored fun—those elements that students find the most surprising when first visiting nCino. But to really understand how phatic communication works in specific communities of goodwill, researchers and students need to become a part of that network. Ethnomethodological approaches to research in the workplace can help both researchers and students explore these communities in authentic ways.

■ Methodological Contexts

To explore how writing in the workplace is changing under these networked conditions, I spent several years visiting MNCs in Wilmington, North Carolina and Kraków, Poland. This project emerged from my efforts to create more collaboration between professional writing students and employees in MNCs. Providing UNCW students with more cross-cultural experience (both remotely and as a study abroad) prepares them for writing in the global workplace, which is increasingly collaborative, digital, and cross-cultural. Some activities involved

- virtual visits from writers in Kraków, Poland;
- tours of nCino, a software company in Wilmington;
- student analysis of texts from MNCs;
- applied learning projects with MNC partners; and
- undergraduate research projects.

The main reason I chose nCino and Kraków, Poland, is because those are the communities I am already networked with through classroom collaborations, field trips, conferences, and study abroad trips, all of which allow students to experience community in new ways (Cummings, 2021).[1] Kraków in particular is

---

1. To learn more about the writing community in Kraków, Poland, see Marsh, 2017 and Johnson, 2017.

a special place to study workplace writing because many MNCs have developed European headquarters there due to the low cost of living in Poland, as well as the high-quality employees available there. In fact, *Soap!*, one of the most well-known conferences on content writing in Eastern Europe, is held in Kraków and is famous for its tight-knit community. This is how I first became interested in how writers in these environments build communities. This project was also interrupted by the COVID-19 pandemic in 2020 and relies mostly on eight Zoom interviews made during that time. That said, I will be drawing data from all these sources (each of which are covered by separate IRBs).[2]

Being a part of these communities of goodwill builds trust between the researcher and participants. In a typical interview, participants might be tempted to paint a positive picture of their company or skip over negative examples from their experience. But when they know and trust the researcher, they are more likely to share both the good and the bad. This is especially important when studying phatic communication, which often involves informal and personal elements that might not be immediately obvious to an outsider. That said, this project focused mostly on how employees successfully built company culture using the technology around them, so that students can observe successful practices not visible in the writing classroom. Being a part of these communities means participating in how the cultures, or social orders, are being built, thus making ethnomethodology ideal for identifying these moments of agency.

According to Barbara Schneider (2002), ethnomethodology assumes that "all social order is organized from within the social situation." In other words, the social structures that constrain writers are not imposed from the outside but emerge from the writing situation itself. Structure and agency are constitutive of each other, and writers are constrained by social structures while also participating in their creation or reproduction. Ethnomethodology, then, is a way to identify interactive points of agency available to writers in the workplace that might otherwise be hidden by a more all-encompassing understanding of social organization. Simply put, workplace writing is best understood as interaction that creates community and culture, not just communication. Of course, MNC values and mission statements establish shapes and boundaries, but ultimately, it is the workplace writer that makes those values and missions reality. For many in the field of technical communication, ethnomethodology has a practical bend (Rooksby & Ikeya, 2011). The goal is not to find hidden structures but to examine the interactions around writing and how people think about them, which enables both researchers and practitioners to improve technologies, methods, and processes.

The goal of an ethnomethodological study is to have writers identify and reflect on how they experience writing, often focusing on the interaction between

---

2. IRB# 20–0125 Exploring Phatic Communication in Multi-national Corporations, IRB# 19–0209 Global Communities of Writing: An Ethnographic Study of Tech Writing in Poland

structure or social context. Typically, ethnomethodology relies on two methods of analysis, either interviews where writers discuss the decision-making around writing or think-aloud protocols where writers speak their thoughts out loud during the writing process (Schneider, 2002). For example, an early ethnomethodological study by Stephen Doheny-Farina (1986) traces the development of a new mission statement at a nearby organization, mapping out the interaction around the document and how it influenced the shape of the growing company. At that time, most of this interaction happened in a board room. How this works today looks much different and requires us to adapt these methods to more networked and digital environments. Though this chapter does not focus on a single document, my goal is to explore how workplace communities understand the networked nature of their writing by specifically looking at the discourse that happens outside and around the more formal forms of writing. At first, these phatic forms of communication look incidental and irrelevant, but this chapter will argue that they are necessary for understanding how teams and members create the community and contexts around them.

Most of the interviews for this chapter focused on writers and content specialists at nCino because I had already met or worked with most of these interviewees. Though the methods I use cannot be considered true ethnography, as I did not spend extensive amounts of times in any single location, I am taking what's been called an ethnomethodological approach. But instead of understanding the ethnographic site as an office building, the research site is an extensively networked community of writers and communicators that cannot be contained by a single location. The nexus of research in workplace writing often revolves around the individual, when most writing—at least in MNCs—is highly collaborative and distributed. To truly understand workplace writing in the 21st century, we need to understand the workplace as a network, not just a physical location.

■ New Collaboration Models in the Workplace

Phatic forms of communication are embedded and shaped by new organizational models that have been developing for decades. Since the 1990s, scholars in technical communication have noted a shift in organizational structures that redefine writing in the workplace as a participatory and distributed activity that restructures power dynamics and how meaning is created (Slack et al., 1993). Globalization has created a faster form of capitalism requiring corporations to decenter power, flatten hierarchies, and create more fluid work processes (Henry, 2006). Workers must take more responsibility for the organizational discourse produced in corporate networks, adapting quickly and collaborating with effective communication around writing (Gee & Lankshear, 1996). In other words, many MNCs have found that giving employees ownership of their workflows not only increases productivity, but also quality. This requires both researchers and practitioners to look beyond a transmission model of communication, which focuses mostly on information, to see how knowledge and discourse is created through networked interaction. New technologies and services require constant and quick innovation, which happens best in these flattened, collaborative networks—at least, according to many of the project management philosophies now being deployed in MNC workplaces.

To leverage these new organizational models, successful companies in the software and technology fields have restructured their team organizations around *agile* project management principles that encourage a more human-centered response to systemic problems and constant change. Unlike our traditional understanding of text, documentation and products in software and technology are never finished, so MNCs need to account for the constant change and diverse user contexts that come along with growing technology. Agile approaches to project management focus less on a unidirectional workflow (often called "waterfall") and more on an iterative process that remains adaptable and flexible. It is better to draft a small section of a document, a small piece of code, or an interface sketch for immediate feedback, rather than drafting an entire text or product only to find out you are way off track.

Agile is one of the primary project management systems used to create more user-based designs through short, iterative cycles called sprints (Pope-Ruark, 2015). The four guiding principles can be found in the Agile Manifesto:

1. Individuals and interactions over processes and tools
2. Working software over comprehensive documentation
3. Customer collaboration over contract negotiation
4. Responding to change over following a plan (Agile Software Development, 2001)

Though the purpose of this chapter is not to delve into the details of agile project management, these guiding principles clearly show how the shift in workflow moves from product-oriented to process-oriented, requiring more networked forms of communication. The introduction of agile into these organizational structures has created a culture of innovation around the collaborative and distributive writing process that ultimately promotes community.

Take for example Jamf, an Apple-based software company created in 2002, with their European headquarters in Katowice, Poland. Certainly, there is a traditional corporate hierarchy with CEOs on top (Jamf, n.d.b). But if you look at the online profiles for the senior leadership team, you will see a "Fun Facts" section on each page. We know, for example, that Dean Hager, the CEO, grew up in a small farm town, has swum from Alcatraz to San Francisco and has been hit by a car twice (but still loves biking) (Jamf, n.d.a). Of course, none of these facts are useful in a strictly business sense, but they invite readers to see a more flattened hierarchy where CEOs share their "humanity." According to David at their Katowice, Poland headquarters, Jamf prides itself on building the company based on people, where teams are the "smallest unit of organization," giving each person a strong sense of ownership. This is what project management specialists call a "horizontal team culture" (see Figure 3.3).

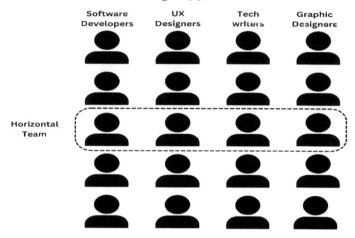

Figure 3.3. Agile team structures (Hawks, 2017).

Rather than managing a large team or department as seen in traditional organizational charts, each manager has people in different teams (or departments), allowing for more cross-functionality that encourages knowledge transfer (David at Jamf). Since most texts circulate extensively through these team networks, no single individual is to blame for a faulty text, and everyone celebrates success together. For example, at nCino, every team has a name and mascot, and they often celebrate together when successfully completing a project. But if something doesn't go right, they don't waste time blaming people; they discuss what went wrong and how they might fix it for next time. Working in these environments requires a good deal of critical thinking and reflection skills.

Though originating in the software industry, where documentation and code is constantly being written, other industries, including education, are adapting Agile and other forms of lateral project management for their own purposes. To understand how writing in the workplace has changed in MNCs, we need to contextualize communication within these more networked environments. Effective employees need to do more than communicate to their immediate supervisor or departmental team (vertically); employees need to communicate in all directions—horizontally, vertically, diagonally, etc. This is true even for employees not directly integrated in the Agile structures. Even in organizational contexts where Agile is not being explicitly deployed, understanding Agile helps us understand these new writing contexts as they develop in different ways across the workplace world. For these systems to work effectively, participants must become adept at creating and maintaining networks. Using forms of communication less focused around work becomes a key feature of workplace writing and helps create bonds that make these new project management systems work.

■ Phatic Use of Technology

Of course, phatic forms of communication are nothing new in the workplace. Several studies have already shown the importance of interaction when collaborating, especially in environments that require more innovation. For example, John Rooksby and Nozomi Ikeya (2012) note key interactions in conference rooms (especially around whiteboards) that contributed to successful sessions:

- paying attention to each other
- maintaining a shared focus
- sketching out ideas
- being open to each other's ideas
- seeking agreement and acknowledging disagreement
- maintaining a sense of humor

None of these interactions are strictly about conveying information; they are more about keeping communication channels open and promoting interaction between participants, because innovation and new ideas tend to emerge from these collaborative environments.

Often, this phatic work means leveraging tools and technology in new ways. In her study on more cross-cultural situations, Tiina Räisänen (2020) found that participants draw on the available means around them to create interaction, develop rapport, and get things done (pp. 170–176). Multimodal resources have become important tools to help participants create more interaction through active listening, back-channeling, and textual/visual brainstorming (Räisänen, 2020, p. 173). In other words, objects and technology around employees participate in the "production of action, social meaning, and subjectivity" of these writing communities (Räisänen, 2020, p.176). The ways employees use whiteboard technology illustrate how available technical means can both convey information and serve phatic purposes.

At nCino, nearly every whiteboard and even window becomes a potential space for interaction and collaboration. These are considered important spaces for sharing information, making new connections, and developing new ideas. But for most employees, they are ephemeral spaces that augment other more digital means for managing knowledge. Becka, a technical writer at nCino, admits that she avoids using whiteboards for project management. Important information can be accidentally erased, so she keeps or transfers important information into a digital project management system called Jira. From a technical writer perspective, it's important to have what is often called "a single source of truth," or a place where all the important technical knowledge can be accessed.

If you walk through the halls of nCino, though, you'll also see that whiteboards serve important phatic functions, unrelated to knowledge and information. Brianna, a senior knowledge platform manager, sees the whiteboard as an interactive space between her and a content specialist that shares her cubicle:

Whenever we want to talk through something or strategize, we go to the whiteboard. So, if you were to go into nCino, you would see that our whiteboard is completely covered because we are whiteboard people. I'm also a visual person. So, I like to draw things out. And she does too.

Whiteboards also serve as a space to build community. For example, when Brianna walks over to see a friend in another building, she'll often leave a little message on the friend's whiteboard. When there are new hires, employees will leave a welcome message on their whiteboard, along with stickers and other fun stuff. According to Brianna, sometimes employees even leave little jokes or pranks on each other's whiteboards. Chase, a graphic designer manager, says he's never seen a serious note on a whiteboard in his department. His team mostly uses them for fun. Many of these activities have moved into Miro, a digital whiteboard app used for brainstorming and organizing projects. In Figure 3.4, you can see how participants added fun memes alongside various brainstorming notes.

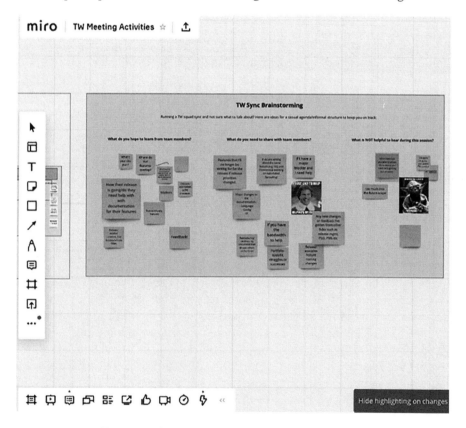

Figure 3.4. Digital whiteboard used for remote work.

During my interviews with employees at nCino, physical proximity played a key role in keeping channels of communication open and building community, even though much of that still happened in digital spaces. Since the 2020 COVID-19 pandemic began just as I started this project with nCino, most of my interviewees talked about how they felt the absence of their office space while working remotely. They missed the ability to "pop your head over the cubicle" to say hello or just chat. Even if you did not end up talking to any neighbors, there was some comfort in knowing that you could. Several participants also mentioned how "chat breaks" were important to their creative process. Occupying one's mind with something else often helped inspire new ideas. During the spring lockdown in 2020, they tried to simulate these kinds of interactions with Slack calls and video meetings, but these lose the kind of spontaneity and informal atmosphere that comes in the office. Because nCino is designed for collaboration with an open office layout, employees could just turn around and talk to someone about a question or issue, instead of having to schedule a time or bug them via email or chat. Becka noted that "there's definitely something to be said for communication that can happen without the need to have it scheduled and just have it flow whenever you feel the need for it." This kind of "flow" can only happen when strong collaborative networks are cultivated and maintained.

Scholars have already pointed out the difficulty of maintaining distributed work groups in online contexts. Building trust is essential for these networks to work (Vealey, 2016). We often ignore that working remotely or online can have negative consequences, for example, triggering feelings of isolation or even paranoia (Larbi & Springfield, 2004 Rice-Bailey, 2014). These are far from network-building attributes. Danielle, a senior marketing analyst, misses the opportunity to laugh or catch up in the mornings before getting down to work, but says that much of this has shifted to Slack, a popular enterprise social network (ESN) that workplaces use as a messaging app (like Facebook just for the workplace). Danielle mentioned that she would be worried that she is missing out on something if she were the only one working remotely. But since everyone is working remotely, she doesn't feel that way. That said, she thinks employees at nCino will be more considerate of remote counterparts once the pandemic is over. In a separate set of interviews, employees at Electrolux in Poland noted that they met international collaborators "face-to-face" for the first time as a result of the pandemic because they were forced to use video chat in Microsoft Teams.

Though this project did not start as a study of digital communication and collaboration during a pandemic, everyone across the world was forced into remote work situations just as I began the core elements to this study. I still do not consider this a study specifically focused on remote work during pandemics. That said, having a pandemic highlights many of the digital practices that MNCs are already using to create collaboration and community, as well as opportunities to reflect on and enhance these tools and strategies. Given the importance of nonverbal communication, adapting multimodal resources in digital spaces is key to effective collaboration, pandemic or not. The same can be said for phatic communication. What was done on whiteboards or across the cubicle walls must now be done digitally. The interactive elements that can be found in conference rooms can also be deployed in ESN environments (see Table 3.2).

Table 3.2. Transference of Phatic Elements to ESN

Interactive element	In person	In ESN
Paying attention to each other	Interjections, eye contact, not checking phones	Short acknowledgement, emoji
Maintaining a shared focus	Using whiteboards, sticky notes, etc., create group focus	Kanban boards, Jira, tickets
Sketching ideas	Sketching, drawing, creating flowcharts	Jira, screenshots, captured drawings
Being open to other's ideas	Asking questions, giving the floor, tentativeness	Slack messages and calls, soliciting questions on Blue Jeans, emojis (😊)
Seeking agreement	Talking directly about disagreement, finding common ground, considering company mission	Direct messages, asking questions
Maintaining a sense of humor	Making jokes, laughing at mistakes	Gyphs, emojis, created emojis

According to most interviews with nCino employees, physical interaction in social spaces was a key element in maintaining connections, but it was undergirded by several informal back-channels like Slack. During the COVID-19 pandemic, most interviewees discussed the challenge of maintaining these core interactions from a distance, and much of this shifted to Slack. These collaborative spaces have become key spaces for building, resisting, and changing company culture and community, while also getting work done.

■ Taking Responsibility for Workflows and Networks

The flattened hierarchies and virtual team structures that we find in MNCs like nCino give employees more responsibility and self-accountability. During the stay-at-home order in 2020, employees did not feel pressured to "be online" or "clocked-in" during certain times of the day or even for a particular amount of time. There was no sense of management looking over their shoulder making sure they were not wasting company time, because employees had accepted their share of responsibility. But employees must be even more intentional about creating those networked interactions that keep communication and collaboration going. Doing this in fun ways is a key motivator for cultivating these networks. Moriah Yancey describes this in her interview:

nCino is just a very open and fun place to work. They want you to have fun while you're working, and I've seen productivity that I've never seen before just by working in a place that values having fun and having the space to just . . . It doesn't have to be just beat, beat, beat, beat, beat. You know, no one's eyeing me at any one time when I come in or watching how long I take a lunch. There's a lot of accountability that you have to take with yourself. And people trust you irrevocably to just do your job, no matter what. No one is questioning you.

In short, nCino employees are responsible not just for the work they do, but also for creating and maintaining the relationships that improve the quality and efficiency of their work. During these interviews, it became clear that ESNs like Slack were key to deploying phatic forms of communication before the pandemic. With the loss of physical phatic channels, these ESNs have become the primary way employees keep communication channels open. Though employees did mention the importance of video meetings in Zoom or Blue Jeans, these were not necessarily the main tool for this kind of communication, because these needed to be scheduled ahead of time and tended to focus on business. nCino did try to emulate their Friday "cocktail hour" on video chat with mixed results.

When formally asked to describe methods of keeping communication channels open, the first thing most interviewees addressed was work-related communications. As one would expect, getting input about projects, working together on new ideas, and finding the knowledge needed to complete a task are key elements to collaborating online. In a vertical team structure, interaction is key to pulling information together and organizing that information for different purposes. This usually means that workplace writers are controlling the writing process and are responsible for making sure that the process is working smoothly. This sometimes means innovating the writing process, using tools in new ways, or simply making connections through the available means within these tools.

These innovations might be something as simple as developing a peer review system. For example, during the development phase of the tech writing department in Kraków branch of Motorola, the writers realized themselves that their writing would be more consistent and efficient if every piece of content was peer-reviewed a few times. They created a simple worksheet to track the peer-review process, which eventually led to the adoption of a more complicated content management system (see Figures 3.5 and 3.6).

Taking ownership of the writing process can range from simple additions like this to more complicated technological solutions. For example, in several interviews, Pawel Kowaluk discusses how he made his work less tedious at Guidewire by creating coding scripts that helped him reuse content across delivery systems.

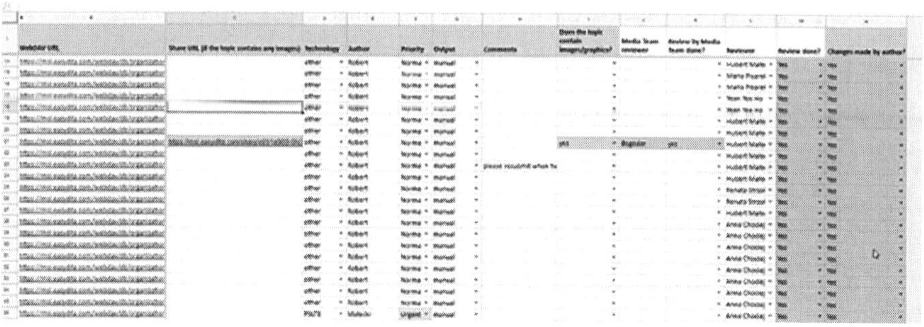

Figure 3.5. Peer review worksheets.

Taking ownership of the writing process also means keeping lines of communication open and creating goodwill. For example, a more specialized collaboration software called Jira is an important space at nCino where tasks can be shared, commented on, and tracked. As with many collaborative tools today, the key affordance of Jira is the ability to network across departments and teams around specific projects. Under vertical team structures, projects may or may not be owned by a single team, but even though responsibility lies with one team, the resources and knowledge certainly are not contained therein. Moriah talks about how she needs to have subject knowledge experts comment on drafts of articles she is working on, and Jira allows her to solicit and track those comments. Additionally, this process helps these experts see what other people have written, so that no one is "doubling-back." She's even seen conversations with themselves in the ticket:

> Oh, she forgot to add this. Oh, she probably didn't have the information about that. Oh, I don't think we ever talked about this beyond a small group. So let's put all the information here or tag her to the ticket that it's on.

She also mentioned that sometimes they'll even answer questions that previous people left.

Before the pandemic, collaborative spaces like Jira enhanced face-to-face sessions by allowing the same kind of whiteboard interactions in digital spaces. Since the move to universal work at home, most of this interaction has shifted to these spaces. Teams can use these tools to maintain focus, pay attention to each other, explore ideas, and seek agreement on projects. Though these can be done on video conferences, those are much more difficult to organize than random meetings in the office. Other ways of cultivating relationships through fun and interactivity happen a lot more in Slack.

■ Understanding Phatic Communication through Emojis

Invariably, when asked if they ever saw off-topic conversations in these spaces or fun interactions, interviewees would excitedly talk about emojis and different

Slack channels that are just for fun. Though there are certainly work-focused channels at every level, nCino has hundreds of extra channels not related to work, ranging from cat lovers to pandemic baking. In professional writing, emojis have a reputation for being trite or unprofessional, but in these MNCs, emojis are thriving. Several of the interviewees mentioned an initial reluctance to use emojis, seeing them as "cutsie" or useless. But workplace writers soon find out that emojis make phatic forms of communication easier, as described by Becka:

> It saves a ton of messages that are just like, "Great,""Sounds good," "Thank you,""No problem." Like that sort of little polite response that will give people whenever someone's agreed to do a task for someone else. So you can just like respond to a message with like thumbs up or like smiley face.

To be an effective writer in today's workplace, you have to know not only how to use emojis, but how to read them. At nCino, you even need to know how to create new emojis.

Of course, this means adding inflection to short messages that might be misinterpreted. Each interviewee could give an example of miscommunication on Slack. For example, Becka recounts a time when a fellow employee sent a message in a very public Slack channel, explaining how another employee had done a spreadsheet wrong. According to Becka, he's never been a rude person, but the message came across mean and ungrateful … and he didn't use any emojis. Not only did this message endanger open channels of communication, it also stained his ethos, especially for people who had never met him. Learning to interact in these spaces is now key to the success of new workplace writers. Brianna remembered a time early on in her career when she tried to be super formal on Slack, adding to her message something like "at your nearest convenience." This came across as "sassy" or "snarky." She has since learned the range of formality differences that occur between communications like email and Slack messages. A phrase like "at your nearest convenience," can easily be replaced by an emoji that will be taken less personally.

Becka uses smiley faces a lot to fill in gaps left by the lack of facial expressions in physical communication. She even has several smiley faces that communicate different levels of happiness.

> But I think that adding emojis cannot replace what was gone, but to a certain degree, help communicate a little bit of what's missing. So if you're saying something that someone could interpret as harsh and then you just add a smiley face. … I definitely use a ton of smiley faces when I'm asking people to do things for me. And I think it comes off a little bit friendlier and at least in my opinion, reminds everyone that we are actually on the same team. We're all trying to create a good product. I'm just trying to do my job. You're just trying to do yours. I'm not mad at you. I just want you to do this for me.

Emoji Scale of Happiness

(sad panda): feeling sorry for you or myself

(double facepalm): blatant annoyance

(grimacing): gritting my teeth through something I don't want to do, but it's not worth complaining about because it's my job

(upside down face): annoyed about something, but I'm pretending like everything is fine

(potato smile): express bonding through sarcasm or irony, sometimes over something annoying

(slightly smiling): add warmth to a request to communicate teamwork or friendship and reduce the chance of misinterpretation

(relaxed): humbly accepting a compliment (signified by blushing)

(grin): general happiness or excitement

(party blob): both happy and proud, usually of a completed task

(joy): laughter, reaction to something funny

(tada): congratulations (edited)

Figure 3.6. Emoji scale of happiness.

In Figure 3.6, Becka laid out her most-used "happiness" emojis, set up as a range from less happy to the most happy. Some of these are standard emojis, some are Slack-only emojis, and some were created by her or another employee. Each of these is a slight gradation that she has found useful in keeping people apprised of her status, while also bringing some humor to the situation.

In her work as a knowledge platform manager, Brianna uses spaces like Slack to "invest back" in the authors that contribute to her knowledge base. To coach authors who may not be professional writers, she likes to add emojis to her comments that soften any criticism or encourage the writer to revise or write more articles. For example, Jira allows emojis and Moriah noted that emojis were a great way to add inflections to comments. Oftentimes employees that know Moriah well will leave a joke. Figure 3.7 shows where a fellow tech writer left "BABAYYYYYYYYYY!" in the notes section, referencing a catchphrase they often use together. Whenever they see each other, she always says, "What it do ba-bee" as a reference to a popular video of a basketball player, Kawhi Leonard, who said that statement shortly after winning the 2018 NBA championship.

Documentation Notes for Tech Writer:	SOME NEW CUSTOM LABELS BABAYYYYYYYYYY!!!!!!!!
TW Ticket Work Needed:	Yes
HTC/HTU Docs Update Required?:	Yes

Figure 3.7. Notes section in Jira.

Emojis are key to creating a team culture at nCino. In Slack, employees can make new emojis, which has become a key element of phatic communication. For example, Moriah is a member of the Potato PotĀto team, which has created a range of potato-themed emojis. Team members have also created posters and shirts. Moriah even dressed up like a potato at one point to celebrate the end of a sprint (a small two- to four-week project; see Figure 3.8). The color-coded potatoes are used to represent work status. For example, the red potato means that you are "blocked" and in need of assistance. The heart potatoes are used to convey caring, thanks, or general affection. The gold and silver potatoes express the quality of a product or functionality.

Figure 3.8. Potato post.

Figure 3.9. Potato emojis.

The name of the team itself references previous teams that were named potato (but each with different pronunciations). In many of these cases, these phatic forms of communication are created by previous interactions. To understand and navigate these networks, you need to be participating. The cultural value "Having Fun" can mean many things, but these employees are clearly building that discourse from the inside out.

■ Phatic Communication within Hierarchy

Though phatic communication is key for lateral and team collaboration, it also serves an important role within the hierarchical structure of MNCs. Flattened hierarchy doesn't mean an absence of hierarchy—it means that channels of communication are open between all employees, not just through the "chain of command." Having these multiple-branched networks in place is key to creating an environment where all employees feel comfortable working with management to solve problems and get work done.

For example, Becka described many meetings where communication was definitely unidirectional (most of which were big video conferences). "All hands" meetings usually involve 100 or more people, and asking questions would "disturb everyone's day." Questions are definitely encouraged on other platforms, especially with managers, but only because they have kept these channels open:

> So, we've already built a relationship of trust, and she reaches out frequently during stressful times and asks me if I'm doing okay or if I need more support. Is there anything she can do for me? I already know that I will be supported by her so it makes it easier to ask tough things.

For managers, this means deliberately asking for questions or even phrasing the questions in specific ways, according to Becka. Usually, her manager will send her a message via Slack, for example: "Hey, I know that release time is really intense. Here are some things that you should be doing. If you have any questions, please reach out to us. We're here to help you." Such messages convey very little information, but keep communication channels open, while also developing an ethos of goodwill. When working in the office, Becka feels comfortable just coming by her manager's desk to talk about whatever needs she has. During the pandemic, this has been replaced by "Slack calls" or video chats.

Danielle mentions that she feels like she can be the most direct with her manager because they already have a strong relationship. Being direct about criticism, problems, or ideas is a key interactive element that helps participants find points of agreement and common ground. This process is much more efficient and clearer than having to constantly "sandwich" criticism with what Danielle calls "niceties" that she is more likely to use with people outside her immediate team. But the ability to be direct is supported by the hard work of building and maintaining the relationship between her and the manager.

> Many times, people in the professional setting feel like gossip is negative when I'm talking about how I'm frustrated with some other person or I'm talking about something that somebody said, and whether it's humorous to me or offensive. Either way, you want to go with it. People think of that as breaking down the morale, but if I didn't have that relationship with my manager and I wasn't able to have those kinds of conversations with him, where we're honest and just have a little bit more fun with it, we wouldn't be as good at our job.

Because they understand their shared goals and have spent time talking about unrelated topics, the tough aspects of collaboration become more manageable. Skilled use of phatic communication is key to creating this kind of openness.

How managers strategically deploy phatic communication was noticeable in the two interviews with managers. When asked about how they might talk about personal topics in work channels, they had less to share, even though they do discourage this kind of openness. Katie, manager of knowledge and technical writing, made it clear that she didn't want to force employees to be open or to have fun, if they aren't interested:

> I would never want someone on my team to feel like they have to share something personal or difficult or even super-exciting or great going on outside of work. We don't have to be a place that combines work, family, and personal life . . . or where we need to bring our full self to work no matter what, even if it doesn't feel comfortable. That's not what I'm saying. But we do try to have an atmosphere where it is safe to be yourself at work and to share experiences so that your team can celebrate those good things with you and help you with the more difficult things.

When talking about having fun with employees, Katie described an intentional effort to keep the fun contained in particular spaces, for example, at social gatherings put together by nCino (like volleyball tournaments and cocktail hours) or specific Slack channels meant for fun. How she participates with other employees on Slack is related directly to how those relationships have been cultivated in the past:

> As a manager, I want to make sure that I'm having fun and showing my personality, but also I'm not necessarily going to be the first person flooding a channel with funny GIFs or something like that. When I'm talking to people, fellow managers or people that I'm really close to, I've tried to show my sense of humor and be myself. But also, I'm not necessarily going to participate in the same way as other tech writers.

Katie definitely participates in the fun but keeps it mostly in dedicated Slack channels. For example, she created a Slack channel for baking at home during the pandemic stay-at-home order. Like many of the other interviewees, she also cultivates deeper relationships in non-work spaces, like Instagram. Most of her personal connections on Instagram existed before she became a manager. Though she gladly connects to employees in these spaces, she avoids sending her own connection requests, so as not to think this kind of connection is a required part of their job.

The layering of networked relationships was true of all the nCino employees that I interviewed, but often strategically so. For example, one Black participant uses a group chat for building relationships with other Black workers. Her work team also has a Snapchat. Both of these are outside the nCino communications network. Though most of these interactions are personal, venting does occur in these spaces, and being off network offers an "extra layer" of security. But phatic communication functions differently in each of these spaces. For example, to be an active participant in the team Snapchat, participants need to be up-to-date on pop culture and slang. Making jokes is key to these interactions. But in the Black group chat, the topics focus around experiences of race and being a professional. Topics are usually much more serious, like the process of getting a mortgage. Though each network requires cultivation, participants need to have a deep rhetorical awareness about what kinds of interactions will keep that network growing.

In the end, writing in the workplace is complicated—technologically, linguistically, and rhetorically. Writers need to navigate multiple levels of interaction and formality and carefully balance an ethos that shows personality, but also keeps things professional and respectful. Most of all, to keep these networks productive, writers need to develop a habit and discipline of cultivating these networks daily. Sometimes this means having fun, sometimes it means checking in, and sometimes it just means letting people know that you are present.

■ Conclusion

The scope of this particular chapter is limited to a few people in a specific MNC, but we need to continue researching how these networks are intertwined within other networks. nCino doesn't just have networks in Wilmington; they also have them in Canada, London, Australia, and Japan. Most of the employees I interviewed work with nCino employees in these areas on a regular basis. Because of their proximity, most of my data has been drawn from a more recent project involving nCino. They have also hired several of our English majors, making it easier to participate in their networks. But much of my experience is contextualized by my collaborations with companies like Motorola Solutions and Jamf in Kraków, Poland (some of which I've used in this chapter). Most of what I've observed at nCino and in my conversations with nCino employees I have also observed more informally in these Polish contexts to varying degrees. Though certainly influenced by local cultures, these workplace cultures still play a dominant role in shaping communication and collaboration across these networks, an element of this study worth further research.

If we think back to my students' visit to nCino and their hesitancy to accept nCino's ethos of fun, it is easy to see now how this might be. Naming conference rooms after locations in Wilmington, having surfboards in the corner, or creating an nCino emoji may seem trite. But that is because we have not been participating in those networks. The interaction between employees is ultimately what brings meaning to these phatic forms of communication. To most nCino employees, it no longer makes sense to separate "having fun" and "bringing your A-game":

> That's why I feel like that interplay with "bring your A-game" and "have a good time" is necessary. One would be unintelligible without the other. (Danielle)

Because of how MNCs are flattening their organizational structures, all employees are participating in the creation of company culture … and they are having fun doing it. For example, there are many variations of "Barry," an employee-created emoji that makes its rounds around the company (see Figure 3.10). Take your work seriously … but not too seriously.

Figure 3.10. Barry logo emoji.

Though further research is required, the organizations that will best survive the pandemic aftermath will likely be those with networks of interaction in place. If employees are actively cultivating relationships and channels of communication, then the shift in circumstances simply means a shift in available means. In the end, most of the employees that I talked to felt that nCino as a company (and themselves as individuals) had successfully shifted their complex collaboration into digital spaces. No, it was not the same, and they missed many of the office elements that enable in-person networking, but they were still "bringing their A-Game":

> We are doing the same types of things just in a totally different format. So, we really haven't lost any of our meetings or our structure or connection to each other. It's just been changed into this sort of two-dimensional structure.

A workplace writer has to know how to use writing to keep channels of communication open and how to use these spaces to have fun and grow relationships. But these workplace writers must also have the ability to be flexible as circumstances and technologies change, managing multiple networks simultaneously, often with different levels of closeness or intimacy. As we've all learned so far in this century, circumstances can change drastically. The available means we have to get work done can also change fast. Phatic forms of communication are key to enabling the flexibility to adapt to these changes together.

■ References

Agile Software Development. (2001). *Manifesto for agile software development.* https://agilemanifesto.org/.

Cummings, Lance. (2021). Internationalizing professional writing programs through online study abroad and open networks. *Computers and Composition, 60,* 12640. https://doi.org/10.1016/j.compcom.2021.102640.

Darrah, Charles. (1994). Skill requirements at work: Rhetors versus reality. *Work and Occupations, 21*(1), 64–84. https://doi.org/10.1177/0730888494021001003.

Doheny-Farina, Stephen. (1986). Writing in an emerging organization. *Written Communication, 3*(2), 158–185. https://doi.org/10.1177/0741088386003002002.

Gee, James P., Hull, Glynda & Lankshear, Colin. (1996). *The new work order: Behind the language of the new capitalism.* Westview Press.

Hawks, David. (2017, December 13). Agile team structure. *Agile Velocity.* https://agilevelocity.com/agile-team-structure/.

Henry, Jim. (2006). Writing workplace cultures—Technically speaking. In J. Blake Scott, Bernadette Longo & Katherine V. Wills (Eds.), *Critical power tools: Technical communication and cultural studies* (pp. 199–218). SUNY Press.

Jamf. (n.d.a). *Dean Hager.* Retrieved November 14, 2023, from https://www.jamf.com/about/leadership/dean-hager/.

Jamf. (n.d.b). *Leadership.* Retrieved November 14, 2023, from https://www.jamf.com/about/leadership/.

Johnson, Tom. (2017, October 31). The untold story of Techwriter.pl: A Polish website about technical communication for technical writers, trainers, and translators. *I'd rather be writing.* https://idratherbewriting.com/2017/10/31/untold-story-of -techwriter-pl-poland/.

Larbi, Nancy E. & Springfield, Susan. (2004). When no one's home: Being a writer on remote project teams. *Technical Communication, 51*(1), 102–108.

Malinowski, Bronisław. (1923). The problem of meaning in primitive languages. In C. K. Ogden & I. A. Richards (Eds.), *The meaning of meaning: A study of the influence of language upon thought and of the science of symbolism* (pp. 296–336.) Harcourt Brace Jovanovich.

Marsh, Ed. (Host). (2017, June 27). Be like Thomas Pynchon with Pawel Kowaluk (No. 16) [Audio podcast episode]. In *Content content.* http://edmarsh.com/2017/06/27 /like-thomas-pynchon-pawel-kowaluk-content-content-episode-16/.

nCino. (n.d.). *Culture and careers.* Retrieved November 14, 2023, from https://www .ncino.com/culture-careers/.

Pope-Ruark, Rebecca. (2014). Introducing Agile project management strategies in technical and professional communication. *Journal of Business and Technical Communication, 29*(1), 112–133. https://doi.org/10.1177/1050651914548456.

Porter, James. E. (2017). Professional communication as phatic: From classical *eunoia* to personal artificial intelligence. *Business and Professional Communication Quarterly, 80*(2), 174–193. https://doi.org/10.1177/2329490616671708.

Räisänen, Tiina. (2020). The use of multimodal resources by technical managers and their peers in meetings using English as the business lingua franca. *IEEE Transactions on Professional Communication, 63*(2), 172–187. https://doi.org/10.1109/TPC .2020.2988759.

Ranade, Nupoor & Swarts, Jason. (2019). Humanistic communication in information centric workplaces. *Communication Design Quarterly, 7*(4), 17–31. https://doi.org /10.1145/3363790.3363792.

Rice-Bailey, Tammy. (2014). Remote technical communicators: Accessing audiences and working on project teams. *Technical Communication, 61*(2), 95–109.

Rooksby, John & Ikeya, Nozomi. (2011). Collaboration in formative design: Working together at a whiteboard. *IEEE Software, 29*(1), 56–60. https://doi.org/10.1109/MS.2011.123.

Schneider, Barbara. (2002). Theorizing structure and agency in workplace writing: An ethnomethodological approach. *Journal of Business and Technical Communication, 16*(2), 170–195. https://doi.org/10.1177/1050651902016002002.

Shannon, Claude E. & Weaver, Warren. (1948). *The mathematical theory of communication.* University of Illinois Press.

Silber, Kenneth H. & Foshay, Wellesley, R. (2009). *Handbook of improving performance in the workplace, instructional design and training delivery.* John Wiley & Sons.

Sims, Brenda R. (1996). Electronic mail in two corporate workplaces. In Mark Warshauer (Ed.), *Electronic literacies in the workplace,* NCTE, 41–64.

Slack, Jennifer D., Miller, David J. & Doak, Jeffery. (1993). The technical communicator as author: Meaning, power, authority. *Journal of Business and Technical Communication, 7*(1), 12–36. https://doi.org/10.1177/1050651993007001002.

Vealey, Kyle P. (2016). The shape of problems to come: Troubleshooting visibility problems in remote technical communication. *Journal of Technical Writing and Communication, 46*(3), 284–310. https://doi.org/10.1177/0047281616639478.

4. Freelancers as a Growing Workplace Norm: Demonstrating Expertise in Unfamiliar Communities of Practice

Brian Fitzpatrick
GEORGE MASON UNIVERSITY

Jessica McCaughey
GEORGE WASHINGTON UNIVERSITY

Abstract

In light of the increase in freelance, contract, and gig economy labor, due in part to the COVID-19 pandemic as well as other societal and economic shifts, the state of the traditional workplace has shifted. So too have the ways in which project teams work together in this new environment. This chapter, using Jean Lave and Étienne Wenger's (1991) concept of communities of practice, seeks to identify and explain the unique challenges that organizations and freelance/gig workplace writers face when it comes to onboarding, communication, and enculturation (Wardle, 2004). The chapter also pulls from interviews from the authors' Archive of Workplace Writing Experiences project, examining two successful professional freelance writers—a commercial director and an illustrator—to consider the ways in which these professionals navigate the difficulties of constantly changing employers and collaborators, each with their own unique communication styles, work cultures, and expectations. In the absence of the stability of a traditional and more permanent work environment (and the community of practice which might accompany it), these freelance workers rely on high levels of skill transferability, flexibility, and multiple complex literacies in their communication and writing, often taking experiences from each gig and applying them expertly to the next. Ultimately, this chapter considers how transfer studies and rhetorical adaptability might aid both organizations and gig workers in smoother and more successful future collaborations as the freelance and gig economies continue to grow.

Keywords

gig economy, freelancers, workplace writing, transfer studies, communities of practice, COVID-19

From social changes and advancements in technology to the pandemic, the past several years have seen long-standing structures and standards of "workplace" shift dramatically. Specifically, in terms of how we work together, project teams have become much more common than they used to be, and team members are much more likely to be spread out geographically (U.S. General Services Administration, 2009), communicating both synchronously and asynchronously (Li et al., 2009, p. 3). According to Clay Spinuzzi (2015), in his book *All Edge: Inside the New Workplace Networks*, we see this "projectification" (p. 32) proliferate across industries, with project teams meeting, joining, and then disbanding when projects end. With this shift, organizations become less traditionally organized and more of what he refers to as "adhocracies," which "represent a structural shift in organizations, and society in general, from hierarchies to networks" (Spinuzzi, 2015, p. 16). This "different kind of workplace" (Spinuzzi, 2015, p. 16) is "increasingly viable and common," but still emerging and taking form, which means that we are not only struggling to see, understand, and support it (Spinuzzi, 2015, p. 15), but also to understand the ways in which these adhocracies complicate workplace writing practices. Because of these short-term and transitory collaborations, organizations are unable to reap the benefits of longer, more stable communities of practice (CoPs) and the learning and writing knowledge that come from them. Further, the move towards work-from-home during the COVID-19 pandemic has exacerbated this timeline and further strained and complicated already rapidly changing structures of communication. As Jennifer Bay and Patricia Sullivan (2021) predict, more blurring of the personal and professional in home spaces, workers and organizations find themselves forced to reconcile the challenges of professionals navigating workplace communication in real time.

With these shifts, we see workers far less tied to physical structures and employers more willing to hire remote and temporary workers regardless of geography, especially due to the pandemic-induced instability so many organizations face. This significant growth of freelance labor—temporary workers moving in and out, communicating with all levels of the organization—changes how we see traditional employee-employer relationships, as well as the writing that happens within them. In 2019, 35 percent of working adults freelanced in some capacity. This percentage, which increased each of the past five years, is expected to continue to grow (Freelancing in America, 2019). And according to one recent survey, COVID-19-related job loss during the pandemic has caused two million Americans to make the shift to freelance work (Berliner, 2020). Freelancing incomes make up nearly one trillion dollars, or nearly five percent of the total U.S. GDP (Freelancing in America, 2019). As a point of comparison, this is a higher percentage of the GDP than comes from the construction industry. Many of these temporary workers are operating in lower-skill "gig economy" situations—driving car-sharing services, delivering food through services like Uber Eats, or perhaps putting together furniture though a contracting service such as TaskRabbit. But many more are performing what is usually defined as "skilled" services (Freelancing in America, 2019). Such skilled work might include graphic design, business consulting, or technical consulting. And as one might expect, most workplace communication, particularly for freelancers, takes place through written texts (Corbel, Newman & Farrell, 2022). While temporary employees like the ones we consider here might not traditionally be thought of as technical or professional communicators, in fact we see them as such, particularly in the context of freelance work, where consultants often take on everything from proposals and bidding to technical requirements. Further, it is important to note that it's not only that freelancers make up a significant percentage of the modern workforce; freelance work itself touches nearly everyone in the working world in one way or another. Whether a full-time, traditional employee is in direct contact with a freelancer on a daily basis or not, their work is almost assuredly impacted by such independent workers. The communication and labor that these freelance workers engage in influences significant portions of modern labor more broadly.

The two industries with the largest percentages of freelance workers are art/ design and entertainment (A Report Named Freelancers Union and Upwork, 2019). Here, we present two case studies of highly skilled, full-time freelancers from these industries. First, we explore the work and experiences of an illustrator. She is a self-taught artist who made the shift to freelance work in the past five years. She sells her artwork, collaborates with larger brands, and has published several illustrated books, including a guided self-help journal. The second case study focuses on a television commercial director. He studied creative writing and now works as a freelance writer and director of documentaries, short films, and television commercials, including several high-profile national campaigns. These interviews have been drawn from a larger pool of interviews with workplace writers across industries in the United States and Canada in a project titled The Archive of Workplace Writing Experiences. These interviews, collected and available for use as classroom resources online (www.workplace-writing.org), explore the writing, learning, and related experiences of these professionals. Like most of the working world today, the interviewees—and particularly these freelancers—rely on writing to do much of their work, even though their work products may not primarily be written texts.

Interestingly, both the illustrator and the commercial director estimate that writing makes up approximately 70 percent of their time. For the illustrator, such writing is primarily pitches, proposals, and contracts (she notes that she spends much additional time conducting research, and that she spends "maybe ten percent of my time . . . actually making work"). The director's writing is largely emailing, but also creating pitch decks ("where we show our ideas in as beautiful and comprehensible a way as possible, with images and words"), offering and responding to notes on various projects, and script-writing. Our research questions center around what differentiates the writing and communication of these workers from the communication practices of professionals in more traditional full-time employment situations, as well as how these freelance workers navigate the changing contexts of "workplace" and "workplace writing." These case study interviews explore these concepts, as well as issues of authenticity in writing across client organizations via personal voice and branding, and the ways in which these freelancers perceive their own development and authority as written workplace communicators.

The number of highly skilled freelance workers continues to grow, yet very little scholarship exists about their communication practices. In this chapter, we examine the writing demands placed on these freelance workers looking to thrive in a new economy. In doing so, we consider a lens initially developed to better understand more traditional workplaces: Jean Lave and Ètienne Wenger's (1991) community of practice. Briefly defined, "Communities of practice are groups of people who share a concern or a passion for something they do and learn how to do it better as they interact regularly" (Wenger, 2011). Organizations and teams in this way develop a set of shared practices, and in this chapter, we explore the ways in which freelancers are or are not enculturated into such communities of practice. At its core, the study and application of communities of practice can demonstrate for us the ways in which such groups, or organizational teams in workplace settings, develop and reproduce, particularly through the roles of the newcomer and the seasoned professional. This, of course, changes when freelancers are involved—and we see now that they're nearly always, in some ways, involved.

Others have critiqued communities of practice, and some even in the context of similar adhocracy-like working contexts. For instance, Lave and Wenger originally conceived of CoPs being in the same location, but this is no longer the case, of course. Many communities of practice are spread out over substantial geographic distance, which surely changes the ways in which communication practices develop and are learned (Li et al., 2009, p. 3). Relatedly, in examining groups and project teams similar to the adhocracies Spinuzzi addresses, Lars Lindkvist (2005) offers a variation on Lave and Wenger's term: "*collectivities* of practice." She writes about "temporary organizations or project groups within firms consist[ing] of people, most of whom have not met before, who have to engage in swift socialization and carry out a pre-specified task within set limits as to time and costs" and the ways in which such a situation makes it extremely difficult to "establish shared understandings or a common knowledge base" (Lindkvist, 2005, p. 1190). Her term, *collectivities of practice*, might also rightly include freelancers.

Further, research that does exist about freelance workers mostly centers around the gig economy, or the seemingly less-skilled workers we mention above. One interesting study in this area also looks at—and also critiques—Lave and Wenger. Irena Grugulis and Dimitrinka Stoyanova (2011) examine this idea of community of practice as it relates to freelancers in their ethnographic research, conducted at a TV production company that, like many other similar organizations, relies heavily on freelancers. Their findings showed that the freelancers in this field were typically at the top of the knowledge hierarchy, whereas the newcomers to the industry were typically full-time employees. The authors describe a "missing middle," meaning that "experienced workers who would normally be central to skills development are simply not available to consult or observe, since they are employed on freelance contracts" (Grugulis & Stoyanova, 2011, p. 342). They point to an omission in Lave and Wenger's definition of organizations as coherent; and we see, too, that this is simply no longer the case in most organizations.

Still, it would be rash to say that traditional workplaces, and therefore CoPs, don't still exist. Rather, it's clear in our research that freelancers are often on the outside of such communities as they perform their work, communicating to and with such groups from this outside space. In the context of freelance workplace writers, a community of practice framework allows us to see these temporary workers as they work to demonstrate expertise across tasks, organizations, and industries. We've made this choice first in an effort to situate and understand freelance workers within contemporary labor, and to examine the ways in which this concept of a community of practice itself changes drastically when we explore the growing workplace writing context of the freelancer. We ultimately demonstrate that this framework is no longer ideal in its current form for understanding how communication practices allow for new versions of communities.

Client Sites as Communities of Practice, Freelancers as the Un-enculturated Outsider

It's well established that workplaces are legitimate learning environments (Billett, 2004; Coetzer, 2007; Engeström, 2001; P. Moore, 2006). Lave and Wenger's (1991) community of practice model has traditionally been a useful framework for examining communication practices within such learning environments. Although Lave and Wenger's (1991) community of practice comes from psychology, many writing studies and professional writing scholars have understandably grabbed hold of it for the affordances it provides in understanding how writers, specifically, learn and develop, not only in workplace CoPs, but also in classrooms and other communities (Henry, 2013; Luzón, 2017; Spinuzzi, 2015). Within these communities of practice, Lave and Wenger identify the concept of "situated learning," or the ways in which practitioners come to understand common practices and conventions over time by observing and participating in shared work with their colleagues (Wenger, 2008). Situated learning allows us to understand the ways in which communication becomes ingrained within groups and requires a period of learning for newcomers. For instance, new junior engineers joining an organization, and therefore a community of practice, will generally have the opportunity to not only be mentored by and observe more senior practitioners, but will also have access to successful documents from past projects, allowing them to gradually integrate from "neophyte" to full participant (Wardle, 2004). In this model, "practice is an ongoing, social, interactional process" in which traditional organizational communities "reproduce their membership in the same way that they come about in the first place. They share their competence with new generations through a version of the same process by which they develop" (Wenger, 2008). It's widely accepted that traditional employees, long-term and—in the past at least—usually on-site, come to understand that there are communication practices specific to their team or department, as well as their larger organization. Over time, they usually learn to successfully participate in them.

Wenger writes that "special measures" are taken with these newcomers or neophytes (Wardle, 2004); during this period, a newcomer experiences what Lave and Wenger (1991) refer to as "legitimate peripheral participation," or a kind of apprenticeship (p. 29). They theorize legitimate peripheral participation as a way for neophytes to come to understand and participate more fully in new communities of practice slowly and with guidance. It is the goal of the employer, viewing their new traditional hire as an investment for the organization, to move the neophyte "inward" from the periphery (Wenger, 2010, p. 132), and eventually fully into the community of practice. These peripheral tasks not only help to introduce the new hire to the skills and necessary expertise of the position, but also allow them to understand, slowly and with smaller stakes, the practices of the communal organization (including communication practices, group dynamics, social practices, and other elements). Imagine, for instance, a newly hired graphic designer in a government organization. They have some specific design skills, surely, and some basic professional communication knowledge. They might know formal letter-writing conventions, for instance, and have what they consider to be strong grammar skills. What they don't know are the ins and outs of the communication within their government organization and, more specifically, their team—two different communities of practice within the same organization. At the broader organization level, there are standards and procedures surrounding communication, both spoken and unspoken, that they will have to learn. At the team or department level, we are likelier to see true legitimate peripheral participation in an effort to acclimatize this new worker slowly but intentionally. They may, for instance, shadow another more seasoned designer. They may be asked to make small design changes on an in-progress design text. The understanding is that they are learning by doing small, but real, tasks on the team. This neophyte's identity is invested in their full future participation, even though their present participation may be peripheral; likewise, it benefits the organization to help the neophyte reach full legitimate participation as quickly as possible in order to reap the benefits of their investment.

But such an environment looks very different for temporary freelance workers than it does for traditional employees, both because of the freelancer's needs and because of the boundaries within and around the client organization. On a very basic and seemingly logistic level, a freelancer might be unaware of, say, the expectations surrounding response time on emails that come in during off-peak hours, or, additionally, how those expectations might change depending on who sent the email—the chief marketing officer, for instance, or the junior copywriter. But of course, there are much larger, higher-stakes differences as well. One major distinction between a traditional new hire to an organization and a freelance-contract hire is that the traditional hire is seen as a novice or neophyte (Wardle, 2004), and the freelance hire is often coming in as a specialist or expert. Lave and Wenger (1991) state that legitimate peripheral participation is central to "belonging" (p. 35), and therefore, we might conclude that without this stage, freelancers *can't* belong. For them, even the baseline idea of the workplace as a learning environment must be challenged. As the freelance worker's time is temporary within the organization, rather than seeing them as contributors worthy of investment, organizations tend to see them instead as "expert mercenaries," there to contribute their specialized skills and move on to the next organization. Traditionally, new full-time employees or group members typically benefit from having "access to the archived material in addition to the experience of and mentoring from experts" (Li et al., 2009, p. 3), but for freelancers, these types of materials are rarely available. Therefore, the freelancer's acclimatization is minimal, yet even more pressing, particularly if they are being brought in to perform a core task which requires authority. They are given little to no guidance, and their participation is not "peripheral" at any point.

Wenger (2008) writes about learning in CoPs that, over time, "collective learning results in practices that reflect both the pursuit of our enterprises and the attendant social relations. These practices are thus the property of a kind of community created over time by the sustained pursuit of a shared enterprise" (p. 45). But of course, the freelancer isn't around "over time." We know that "writing is not easily transferable from one domain of discourse to another, even by highly skilled professionals working within a single occupational setting" (Smart, 2000, p. 245). And so, as we think about these freelancers, it's crucial, and yet seemingly ignored in workplace studies, to begin to understand the ways in which they write, learn, and enculturate to communication practices.

The Contradictions of Gaining and Maintaining Freelancer Identity and Authority

Elizabeth Wardle (2004) draws on Lave and Wenger in exploring ideas of identity and authority for new writers entering specific workplaces, arguing that "if the neophyte is granted some measure of authority by an institution but does not quickly learn the appropriate speech conventions of her new community of practice, she may soon lose the authority with which she began." As Wardle describes, in a traditional workplace, it behooves the organization to ease the neophyte worker inward from the periphery more fully into the community of practice so that both the community (organization) and the new worker can reap the rewards of this time and resource investment. A newcomer would "normally experience a 'grace period' for adopting community practices" (Wardle, 2004, n.p.) before being asked to perform as an expert. This period of legitimate peripheral participation is strategic; it serves the organization's bottom line, as this grace period will ultimately allow for, they expect, more efficient and productive work down the line.

However, freelancers are brought in on an assumption about their ability to perform immediately and fully. Linda Li et al. (2009) point to the "tension between satisfying individuals' needs for personal growth and empowerment versus an organization's bottom line" as possibly the biggest challenge in developing effective communities of practice. And this tension is surely at the forefront of the "problem" of freelancers here; an organization is unmotivated to invest time for the personal or professional development of a freelancer. Because of this, they're not welcomed into communities of practice, and, yet, are expected to participate as if they are a member, however temporarily. Moreover, the stakes for the freelancer are incredibly high: Their livelihood and future work depend on integrating themselves enough to participate seamlessly—or at least close enough to seamlessly as to not cause a disruption.

Freelancers are brought in to be the "expert" out of the gate, even before they enter, in fact, through their written proposals (or, at times, a portfolio) that contributed to their hiring in the first place. Freelancers may not need to establish technical or specialist authority, as it may be immediately granted. Again, a graphic designer, brought into a project without any other graphic specialists, would likely be seen as the sole authority in that skill. Yet freelancers are seen not as community members (or potential members), but as specialized tools with both the expectation of authority and the simultaneous withholding of it. They walk a chronic tightrope: They are, by definition, outsiders, but are often asked to take on positions of authority *inside* established communities of practice. Freelance hires are viewed simultaneously as experts in their area of specialty (illustration, film directing, graphic design, etc.) and are asked to perform central tasks, which might require "full participation" practices, from their position on the periphery while being intentionally kept from any inward trajectory. For the illustrator, a freelance job is never as simple as merely showing up and performing her expertise (illustration) and moving on. The realities of each new project require myriad genres of writing and labor, styles of communication, audiences, and dynamics before they ever get to perform their core task (painting, perhaps, a spread for a magazine). Communities of practice require both "time and sustained interaction" —luxuries not granted to the freelance consultant; their ability to create and maintain authority may lie with their ability to assert enough expertise and authenticity to outweigh any shortcomings in expectations of practice (Wenger, 2011). They have little ability to build additional authority through demonstrating a successful navigation of practices, and yet the freelancer's identity is multi-faceted and complex. Relying on Lave and Wenger's theories about how a (traditional, permanent) newcomer must feel the small work they're doing is important, Wardle (2004) notes, "Joining new workplace communities, then, is not simply a matter of learning new skills but also of fielding new calls for identity construction" (n.p.) This is perhaps even more true for temporary workers.

A writer's history and experiences will, of course, inform not only the ways in which they come to understand communication practices in a client organization, but also how they approach personal professional writing tasks and choices (Kohn, 2015, p. 171). Wardle (2004) notes how easily authority can be overshadowed and eventually disregarded through enough transgressions against expected practices of the community, and so freelancers must create additional opportunities to communicate their expertise. This vocalized authority, born from core expertise (illustration, web development, graphic design) may be incongruent with expected practices, but it is central to communicating a specific expert perspective and must outweigh any perceived incompetence or ignorance of expected practice. In her interview, our illustrator discusses the ways in which her core competency (illustration) offsets any perceived deficiencies in other practices:

> I didn't go to art school, and I didn't go to business school, so I don't know anything about marketing or publicity or [law] or anything like that, and it's just been completely learning as I go and making tons of mistakes, the same mistakes over and over again.... I'm still learning of course, and I think that that artist part of me that just wants to write books and make drawings has a very casual approach to a lot of the legal writing, especially when I talk to my editor and my agent I'm not always capitalizing or using punctuation or formal methods of writing, and I think that as an artist you get away with more. I think people let you be casual because that's you, and you make the work that you make, and they're not going to nitpick if you don't capitalize or things like that. But I think that's been also something to learn when I'm catching myself, because there's a certain professionalism and etiquette that you need to maintain, and I think that's been difficult for me to grow into since I'm not used to doing it.

The freelance illustrator here notes an important moment of negotiation via "boundary interaction" communications (Wenger, 2010, p. 126). She simultaneously acknowledges the ways in which she negotiates her identity (creative, artist) through a casual approach to grammar while also recognizing both the leeway granted to her due to her expertise as well as the importance of moving (negotiating) her writing closer to the expected business and legal writing practices of her field, thus reducing the incongruity between the two types of writing practices. Still, as "authority ... must be maintained through individuals' speech and actions," it is vital that her expertise be communicated clearly and frequently (Wardle, 2004), lest she risk losing credibility in the eyes of her editor or agent.

Similarly, our commercial director speaks to this need to balance his identity and authority between what is expected and what feels most authentic to his expertise:

Most of the commercials that I write are silly or absurdist, so when I'm scripting, I try to let myself go as weird and silly and open as possible. But then when I'm talking to a client, I have to obviously button myself up and be very direct, straightforward, and professional. So, it's a lot of tone shifting when I'm actually doing the writing.

We see here that the freelance director can explicitly make distinctions between these various identities, recognizing which "voice" to show and when. He references an absurdist sense of humor, but notes that in order to be taken seriously in this client community, such silliness needs to live only on the page.

Continuing, the commercial director speaks to this understanding that he is, in fact, working for a client with its own vision (or multiple visions) that may, in fact, be in conflict with his own:

> You're always contracted for two revisions, but you always go until at least five—[clients without creative experience] keep sending emails with each revision, where they're winnowing down what they want, you're winnowing down and fighting for what you think is really important, and making sure that you're navigating that space where, there's a lot of times that . . . people can lose the thread of what was even good about it, so the onus is always on me to maintain . . . whatever the crystal was inside . . . to make sure that it's unbroken when it gets to the final destination.

The director demonstrates here that he is working to maintain his own vision while also struggling to satisfy the non-expert client's desires. Ultimately, creating and submitting work that represents his own aesthetic—the "crystal," as he calls it—is essential to him. This is at least somewhat tied to his portfolio—he wants to be able to demonstrate this cohesive strong work to other clients—but it's also surely tied to his professional identity. And yet, of course, his authority to make sure the crystal "gets to the final destination" and is both personally satisfying and satisfying to his client must be in some conflict with his community of practice. This is especially complex, as, if a freelancer's expertise is questioned for any reason, they risk not being rehired for future projects. Their initial, limited authority can be revoked. Without the necessary authority to succeed, especially as an outsider where even minor deviations from expectations of communication or dynamics can lead to the end of their authority, freelancers run the risk of their contributions being discarded or not taken seriously.

The director speaks further to this challenge, as he recalls his early years as a freelancer and challenges in adapting to unique communication styles:

> Because I didn't take any business marketing or any of those sorts of classes, I was startled by the difference in vocabulary between [my field] and sort of everyone else. These sorts of weird acronyms

that would come up, like ROI and CRM and PPQ, or whatever they are, really threw me for a loop for a while, and it took me a long time to learn that language because there is a very specific language to this industry.... I think that was the biggest hurdle. ... just having completely different lexicons and different words for the same things. And I've been fighting that still, in terms of trying to avoid the business-minded idiomatic phrasings that a lot of people fall into, like "making the ask" or "the burning bush" or "the view from 30,000" or you know, all of those idiomatic crutches that people lean on in business relationships because it feels safer. That was pretty startling to me.

Here, the director not only recalls the unfamiliar phrases and acronyms he had to learn in order to fully participate in client communities, but also the ways in which he battles becoming *too* enculturated linguistically. He points to what we tend to think of as business clichés and suggests that even though he was forced to make sense of certain community practices in order to thrive, he was unwilling to take on all of them. His own identity was at risk in doing so. These freelancers are surely hired, in part, for their particular identities, aesthetics (for creative professionals), and unique ways of thinking, and yet they can't stray too far from the practices of their client communities. As the director stated, "tone-shifting" is constant and requires quick and adept versatility.

And it's here that both of our freelance professionals speak to what we might say is the crux of this identity and authority problem: authenticity, or how these freelance professionals—particularly, we would say, those in creative fields—straddle this line. The illustrator states,

I try to really write from the heart and connect with my audience, and along with that comes the writing that I do on Twitter and Instagram, both social media writing, but I try my best to be relatable and to be authentic instead of somebody that is just trying to sell herself.

As an artist, she describes working to connect with her audience, but as a freelancer, she *must* sell herself, and this is happening not only on social media, but also in her interactions with clients daily and—as we see in the following section—among multiple communities of practice. By this we mean she interacts with multiple teams or organizations as a freelancer at one time, navigating between the norms of these various communities.

■ Navigating Multiple Communities of Practice

In complex workplaces, which we would argue includes those employing freelancers, we also see multiple communities of practice overlap. For instance, our illustrator might be interacting with a magazine's higher-level editorial department, which is one CoP, but also with other in-house designers, photographers, and writers, all situated in other CoPs. In such organizations, the lines between teams become blurry and fluid, and learning and interacting obviously also become more complicated (Gobbi, 2010, p. 160). Traditional permanent employees, too, must traverse multiple communities of practice—the magazine's full-time photographer, for instance, communicates with her team, as well as many other teams, but she has access to these communities in a much more direct and long-term context.

For freelancers, every new project involves multiple new communities of practice. And, of course, sometimes these communities disagree. Our freelance writer-illustrator recalls early challenges in making her work appealing across multiple audiences:

> I probably took 20 ideas [to an agent], and she liked one of them, which is the one we ended up going with. And after that, I basically did writing. . . . And then after that was finished, I created the illustrations that would go along with the manuscript . . . and then after that you do the marketing/publicity side of the proposal, which is talking about yourself, talking about what you have accomplished so far, you basically want to convince the publisher that you have an audience that will buy the book. If they give you the money to write a book, you'll be able to sell it. And so you have to determine your target audience, and other books that are already like it on the market that won't be competitors, but to show them that there is an audience for the work, and you do a complete marketing plan, who you would pitch the book to, possible publications that would feature it, possible influencers that will write about it, the whole thing. . . . It's always a constant battle between writing honestly and authentically and writing something you know will go viral or that people want to read.

We can see the multi-faceted approach to writing and communication she is forced to take, and without experience or membership in a community of practice, the effort is largely an experiment in constructing authority and building one identity while maintaining another, sometimes for multiple audiences at once.

Similarly, our freelance commercial director discusses the complexities of maintaining authority and expertise, here as a script writer among various executive audiences within one organization on a new project:

> I'm in constant conversation with the head copywriter at the agency, the creative director, or the associate creative director at the agency; they're usually my point people on that side. And then on the client side . . . there are also some companies that have creative

directors of their own, so, I guess it would be creative director, copywriter, senior vice president, or sometimes marketing director, or occasionally people have weird, sort of esoteric titles, like thought leader, but it's usually people who are in the upper echelons of whatever company we're dealing with. . . . Sometimes on the client side there are 15 people involved who are all supposed to give notes, and really, one person is leading the team, but person number 13 feels left out, so they always toss a curveball in, and you have to navigate that stuff by again, just charm and a lot of "in our professional opinion" sort of phrasing, where it's like, again, just massaging and making sure that people aren't leading themselves off of a cliff because they think they know what's best.

Herein lies an additional challenge faced by many freelance workers: Without any static community of practice, the target for these workers is ever-moving. Successful interaction with one job does not guarantee success in the next, we know, but also, a successful interaction with one representative at a client site does not guarantee success with another from the same site. What might be a learned experience with one community of practice might not be transferable to the next project and a new community of practice, even within the same organization, or the same industry. In this way, freelancers "accumulate skills and information, not in the abstract as ends in themselves, but in the service of an identity" (Wenger, 2008, p. 215)—an identity largely defined by awareness and adaptability. The freelancer must become a sort of Swiss Army knife worker, able to recognize valuable boundary events and when to "massage" communications, when to defer, when to negotiate or assert their own practices and expertise, and when to acquiesce.

This challenge of engaging with multiple overlapping communities of practice requires that freelance workers navigate several, sometimes distinct, communication styles and, at times, even varying levels of authority, expertise, social dynamics, and vernaculars within each gig and from gig-to-gig. They need to show at least some competence across all of these fronts in order to maintain the authority to perform their core tasks and for their collaborating audiences to value that work. So how, then, do they do this?

Freelancer Development and Learning Outside of Client Organizations

As freelancers are seen as too temporary to participate in significant learning within any of the communities of practice to which they are exposed, it must be considered from where their personal practices develop. Freelancers' collected personal practices may be the product of high-stakes trial-and-error experiences. Whereas the neophyte is gradually oriented and acclimated to the practices of the community, the freelancer has far less time and fewer opportunities ("boundary events"; Wenger, 2010) in which to express their expertise to build and maintain authority. When asked how she overcame early challenges in connecting with and convincing new audiences, our freelance illustrator answered,

> I read a lot. I read other people's pitches. I read contracts. I read advice online on how to write a better pitch, how to write a better proposal. I look at examples, and then I try to apply those. So, it's a lot of just teaching and educating myself from the books and the internet, the sources that I have around me.

Without the shared interactions of the community of practice—of fellow specialists—such freelancers are left to learn and model their practices from their own and others' past experiences (and missteps). Unfortunately, they rarely have the benefit of the "grace period" granted to the neophyte hire to find their place within expected practices. The stakes here for freelancers are high. With each boundary event, they are at risk of the incongruence between their personal practices and the community's practices being interpreted as incompetence, rather than intentional "negotiation" or asserting their own expert voice (Bourdieu, 1992/2003).

Even when freelancers do have access to their own communities of practice, those communities still tend to be centralized around their own technical/personal expertise, rather than communities similar enough to those to which they require access. For example, a freelance graphic designer may get together with other graphic designer friends or colleagues to share experiences about their work, but this kind of community of practice remains distinct from the unique shared competencies of any of the future project teams they might work with. On this subject, the freelance director says,

> I'm in a sort of loose group of writers that meet every week and we discuss either stories or scripts that we're writing, and we're all sort of various different types of professional writer, so that is a type of training, but it's not a formal type of training, and it's totally free except I have to buy guacamole.

Freelancers serve as kind of itinerant specialists, bouncing from community of practice to community of practice, taking with them each experience, yet not necessarily finding each one wholly applicable to their next temporary homes. The freelance director may pitch script ideas, discuss different production designers they've worked with, perhaps even share horror stories of companies with whom they've contracted, but without direct engagement and participation with the writing practices of the (contracted) community itself, significant experimentation is required in each interaction. Freelancers' personal professional practices cannot be generated from firsthand enculturation into any of the communities of practice with which they work formally, but instead may be cobbled together from the outside looking in—trial and error, observing successful (and unsuccessful) models, secondhand accounts from peers, etc. When they attempt to apply these practices to each new project (with a new or several new communities of practice), it is for the first time, and incongruencies, which may challenge their authority and perceived expertise, are inevitable. Regarding this kind of trial-and-error approach to entering a new engagement, our freelance writer and illustrator notes,

> For my first book, I made the proposal entirely on my own, and it was a wild shot in the dark, and I managed to submit it to an editor, and it was risky because ... it was as professional and as detailed and in-depth as something that I had ever made. But now, my second time around, I have an agent, and I work with her to perfect a proposal, and just to give you an idea, my first book the proposal was I think ten pages, and with my second [was] about 40. So yeah. It was a lot more well-developed the second time around.

She continues:

> The whole proposal process was absolutely new to me, and I didn't know how to convince other people. So as far as writing, I had only ever learned how to use persuasion in [college] essays basically, always trying to convince the reader of my argument and how it tied to a book and a theme, but I had never learned how to use it in order to talk about myself and my capabilities. So although I had some sort of background on how to be a convincing writer, I didn't feel prepared to apply it the way that I've had to.

The writer-illustrator's livelihood is entirely dependent on her ability to traverse the dynamic expectations of several seen and unseen communities. Even though she had little familiarity with proposal writing and the expectations of the field, she was successful in her first publishing attempt largely by virtue of her technical capabilities. She admits that when she gained some access to an agent (a representative of a large-scale community of practice, or several), she gained a better understanding of how to enact these practices in genre, audience, and voice. Her proposal grew from ten pages in her initial attempt to 40 in her subsequent; she thought more about the business side of her work, potential audiences, etc.; she refined her adeptness in communicating her own voice and amplifying the technical expertise which had won her the initial proposal.

Conversely, our freelance director acknowledges his existing competence in navigating and adapting his practices in communication, which he believes gives him an edge over others with more technical skill. He references his experience in undergraduate workshop groups as a main contributor to his ability to successfully communicate, receive, and process feedback in his career:

I was lucky enough to study creative writing and so a lot of my education was workshopping … taking what other people had written, sitting down in a room, … and saying, "You know what, the opening was great, the middle I kind of lost you, but by the end, you had me and I think if you spend another week and a half … this thing will really sing." And having that basis of knowledge as to how to speak to people in a critically constructive way that finds what's good, tries to slough off what's bad, and really help them find their vision while also hearing that same kind of criticism about my own work—that I think was the most important aspect of my college education in terms of moving into the professional world. Finding ways to be critical of people and also to exalt them, and basically having that as my schooling, has made me a better coworker than I would have been if I didn't have it. … . I think the big hurdle in workplace writing is not can everything be harmonious … but can you solve a problem exclusively with your writing? Like can you identify something that's wrong, get in touch with the right person who can fix it, and make them understand exactly what the problem is, without ruffling their feathers or making them concerned about something?

… Without the creative writing study that I did in college, I wouldn't have a career. It is the reason that I am able to communicate with any sort of alacrity and why I've been able to move through my career very quickly in a way that I didn't even expect. … A lot of the people that are in the same field as me might actually be better at the tangible parts of the job, like being a director and being on set, but I'm much more likely to win the job because I'm a more persuasive writer.

Despite acknowledging that others may have greater technical skill, our freelance director recognizes that his early success comes from being able to do what some other peers cannot—perceive and adapt to communication standards and expectations. Whereas the illustrator's technical capabilities overshadow any perceived incongruities or expectations among proposal/business communities of practice, the director feels his participation in prior writing communities of practice gives him an advantage over those who may have more technical acumen, yet lack persuasion and adaptability. This is, of course, not to say that either freelancer would likely be successful if they were genuinely deficient in either their communication or their technical prowess. But the fact that a particular acuity in one skill may compensate for greenness in another may give insight into how much leeway a hiring client organization will give to those that cannot (for lack of access) meet the expectations and standards of their particular community of practice.

Both the illustrator's first proposal and other well-received work and the director's reference to his success in moving up relatively quickly as a freelance professional demonstrate early success in our two cases. Without such initial "break-in" success and exposure to, even peripherally, the practices of their industry, one wonders if a freelancer might perpetually struggle to adjust their practices to fit with the communities and client organizations to which they aspire to enlist, even briefly. And yet, both of our interviewees, and countless freelance workers, find success among these myriad challenges of authority, identity, and practice through, it would seem, a strong awareness and pliancy in their approach to their work, writing, and communication.

Both the illustrator and director obviously are quite skilled in their work, and their success is a testament to that. However, each of these freelancers recognizes a "rawness" in a portion of their personal practices; yet their strengths, be they technical or practical, have helped offset that rawness (in the eyes of their client organizations) and allow them to establish authority and prove their capabilities. While aptitude (technical or linguistic) might get their foot in the door initially, what they are learning from "brushing-up" against established communities of practice in each new experience seems vital to their sustained success. According to Stephen Billet (2004), "when individuals engage in everyday thinking and acting, more than merely executing a process or task, their knowledge is changed in some way, however minutely, by that process" (p. 314). These freelancers are coming into projects with specific skill sets and through experience and (even tangential) contact with communities of practice, are deepening their skills to become more well-rounded contributors and more attractive future hires.

■ Conclusion

It's important to pause here and note too that there is, of course, successful communication between freelancers and clients all the time. Both of our freelancers here, in fact, when asked if they consider themselves to be successful communicators, state that they do, at least to some extent—even as they voice these very real and constant challenges. And it feels obvious that we wonder here, how, and why? Are our two freelancers particularly adaptive? Or are they so talented in their specific areas of expertise that they are granted that authority if they're communicating "well enough"? We see that the process of collaborative work for freelancers is wildly different than when it is comprised solely of permanent employees. The framework of communities of practice, while it illuminates many of the challenges freelancers face, doesn't work to help us genuinely understand how they *do* develop their communication practices. Issues we address above, including identity, authority, enculturation, and learning and development, all require further research; here, we are pleased to offer a glimpse of this world and its communication challenges, but this initial case study set is quite limited. Further, although here we focus on "skilled" freelancers, we also hope that future scholarship will work to make sense of how communication practices for those workers more squarely in very temporary, gig-based contexts perform nuanced and, we might guess, complex communication through written texts.

Finally, as we move forward, we recommend a new framework for studying freelance workers, alluded to briefly above: transfer. Early transfer scholarship—in fact, *all* transfer scholarship—tells us that the act of transferring knowledge and skills, particularly when it comes to writing, is a "complex phenomenon" (Moore, 2017, p. 6). The ways in which writers learn and develop in one context do not naturally transfer to other contexts—and we hypothesize that this would be particularly true for those communicators, like freelancers, who by nature move frequently between writing contexts. While our understanding of transfer is still limited and somewhat piecemeal, we know that certain activities and ways of thinking contribute to transfer. And freelancers offer us a powerful and potentially very valuable set of participants to begin to see how transfer works at a micro and temporary level. Chris Anson and L. Lee Forsberg (1990), in their early, but illuminating transfer study, found a consistent cycle for new workplace writers: expectation to frustration and/or disorientation, and eventually to transition and resolution. This last stage likely coordinates with the point when a writer in a new context, usually workplace, begins to become, as Wardle (2004) would say, enculturated. But freelancers, of course, have limited time, guidance, and community to reach resolution. We anticipate that examining the stopping point, so to speak, for freelancers in this process would yield insights both for the individual workers and their hiring organizations. Additionally, as some freelancers *do* adapt and learn and some are, of course, very successful communicators—some certainly reaching "resolution," even if they do move on to a new gig soon after—transfer offers us the chance to begin to learn how, and why.

As this growth in freelance and gig labor is expected to continue to increase in the coming decade, workplace writing scholars must acknowledge that the contemporary workplace includes such contract work to a larger degree than ever before. As a field, we must pay more attention to the multiple, complex literacies required in the freelance market. Freelancers must be extremely adaptable in their writing practices, as they perpetually exist in the precarious position of simultaneous expert and novice. They are constantly aware of the temporary nature of their position, and so their ultimate goal is a successful project, rather than full participation in the organization. Just as these hiring organizations do not desire a freelancer's enculturation into their communities of practice, the freelancer may only seek enough guidance to successfully complete their tasks. Their work with one organization, as a part of their larger portfolio, is in many ways their ticket to their next job. Understanding the ways in which this happens across freelance areas of expertise and client industries will shed new light on how freelancers and client organizations can collaborate more efficiently and successfully as modern workplace writing continues to evolve.

■ References

Anson, Chris M. & Forsberg, L. Lee. (1990). Moving beyond the academic community: Transitional stages in professional writing. *Written Communication*, *7*(2), 200–231. https://doi.org/10.1177/0741088390007002002.

Bay, Jennifer & Sullivan, Patricia. (2021). Researching home-based technical and professional communication: Emerging structures and methods. *Journal of Business and Technical Communication*, *35*(1), 167–173. https://doi.org/10.1177/1050651920959185

Berliner, Uri. (2020, September 16). *Jobs in the pandemic: More are freelance and may stay that way forever*. NPR. https://www.npr.org/2020/09/16/912744566/jobs-in-the-pandemic-more-are-freelance-and-may-stay-that-way-forever.

Billett, Stephen. (2004). Workplace participatory practices: Conceptualising workplaces as learning environments. *Journal of Workplace Learning*, *16*(6), 312–324. https://doi.org/10.1108/13665620410550295.

Bourdieu, Pierre. (2003). *Language and symbolic power*. Harvard University Press. Original work published in 1992.

Corbel, C., Newman, T. & Farrell, L. (2022). Gig Expectations: Literacy Practices, Events, and Texts in the Gig Economy. *Written Communication*, *39*(1), 66–96. https://doi.org/10.1177/07410883211052941.

Coetzer, Alan. (2007). Employee perceptions of their workplaces as learning environments. *Journal of Workplace Learning*, *19*(7), 417–434. https://doi.org/10.1108/13665620710819375.

Engeström, Yrjö. (2001). Expansive learning at work: Toward an activity theoretical reconceptualization. *Journal of Education and Work*, *14*(1), 133–156. https://doi.org/10.1080/13639080020028747.

Freelancing in America: 2019 Survey. (2019, October). https://www.upwork.com/i/freelancing-in-america/2019/.

Gobbi, Mary. (2010). Learning nursing in the workplace community: The generation of professional capital. In C. Blackmore (Ed.), *Social learning systems and communities of practice* (pp. 145–162). Springer. https://doi.org/10.1007/978-1-84996-133-2_9.

Grugulis, Irena & Stoyanova, Dimitrinka. (2011). The missing middle: Communities of practice in a freelance labour market. *Work, Employment and Society*, *25*(2), 342–351. https://doi.org/10.1177/0950017011398891.

Henry, Jim. (2013). Fitting into contemporary organizations. In Johndan Johnson-Eilola & Stuart A. Selber (Eds.), *Solving problems in technical communication* (pp. 75–97). University of Chicago Press.

Kohn, Liberty. (2015). How professional writing pedagogy and university–workplace partnerships can shape the mentoring of workplace writing. *Journal of Technical Writing and Communication*, *45*(2), 166–188. https://doi.org/10.1177/0047281615569484.

Lave, Jean & Wenger, Étienne. (1991). *Situated learning: Legitimate peripheral participation*. Cambridge University Press.

Li, Linda C., Grimshaw, Jeremy. M., Nielsen, Camilla, Judd, Maria, Coyte, Peter C. & Graham, Ian D. (2009). Evolution of Wenger's concept of community of practice. *Implementation Science*, *4*(1), 11. https://doi.org/10.1186/1748-5908-4-11.

Lindkvist, Lars. (2005). Knowledge communities and knowledge collectivities: A Typology of knowledge work in groups. *Journal of Management Studies*, *42*(6), 1189–1210. https://doi.org/10.1111/j.1467-6486.2005.00538.x.

Luzón, María José. (2017). Connecting genres and languages in online Scholarly communication: An analysis of research group blogs. *Written Communication, 34*(4), 441–471. https://doi.org/10/gcjd45.

Moore, Jessie. L. (2017). Five essential principles about writing transfer. In Jessie L. Moore & Randall Bass (Eds.), *Understanding writing transfer: Implications for transformative student learning in higher education* (pp. 1–14). Stylus.

Moore, Patrick. (2006). Legitimizing technical communication in English departments: Carolyn Miller's "Humanistic Rationale for Technical Writing." *Journal of Technical Writing and Communication, 36*(2), 167–182. https://doi.org/10.2190/E1W4-WBXN-HTNC-U7ED.

Smart, Graham. (2000). Reinventing expertise: Experienced writers in the workplace encounter a new genre. In Patrick Dias & Anothony Pare (Eds.), *Transitions: Writing in academic and workplace settings* (pp. 223–252). Hampton Press.

Spinuzzi, Clay. (2015). *All edge: Inside the new workplace networks.* University of Chicago Press.

U.S. General Services Administration. (2009). *The new federal workplace: A report on the performance of six workplace 20:20 projects.* https://www.scottrice.com/wp-content/uploads/sites/906/2012/06/WORKPLACE-2020.pdf.

Wardle, Elizabeth. (2004). Identity, authority, and learning to write in new workplaces. *Enculturation, 5*(2). https://parlormultimedia.com/enculturation/5_2/pdf/wardle.pdf

Wenger, Ètienne. (2008). *Communities of practice: Learning, meaning, and identity.* Cambridge University Press.

Wenger, Ètienne. (2010). Communities of practice and social learning systems: The career of a concept. In C. Blackmore (Ed.), *Social Learning Systems and Communities of Practice* (pp. 179–198). Springer. https://doi.org/10.1007/978-1-84996-133-2_11.

Wenger, Ètienne. (2011). Communities of practice: A brief introduction. University of Oregon Libraries. https://scholarsbank.uoregon.edu/xmlui/handle/1794/11736.

5. Writer Identity, Literacy, and Collaboration: 20 Technical Communication Leaders in 2020

Ann Hill Duin and Lee-Ann Kastman Breuch
University of Minnesota

Abstract

In response to calls to strengthen the connections between academic research and technical communication practice, our research seeks an opportunity to learn from and collaborate with practitioners as a means to tap the expertise of advisory board members and begin to articulate the evolution of our field as we prepare students for work in these industries. A critical purpose of this study is to engage in continued work to address the gap between academic research and technical communication practice and articulate the evolution of our field. We examined this gap by exploring the practices of all 20 technical communication leaders serving on our programs' advisory board, interviewing each member to investigate their writing and technical communication identity, understanding and attention to sociotechnological literacies, and approaches to collaboration. The first phase of analysis included interview transcription and individual coding of common themes; the second phase involved discussion of results and how themes matched across our coding. We then shared results with advisory board members, inviting them to expand on findings through focus group discussions and later, review of an early draft of this manuscript to provide verification of the stated results and implications. Participants described and affirmed a shift in that technical writing and communication is no longer chained to product development but instead is connected to services and processes. Individual genres received less attention from our participants; rather, the workplace writing described by participants is much more about process and systems; they see themselves and the profession as integral partners "at the table." Identity involves multiple identities that are strategic and collaborative; literacy is about content, audience, tools, and usability; and collaboration is remote, involving multiple teams and structures. We apply the insights of these findings to develop and strengthen curricula and professional development opportunities that foster multiple literacies and collaboration to prepare students for the future writing workplace.

Keywords

identity, sociotechnological literacies, collaboration, technical writing and communication, academia and industry

DOI: https://doi.org/10.37514/TPC-B.2023.2128.2.05

Technical communication and composition scholars have long investigated writing in nonacademic/workplace settings, as contributions to these edited collections attest: *Writing in Nonacademic Settings* (Odell & Goswami, 1985), *New Essays in Technical and Scientific Communication* (Anderson et al., 1983), *Writing in the Workplace: New Research Perspectives* (Spilka, 1993), *Nonacademic Writing: Social Theory and Technology* (Duin & Hansen, 1996), and *Digital Literacy for Technical Communication* (Spilka, 2009). These collections depict an evolution of workplace writing in that they describe the multiple contexts and purposes of nonacademic writing (Odell & Goswami, 1985), examine readability and style of scientific and technical writing (Anderson et al., 1983), explore concepts of authorship and collaboration that influence writing in various workplace settings (Spilka, 1993), and conjoin social and technological approaches to the study of workplace writing (Duin & Hansen, 1996; Spilka, 2009). Workplace writing continues to be explored by scholars. For example, in interviews and observations of ten technical writers, Kathy Pringle and Sean Williams (2006) identified "information design" as a critical activity and noted that technical communicators will continue to rely heavily on technology in their work. In a case study of a technical writing team at a biomedical company, Lee-Ann Kastman Breuch (2008) examined the ways that single-source documentation practices challenge notions of individual and collaborative authorship among technical writers. Stuart Blythe, Claire Lauer, and Paul Curran (2014) gathered results from a national survey of technical and professional communicators to share ways Web 2.0 technologies impact the work of technical communicators. Themes in these earlier works include contexts, technologies, power, and authorship in technical communication workplaces.

A critical theme in technical communication scholarship that we are especially interested in exploring is the relationship between academic research and technical communication practice. Specifically, we are intrigued by the perceived gaps between these two realms and by findings that practicing technical communicators desire more clear connections between academic research and their work (Andersen & Hackos, 2018; St.Amant & Melonçon, 2016). For example, Rebekka Andersen and JoAnn Hackos (2018) emphasized that "building stronger relationships [between academia and industry] can . . . provide insights that facilitate effective education and training across the field" (p. 347). As a means to better understand the value and accessibility of academic research to practitioners, Andersen and Hackos (2018) asked 11 seasoned practitioners in technical communication, five of whom serve on editorial review boards, to read 12 peer-reviewed articles and six trade articles. They then conducted interviews to learn about the practitioners' experiences and perspectives. Results indicate that while practitioners assume that academic research applies to them, it is "not communicated in a way that makes the application clear" (Andersen & Hackos, 2018, p. 1). Andersen and Hackos (2018) noted "much agreement . . . in technical and professional communication, that mutually beneficial research can help foster productive relationships between academic and practitioner stakeholders"

(p. 2). However, they articulated a "major barrier to maintaining these productive relationships [as] the challenge of communicating research results ... in ways that are understandable and that make immediately clear the value and relevance of the research" (Andersen & Hackos, 2018, p. 2). They also noted that academic researchers "know little beyond anecdotal stories" (p. 2) about what practicing technical communicators actually think about this research. Andersen and Hackos (2018) emphasized the importance of academic researchers to make practical applications and use cases clear and "to write with a practitioner audience in mind" (p. 1).

Kirk St.Amant and Lisa Melonçon (2016) also addressed the gap between academic research and technical communication practice. To better understand practitioners' perceptions and views as to what research topics merit focus, what approaches should be used when conducting research, how research might best be shared, and the value of collaborating on research, they conducted 30 asynchronous interviews. They chose practitioners who were familiar with academic research through their "conference presentations, presence within the field, publications, or references from other practitioners" (St.Amant & Melonçon, 2016, p. 350). They used purposive sampling as a means to identify practitioners whose "particular settings, persons, or events [are chosen] for the important information they can provide that cannot be gotten as well from other choices" (Maxwell, 1997, p. 87, cited by St.Amant & Melonçon, 2016, p. 350). Their interview questions addressed technology use, what it means to be a technical communicator, what specific audiences we need to understand in today's workplace/industry context, and current contexts "of the real world" and how these affect technology use. St.Amant and Melonçon (2016) found "major divides between the current academic research being published and the needs for research in [the practitioners'] jobs" (p. 357). They identified two immediate steps: 1) to identify and use venues for sharing research, e.g., to seek out opportunities to collaborate [with practitioners] when engaging in research and to "have practitioners review manuscripts and suggest how to add such applications" (St.Amant & Melonçon, 2016, p. 358); and 2) to "tap industry advisory boards" (St.Amant & Melonçon, 2016, p. 360).

In response to calls to strengthen the connections between academic research and technical communication practice, our research seeks an opportunity to learn from and collaborate with practitioners as a means to tap the expertise of advisory board members. A critical purpose of our study is to engage in continued work to address the gap between academic research and technical communication practice and articulate the evolution of our field. Therefore, we specifically examined this gap by exploring the practices of all 20 technical communication leaders serving on our programs' advisory board.[1] Our Technical Communication Advisory Board (TCAB) is an intergenerational group of business leaders

---

1.   This study was reviewed by the University of Minnesota Institutional Review Board, #00008822, and was determined to be "not human subjects research."

whose engagement with our undergraduate and graduate programs is twofold: to provide exemplary networking and experiential learning opportunities for students and to enrich the curriculum and visibility of our programs and students. Students interact with these members through "Connect" events, research showcases, mentor programs, panel presentations, and class visits. TCAB members work in companies including Maximus, Meditech, Mosaic, ComTech, 3M, Wells Fargo, Graco, Medtronic, Unisys, Dashe & Thomson, Facebook, and Boston Scientific or lead their own businesses related to technical communication. Three of the 20 members serve in higher education roles. Our students and programs have benefited greatly from TCAB member expertise and direction since this advisory board began in 2014. Members are instrumental in curricular development (Duin & Tham, 2018); mentoring (Breuch et al., 2022); and promoting strategic direction, e.g., to foster practice with global virtual teams and translation management (Duin & Palumbo, 2021; Palumbo & Duin, 2018).

Through our interactions with advisory board members, we have noticed the growing importance of aspects such as writer identity, sociotechnological literacies, and collaboration; therefore, we have designed this study to learn more about these aspects of practice, in an effort to continue work toward bridging a gap between academia and industry settings of technical communication. However, while the TCAB vision statement includes the goal that this work will also "increase the effectiveness of our TCAB members with their industries," we have not to date interviewed each member individually as a means to understand each member's evolving technical communication identity, literacies, and collaboration practices and to begin to articulate the resulting evolution of our field and increase effectiveness as we prepare students for work in these industries.

In previous research, each of us has studied technical communication identity (Breuch, 2002; Duin & Hansen, 1996), sociotechnological literacies (Breuch, 2002; Duin & Hansen, 1996; Duin & Tham, 2018), and approaches to collaboration (Breuch, 2008; Duin et al., 2021). While we have developed theoretical and pedagogical direction for research and teaching, this study taps practitioner expertise in 2020. We used this opportunity to interview each member to investigate their writing and technical communication identity, understanding and attention to sociotechnological literacies, and approaches to collaboration. Our specific research questions include the following:

- What do contemporary workplace writing spaces look like, and how do they impact writer identity?
- What literacies are required for contemporary workplace writers?
- What new types of collaborations are required in workplace writing?

Conducted amidst the exigency at the beginning of a pandemic, this study may provide a most unique chance to illuminate our understanding of writer identity, literacy, and collaboration for 2020 and beyond.

Identity, Literacy, and Collaboration in Technical Communication

We begin by reviewing key resources in support of examining identity, literacy, and collaboration to provide more context for our study and research questions.

Identity

We see identity as a key factor in understanding academic and industry perspectives of technical communication. By *identity*, we mean understanding the ways technical communicators define their work, whether through work contexts, job titles, practices, workplace communities, or field-based issues and questions. The most extensive mapping of the identification of the field of technical communication to date continues to be that by Carolyn Rude (2009), in which she examined 109 books that address technical communication to identify explicit or implicit statements about purpose or research questions: "Research questions, more than research methods or topics, define a field internally and externally by pointing to the knowledge making that is unique to the field" (p. 175). To launch discussion, she mapped studies around a central research question—"How do texts (print, digital multimedia; visual, verbal) and related communication practices mediate knowledge, values, and action in a variety of social and professional contexts?"— and sub-questions under four related areas: disciplinarity, pedagogy, practice, and social change (Rude, 2009, p. 176). Rude (2009) concluded that "The field's identity, however, resides not just in best practices for career practitioners but also in the knowledge that transcends practice. The identity and value of the field also reside in what it contributes to the world beyond better practices" (p. 205). Rude (2009) advocated for a shared sense of our common goals, of our identity, writing that "a shared sense of our common goals in research could contribute to the field's visibility, identity, status, and sustainability" (p. 207).

The Society for Technical Communication (n.d.) defined the field as being broad, with the "value that technical communicators deliver" being twofold: "they make information more useable and accessible to those who need that information, and in doing so, they advance the goals of the companies or organizations that employ them." The partial list of identities includes technical writers and editors, indexers, information architects, instructional designers, technical illustrators, globalization and localization specialists, usability and human factors professionals, visual designers, web designers and developers, teachers and researchers of technical communication, and trainers and e-learning developers. Similarly, Tom Johnson, in his August 9, 2018 blog post to https://idratherbe-writing.com/, emphasized the importance of supplementing tech writing with a hyphenation as a means to indicate the breadth of one's identity. Examples from his list of 28 identities include technical writer/content strategist, technical writer/usability specialist, technical writer/DITA specialist, technical writer/

information architect, technical writer/project manager, and technical writer/web analytics and SEO. Each of these sub-identities includes a set of literacies—social and technological skills and competencies—that distinguish the specific sub-identity.

Drawing on research literature in the field surrounding the changing workplace for technical communicators, William Hart-Davidson (2013) identified three major work patterns and identities: information design, user advocacy, and content and community management. As information designers, technical communicators must "learn to make texts that transform" (Hart-Davidson, 2013, p. 61); as user advocates, they must "get to know users, or better yet, get them involved" (Hart-Davidson, 2013, p. 62); and as content and community managers, they must "improve ... coworkers' abilities to write together" (Hart-Davidson, 2013, p. 64). Hart-Davidson also highlights the work of Katherine Kellogg, Wanda Orlikowski, and JoAnne Yates (2006) called "boundary crossing," in which they note that successful boundary crossing involves strategic knowledge sharing to establish common ground along with specific methods for sharing "routines, languages, stories, repositories, and models" (p. 24). Successful boundary crossing also involves development of sociotechnological literacies.

■ Sociotechnological Literacies

In technical communication, discussions of literacy have primarily focused on technological literacy and, most recently, code literacy as a means to prepare students for the workplace (Duin & Tham, 2018). Stuart Selber's (2004) initial work to reimagine computer literacy through functional literacy (students as effective users of technology), critical literacy (students as informed questioners of technology), and rhetorical literacy (students as reflective producers of technology) provided a solid framework for organizing local learning environments that "integrate technology meaningfully and appropriately" (p. 1). Marjorie Hovde and Corinne Renguette (2017), drawing on the work of Selber and other technical communication scholars who have addressed technological literacy (Breuch, 2002; Brumberger et al., 2013; Cook, 2002; Northcut & Brumberger, 2010; Turnley, 2007), consolidated subsequent scholarship into functional, conceptual, evaluative, and critical levels of technological or digital literacy.

Looking outside our field, Peter Stordy (2015) articulated digital literacy as "the abilities a person or social group draws upon when interacting with digital technologies to derive or produce meaning, and the social, learning and work-related practices that these abilities are applied to" (p. 472). Developed in the UK through an extensive review of articles, reports, frameworks, specifications, and standards as well as interviews, the Joint Information Systems Committee (JISC) Digital Capability Framework (2019) defined digital literacies as "the capabilities which fit someone for living, learning and working in a digital society." In this framework, digital literacy capabilities include ICT (internet and communication technology) proficiency; data and media literacies; digital creation, problem solving, and innovation; digital communication, collaboration, and participation; digital learning and development; and digital identity and wellbeing.

According to Lesley Gourlay and Martin Oliver (2016), use of JISC and other frameworks that seek to define digital literacy "based on capabilities or features of learners" may cause us to lose sight "of important aspects of student engagement with technologies" (p. 78). Gourlay and Oliver preferred the European Union's DigEuLit project definition provided by Allan Martin and Jan Grudziecki (2006):

> Digital Literacy is the awareness, attitude and ability of individuals to appropriately use digital tools and facilities to identify, access, manage, integrate, evaluate, analyse and synthesize digital resources, construct new knowledge, create media expressions, and communicate with others, in the context of specific life situations, in order to enable constructive social action; and to reflect upon this process. (p. 255)

This definition is useful as we examine literacy as articulated by technical communication leaders in the workplace since it notes the importance of awareness, attitude, and ability along with the use of tools; it includes context and the importance of enabling constructive social action along with reflection. In short, it integrates technological and social literacy (Duin & Hansen, 1996; Spilka, 2009).

A critical goal in preparing students for writing in the technical communication workplace is to

> teach students how to write for social contexts within a technological world, how to write for a world where an understanding of communicating across distance is imperative, how to write for audiences that inhabit virtual communities and workplaces.... A crucial goal ... is to recognize the importance of sociotechnological issues. (Duin & Hansen, 1996, p.10)

Understanding of workplace contexts and authorship, analysis of power and politics, and connections of academic and nonacademic/industry sites via emerging technologies result in increased relevance and sociotechnological literacy. Scholar-instructors of technical communication "must equip [technical] writers with anthropological, social science, and linguistic skills ... that will enable them to analyze their sociotechnological writing environments as well as participate in them" (Duin & Hansen, 1996, p. 13). Such baseline literacies allow technical writers "to enact change rather than depend on either academia or the professional site to alter it" (Duin & Hansen, 1996, p. 13). Participating in sociotechnological writing environments requires seeing collaboration as a foundational competency in technical communication.

▌ Collaboration

Technical communicators must be prepared to collaborate with engineers, subject matter experts, and programmers; they must be adept at using collaborative software and working with global virtual teams. In the move from the use of the desktop to mobile technologies to social media to desktop videoconferencing and online collaboration platforms, technical communicators increasingly work in collaboration with others and with the evolving technologies supporting such collaboration.

Isabelle Thompson (2001) located critical differences in how collaboration is considered in the academy and in industry after conducting a qualitative content analysis of articles on collaboration in technical communication. In workplace terms, Rebecca Burnett and colleagues (2012) asserted that "collaboration is important because virtually all workplaces rely on group-based decision making and projects, often increasing creativity, productivity, and the quality of both process and product" (p. 454). Empirical studies of writing in workplace settings (e.g., Allen et al., 1987; Cross, 2001; Jones, 2007; Lay & Karis, 1991; Winsor, 2003) further clarify the nature of workplace writing collaboration. In their work to synthesize the rhetoric, science, and technology of collaboration, Ann H. Duin et al. (2021) consolidated a guiding framework for understanding, teaching, and practicing technical and professional communication (TPC) collaboration. They emphasized the need for exposure to and practice with the complex contexts of workplace collaboration along with understanding of innovative approaches such as Agile project management and design thinking.

Ann Duin et al. (2021) shared that Jessica Behles, in her 2013 survey of the use of collaborative writing technologies by technical communication practitioners and students, identified wikis, online word processors, learning management systems, SharePoint, and Google Docs as tools used daily by practitioners. TPC professionals indeed get things done through the use of social, collaborative, and virtual tools, and a myriad of such tools now crowds the marketspace (Software Advice, n.d.). Abram Anders (2016) examined a prominent team communication platform (TCP), Slack (https://slack.com/), used by one million people at the time of his study, and now (in 2020) used by over 12 million people a day (https://slack.com/) across all types of industries and organizations. In his analysis of 100 self-published blog posts by Slack users, he found the platform to support knowledge sharing and collaborative workflows: "The communication visibility afforded by TCPs ... had direct impacts on collaboration processes. Users noted that communication visibility—especially when supported by compartmentalization of groups, projects, and topics—enabled more distributed and self-organized styles of collaboration" (p. 247). The use of Slack also resulted in greater engagement and presence, context awareness, generative role-taking, leadership awareness, and synchronicity. As Anders (2016) quoted a user, "'It [Slack] compresses a lot of the stuff you might otherwise do in meetings into a

Slack channel, so that information is visible to everyone it should be visible to, and it saves people time: They don't necessarily have to meet but can stay updated on a project's status'" (p. 252).

As we consider the future of collaboration, we also must recognize our increased collaboration with artificial intelligence (AI) agents and nonhuman collaborators. In industry, Microsoft, Salesforce, and Oracle have integrated AI into their enterprise collaboration platforms, including Slack (Fluckinger, 2019). In a recent *Harvard Business Review* article on collaborative intelligence, H. James Wilson and Paul Daugherty (2018) found from their research of 1,500 companies

> that firms achieve the most significant performance improvements when humans and machines work together. Through such collaborative intelligence, humans and AI actively enhance each other's complementary strengths: the leadership, teamwork, creativity, and social skills of the former, and the speed, scalability, and quantitative capabilities of the latter. (p. 117)

A recent Deloitte analysis further supported this theme, finding "superteams" in which AI is integrated into teams "to produce transformative business results," with 70 percent of respondents reporting exploration and/or use of AI (Volini et al., 2020).

In summary, the 2020 technical communication landscape—its identity, literacy, and collaboration—evolved at lightning speed. We articulate this dynamic evolution through engagement with 20 technical communication leaders in 2020.

■ Method

We conducted 20 one-on-one synchronous interviews with our Technical Communication Advisory Board (TCAB) members. All 20 of our TCAB members participated; we attribute this full participation to member commitment to their advisory board roles. Interviews ranged from 30 to 60 minutes and addressed four questions involving identity, sociotechnological literacies, collaboration, and any other comments about workplace writing. Interview questions included the following:

- Please describe your work and "identities" as a technical communication professional.
- What social and technological literacies are most important as part of your work?
- Please describe your collaborative work. How has collaboration changed for you over the years? More recently?
- Please share any other points with us regarding the "writing workplace" of 2020.

We transcribed the interviews with assistance from auto-transcription connected to Zoom. Two student transcribers reviewed the transcripts and edited them for any corrections. Each interview transcript was viewed as one unit of analysis.

We as co-authors coded each interview transcript in two phases, as described by Johnny Saldaña (2013). The first phase involved coding each transcript individually for common themes, similar to "structural coding" described by Saldaña. Coding in this phase was open-ended and involved identifying themes directly in the transcripts as well as in a spreadsheet to indicate the frequency of each theme across interviews. Then, each co-author calculated frequencies in two ways: (1) number of times each theme was mentioned within each interview and (2) total number of interviews in which the theme appeared. Each co-author created a spreadsheet with this information.

The second phase involved discussion of first-phase results and a discussion of how themes matched across the two coders. This second phase of coding most closely matches Saldaña's (2013) "pattern coding," a common second-phase coding approach to solidify patterns across data. This second phase also involved inter-rater reliability, which was conducted by comparing themes and frequencies. We compared spreadsheets and identified similar themes through color coding. Our second phase demonstrated that frequency of theme mentions had high agreement, at 80 percent, with agreements around 14 categories of themes. Disagreements existed around (1) how to address "work" and "identity" themes, (2) identifying sub-themes within the larger categories, and (3) reviewing themes mentioned fewer than two times. As co-authors, we discussed and resolved these disagreements by including "work" as part of the broader category of "identity." Sub-themes were discussed for commonalities. We also added an "other" category for themes mentioned fewer than two times. Our identification of 14 categories or patterns of themes remained steady throughout this phase. Agreement about the number of times a pattern or category appeared across interviews was high, at 90 percent. Disagreements about patterns were identified as having more than two counts difference in the number of interviews in which a pattern or category appeared. These differences were discussed and resolved. Our findings resulted in 14 high-frequency categories related to identity, literacies, and collaboration, with an additional "other" category.

After interview analyses, we shared results with members, inviting them to expand on findings through focus group discussions. During the focus group discussions, we asked the following questions: What are the implications stemming from these results? Implications for your current and future work and identity as a technical communicator? Implications for TC field? Implications for your future colleagues (i.e., those we teach)?

Eleven of the 20 TCAB members participated in one of the two focus groups (held using Zoom). We each kept notes, sharing and discussing them with each other to determine overarching themes and begin drafting. We shared a pre-final draft of this chapter with all TCAB members for final comment and verification of findings and implications for workplace writing.

■ Results and Discussion

Overall, participants in this study described and affirmed a shift in technical writing and communication work. That is, technical writing and communication described by these participants is no longer chained to product development but instead is connected to services and processes. Individual genres received less attention from our participants. Rather, the workplace writing described by these 20 technical communication leaders is much more about process and systems; they see themselves and the profession as integral partners "at the table." Our "gist" of the findings is as follows:

- Identity is about multiple identities that are strategic and collaborative.
- Literacy is about content, audience, tools, and usability.
- Collaboration is remote, involving multiple teams and structures.

Further explanation of our coding illuminates these findings. Our coding of interview responses resulted in 163 coded themes (in Phase 1 coding) and 14 high-frequency categories of themes, plus an "other" category for a total of 15 categories (Phase 2 coding). Table 5.1 shows that these categories include (in rank order of frequency of mentions by TCAB members) collaboration, tools, multiple identities, content, usability, strategic thinking, remote work, relationships and networking, educating, cross-functional work, translation, business, soft skills, legal and regulatory, and "other." Each category includes a breakdown of coded themes included in that category. We observed that some participants discussed a theme multiple times during their interview (for example, if translation work was key to their work, they may have mentioned translation multiple times). Thus, instead of reporting by frequency of mentions, we report the number of times each category and related themes appeared across interview participants.

Looking at the top five categories overall, we see that collaboration, tools and platforms, multiple identities, content, and usability were mentioned the most frequently among TCAB members. These categories addressed, primarily, the kinds of work our participants reported doing as regular parts of their jobs. The remaining ten categories addressed nuances of that work, such as strategic thinking, remote work, educating, and soft skills. These nuances demonstrated abilities that our participants noted as necessary for technical communication work today.

We shared these results with focus groups as well, and one participant mentioned that the results reflected three aspects: how people do their work (usability, teamwork), what they do (e.g., content), and the impact of this work (sustainability, usability, strategy). Another member shared that while every individual should understand all 14 categories, it's important "to differentiate through focus on what strengthens you in that list."

Table 5.1. Coding Results From Interviews About Workplace Writing

Categories *	TCAB Members Mentioned	Coded Themes within Categories
Collaboration and teamwork	20/20	Collaboration, teamwork roles, teams, virtual team
		Cooperation, essential, global, lead, SMEs, environment
		Project management, people management, planning, Agile
Tools and platforms	18/20	Tool knowledge, media richness, tech use, tools
		Media, technology, Google, MS Teams, Slack, G, JIRA
		Collaborative platforms, using tech to collaborate, confluence
Multiple identities	14/20	Wear many hats, hybrid identities
		Information architect, user interface designer, learning experience designer, guide, chief learning officer, consultant, developer
Content, writing, authorship	12/20	Content, CMS, structured documentation, audits
		Writer, technical writer, writing, authorship/ownership
		Content strategist, design, management, reuse, officer
		Documentation, production, formatting, decisions, systems
		Publication, deliverables, output, version control, templates
		Changing authorship/ownership, identity
Usability / UX, audience	12/20	Usability testing, user partner, UX/UI, advocacy
		Usability, user advocate, satisfaction
		Audience understanding and analysis, people
Strategic thinking, influence	11/20	Strategic thinking, strategy, business partner, adding value
		Critical thinking, persuasion, politics, influence, silo
Remote work	11/20	Remote digital, flexible work, recruitment
		Video conference, video output, Skype, Zoom, teleconferencing
Relationships / networking	10/20	Networking, relationship building, relationships, CRM
		Social awareness, meetings, presence, diversity

Categories *	TCAB Members Mentioned	Coded Themes within Categories
Educating, training, coaching	10/20	Educating, educator, learning, learn, training, coaching partners
		Training, teaching, coaching partners, guide
Cross-functional work, negotiation, credibility	10/20	Cross-functional work, negotiation, w SMEs
		Credibility, trust, recognition, respect, partner, value, confidence
Translation, localization	9/20	Translation, translator, translation manager
		Localization
		Global work (time zones, language, partnerships)
Business, ROI, sustainability	7/20	Budget, ROI, sustainability, forecasting, efficiency
		Business, partner, business case, customer
Soft skills	7/20	Language forms (visual, nonverbal, eye contact)
		Softer skills, empathy, play, analyze, curiosity, diplomacy
		Communication, essential, helper, methods
		TC as listener, listening skills, transparency
Legal, regulatory	5/20	Regulatory compliance, labeling law, legal review
		Standards, ISO, requirements, regulatory, compliance, legal
Other	Varied	Curiosity, marketing, troubleshooting, social web, multitask, databases, readability, Quality control, systems, innovation, story, process

* Categories are displayed in rank order of frequency of mentions by TCAB members.

Results indicate a clear broadening of TPC identities as the TPC workplace evolves. According to these participants, abilities critical to the 2020 technical communication writing workplace include working remotely; collaborating; thinking strategically; building relationships and networks; and expanding understanding of content authoring, tools and platforms, translation and localization, business ROI, legal and regulatory compliance, and usability/audience. Interviews were conducted during the 2020 COVID-19 lockdown; TCAB members stressed how TPC professionals might best prepare for remote work, networking, and continued building of the profession.

To further discuss the results and consider implications, we organize the remainder of our discussion according to our original research questions:

- What do contemporary workplace writing spaces look like, and how do they impact writer identity?

- What literacies are required for contemporary workplace writers?
- What new types of collaborations are required in workplace writing?

What Do Contemporary Workplace Writing Spaces Look Like, and How Do They Impact Writer Identity?

Participants in this study asserted that technical communicators have multiple identities that are related to a collaborative workplace. As an example, one participant described technical writing work not as individual but as part of a team:

> What is expected from a technical writer has changed a lot. The idea that you can just sit in the background and get information and make a PDF is no longer what we do and I just don't think it's a valid way to look at technical writing. It's really changed to be more of a collaboration where we really are part of the team that does the work. We're part of the team that's held accountable. (P13)

Words used by participants to describe identities included "project manager," "trusted partner," "translator," "problem-solver," and "strategic partner." One participant included detail about project management and collaboration as they describe their identity:

> I was hired to be a technical writer and that was right after graduation. So then I was a technical writer for two years and then the technical publications information architect ended up leaving the company, and then it was, well, how do we fill this need? So I stepped in to help manage things and keep the boat afloat, which ended up being managing a lot of translation projects and our translation platform. (P10)

Another participant described a key identity as "problem solver":

> I would say the main identity would be a problem solver. That's what we're finding with our work that we have certain audiences that either can't find the information they want, don't understand the technical information, or it's not working. And so really, we've looked at how to problem solve. . . . So identity wise, we really look at problem solver, and we personify that. We are a communicator next, because we are the glue that holds all of our subject matter experts together. We understand enough about a lot of different pieces of this content ecosystem. (P18)

Current and assumed future roles and the associated workplace writing spaces of participants in this study are clearly collaborative, requiring them to practice *many identities* on many teams, to be skilled in multiple project management methods, and to use multiple tools and collaborative platforms. Members shared about the multiple skills needed and how collaboration leads to increased accountability and problem solving:

> I do wear a number of hats and that's very typical of a technical writer or technical communicator. You will change your hats and sometimes you're writing and sometimes you're editing, sometimes you're providing training and that would include writing. (P20)

> So the kinds of skills you need within your group include requirements analysis, customer relationship management, information design, information architecture, content management, content development or writing, editing, graphic design, system testing of the information for users, usability testing, translation and localization, specific technical subject matter expertise, estimating scheduling and planning, project management, authoring tool expertise, content management tool expertise, and information maintenance. (P12)

One member emphasized that "technical communication has probably, for me, transcended words" and that "*authorship doesn't matter; ownership matters.*" She shared this scenario to illustrate "channeling" collaboration in her writing workplace:

> Who is the author? You know, we really stopped using terms like authors, even when I speak to people I've come to use the term *owner*. Because the owner is really the key person. The owner has to make sure this document is completed, but that doesn't mean they're writing it or they're really authoring it, or really they're touching it at all. Authorship doesn't matter, ownership matters. And so if you create a great proposal, I don't care who wrote it, but who owned it. Who was the person that was responsible for getting this thing produced? (P2)

Another member shared a similar scenario in terms of transcending words and making sure to listen:

> It's not that I don't care what the words are, but it's not my mind that determines what the word should be, but it's listening to the product team and helping the product team figure out what it's trying to say. I'm not writing with my own voice so much as I'm writing what the product voice should be, and I don't think you can arrive at that without being collaborative. (P6)

Participants also discussed the need to serve as a *translator* of technical information:

> And so the students that I'm coaching and instructing, I'm, I'm trying to help them develop skills in communicating this very technical content to mixed audiences and to do that in a way that, you know, essentially positions them as translators. (P14)

In contrast to the Society for Technical Communication's definition of technical communication identity as making information more usable and accessible, and in so doing, advancing the goals of the companies or organizations, these technical communication leaders emphasized that multiple identities play a prominent role in their current and future workplace writing. One member asked, "What does tech comm actually do? Are you just like PDF monkeys where we tell you what to do, and then you just go make pretty PDFs when you're done? Like, I think that's what tech comm was maybe 20 years ago, but it's not what we do today." He and others stressed the identity of being *a trusted partner*:

> We are a part of the product design. We are a part of the requirements and the process at the beginning. We are a part of the development throughout the process. We are part of development and when we get to the end, we are handing off our final deliverables just like they are. We're not a service org. We're a trusted partner. And we have a level of expertise in what's required for the instructions for use, what's required by the different regulatory bodies, what's required by our business partners. (P13)

> I have to have collaborative trust with the R&D specialists that they're telling me what I need to know, and I would say that the more specialized the area is the more you have to trust within your collaborative endeavors. (P19)

These findings confirm Hart-Davidson's (2013) emphasis on technical communicators as information designers and Kellog et al.'s (2006) earlier note of successful boundary crossing that involves strategic knowledge sharing. A number of members spoke of being problem solvers and strategic business partners, articulating the ways in which they changed identity "from being someone that helps people communicate to [someone who] helps someone strategize." One member, a consultant for a wide variety of industries, emphasized identity as being "an *active business partner*":

> In probably the era when DITA was first coming out, you know that, well, we don't need this. We don't need to do that. I think that's changed now, because more organizations have decided that there's some need for structure and that you don't want to invent everything on your own, that there are ideas out there about how to do things and certainly you know managers come to meetings and talk to experts and talk to one another. And we're trying to learn about how to do things, but it's a slow process. (P7)

We need to move the identity from somebody who sort of plays in the background and isn't really seen, to an active business partner who is at the table and helping make decisions, not just in how things are worded or written or laid out on the page. . . . Now we're the user experience designers, and we're all of these other many things that have really brought the technical communicator to the table as a business partner. . . . We need to take ourselves seriously as a strategic business partner, and that means speaking up more. (P5)

What Literacies are Required for Contemporary Workplace Writers?

Many participants articulated this "additional set of skills" in response to the question about sociotechnological literacies. While members discussed "writing" as being an important part of their job, including issues of authorship and ownership, focus shifted to "content" as a way to describe the multiple writing tasks and contexts. For example, participants discussed content management, content strategy, content reuse, and ways that content may be created collaboratively.

I guess, is a literacy around content strategy, the ability to define a means by which we are saying yes or no to the next plausible idea that comes along we could do. That takes work, and it takes practice and an awareness of the importance of that strategy. (P16)

Content was also described as an endeavor involving teams, rather than individual writers, thus affecting shifts in how writing was approached in workplaces.

I mean, a lot of our work, we say in interviews, it's maybe 60 or 70 percent project management. It's not a lot of sitting down and typing. It is a lot of negotiating those schedules, figuring out what the dependencies are, figuring out configuration management. The same content gets leveraged in like ten different manuals. But this version needs to say this, and that version needs to say that. So how do I keep track of all those pieces? (P13)

In addition, the use of *tools* was a common theme in the interviews, including collaborative platforms, structured authoring tools, content management systems, and collaborative technologies such as Google and Slack. Technology was a clear factor in affecting literacies, and the collaborative component certainly underscores the importance of sociotechnological literacies, or the ability to understand the impacts and applications of collaborative technologies.

Certainly right now with COVID-19, technological literacy is really important, but even absent COVID-19, that technological literacy is really important. . . . One really important technical literacy that's embedded within technology is the ability to use technology to curate our data sets that we have to talk about and write about. (P19) I'm starting to see that even within user experience, where there's an increased specialization. You know, you might be very invested in UI [user interface] development and then your digital literacies are going to be prototyping tools, wireframing tools, you know, an expertise with mocking up screens and doing HTML or XML, you know, and actual web building. But if you're more of a strategic user experience researcher, those digital literacies don't emerge as much, and what you need to be proficient at [are] the soft skills of effective user research. (P16)

As the quote above illustrates, literacies were also highlighted in terms of *softer skills*, including problem-solving, networking and building relationships, strategic thinking and communication, working with cross-functional teams, and connecting sociotechnological literacies such as listening, practicing empathy, and clear verbal and nonverbal communication. Soft skills around relationship building underscore the collaborative nature of technical writing and communication described by these participants:

The networking and the relationship building is a very important part of what I do. (P4)

I think one of the things we're looking for is can you build those relationships? Can you establish yourself as a partner? Can you get so people know who you are? (P13)

In addition, soft skills related to listening and problem-solving support the ideas of technical communicators as trusted partners:

Listening is definitely one of those skills that I think is more important than ever. That's part of being present, and I've heard that a lot from people in the field, from managers especially. To listen to others, to understand where they're coming from, to really be able to understand the situation before jumping in to respond or reacting. That's really, really important. (P17) The notion of being able to articulate that solution in a way that adds value to it is huge. And so I think it's changed my identity from being someone that helps people communicate to someone who helps people strategize. (P2)

Inherently part of my job is strategy, and so I spend time on strategy [and] create frameworks for people to engage their work. Some of that might be, how are we looking logically, how are we looking at this problem right, and what do we want to call things? How do we want to label things? (P15)

Some participants explicitly mentioned the soft skill of empathy, both in terms of working with other colleagues and in thinking about end users who would benefit from information designs they were creating.

> I think a capacity for empathy is really important. That either comes naturally or you can systematize it through a process like design thinking. Where you start with empathy and that means, to me, that means understanding a day in the life of your audience and so that you can think holistically about what they need, when they need it, where they need it. How to serve it up, right, so that whatever objective you have in your written piece you're taking the most ideal attempt to serve it up in a way that your inner audience needs it. (P11)

> Certainly that element of being empathetic, advocating for users, is still something that unites all of us. . . . And within the Agile environment, right, we're relying on our designers to be advocates for the user, to promote user-centered design within the Agile environment, and to really be that stand-in, making sure that users are present throughout everything we're doing. (P8)

These responses align with broader definitions of literacy from outside our field, e.g., as Stordy (2015) articulates digital literacy as "the abilities a person or social group draws upon when interacting with digital technologies to derive or produce meaning, and the social, learning and work-related practices that these abilities are applied to" (p. 472). In addition, members clearly recognize the importance of sociotechnological issues, i.e., their understanding of workplace contexts and authorship (see above "scenario" quote), and their ability to be a viable part of business strategy to enact change.

What New Types of Collaborations are Required in Workplace Writing?

As shown in Table 5.1, collaboration was the only theme discussed by all participants in our study, which demonstrated its prevalence among our participants. The greatest amount of input surrounding new types of practices in the workplace writing setting involved discussion of *remote work* as it relates to identity, literacy, and collaboration. One member who has the broadest pulse across Twin Cities' technical communication businesses pointed out that this shift was well in place prior to COVID-19:

> I'm seeing more companies be receptive to remote work. It is a huge shift in just the last several years. For example, in companies like Medtronic or United Healthcare, it is now very common

to work remote. Related to this point, some companies are hiring across the country rather than in one geographical location. They may start with a local search. However, if they cannot find the talent they need, they may have to expand their search outside the immediate geographic area and hire someone who lives wherever. (P1)

Others mentioned being part of a team as a consistent part of the work of technical writers, in addition to working remotely in teams (e.g., "virtual teams"):

There's a sea change happening with collaboration. Especially before coronavirus, more and more people were working remotely. And it's kind of hit a tipping point here where you know, all these people who never worked from home are now being compelled to do so. And it's actually come at a very, the timing has been very fortuitous, because we have these tools like Zoom and Microsoft Teams where these, and Slack, they've kind of been in this, we're kind of on the leading edge of the bell curve. (P8)

So, in this industry, you need to be able to work remotely, independently, and also as a team member because translation always involves multiple people with multiple responsibilities. It could be like a project manager, translators, vendor managers, quality managers, and if the project is large, you might have multiple translators. . . . All this communication is done remotely, but as a team. So from the social perspective, you need to be able to work independently, remotely, but in a team, like a virtual team environment. (P3)

COVID-19 also was on everyone's mind:

I think that navigating [COVID] and even learning about how to do that effectively is going to become more and more important as we go through things like this, to be honest. Right now, since we have to meet, it's usually now more formalized meetings, because people are blocking their calendars, especially if you're home with your family to balance personal and professional life. So I think training and learning more about what the new workplace is or is going to be. I think that's gonna affect workplace writing in my opinion. (P18)

One member articulated his unit's pivot amidst COVID-19 as "experiencing a scene in progress" that involves "brand new assumptions" for users and for getting things done. This exemplifies sociotechnological literacy:

The workplace writing decisions we're making now that might have sounded like business as usual last month, will be viewed with brand new assumptions. Our readers, our users have new things on their minds. They may be preoccupied with attending to sick family members or their kiddos. They might be experiencing unemployment or underemployment. They might be cooped up in an environment where it is harder to achieve the conditions necessary for attention and concentration. . . . I feel as though as a technical communicator it's easy to point to now as an example of why we have been focused on the right thing all along, and now we're all experiencing the hypotheticals we kept talking about. (P16)

And others stressed the continued importance of collaboration in working with others to create content products:

When you collaborate and become more of a communicator or problem solver, you're pushed out of your comfort zone as an actual technical writer. I would love to sit down and just be able to work on documents or videos, but really it's engaging with those around us to create the best product that, and by product I mean document, video, interaction, content, if you will. And so in regards to workplace writing, a lot of that is done now in a group collaborating. (P18)

As a means to verify the stated results and implications from this study, we shared a pre-final draft of this manuscript with TCAB members during mid-June 2020. One member emphasized the role as a communications consultant, coach, and practitioner throughout his work in support of individuals, teams, and groups as they assess their communication goals and improve communication skills. Another member, in response to reading the final section of this manuscript, wrote the following:

I especially think your Epilogue is extremely important right now. I wonder if the concept of social justice could be more expressly correlated with the section describing empathy and soft skills? I'm seeing an encouraging, if overdue, acceleration of the import of concepts of social justice in our work. Accessibility and inclusive design, for example, are becoming central elements of my team's identity. My team has researched necessary modifications to our software to be more inclusive with gender identities. I expect this to continue to become a more paramount element of our identities and key literacies. (P9)

Needless to say, while we were working to articulate the evolution of workplace writing in technical communication, everyone instead was working to make sense of the world.

■ Conclusion

This collection on workplace writing afforded us the opportunity to interview each TCAB member individually as a means to understand each member's evolving technical communication identity, literacies, and collaboration practices and begin to articulate the resulting evolution of our field as we work to increase effectiveness as we prepare students for work in these industries.

In 2006, Pringle and Williams asked, "Has technical communication arrived as a profession?" predicting that technical communicators "will begin participating more frequently in the development cycles of technology" (p. 368). Our results clearly indicate that the technical communicator is expected to be "at the table" performing multiple roles as shown in Table 5.1. Amid a technical communicator's main identities and sub-identities (Johnson, 2018), they are seen as a trusted, strategic business partner. Our results show that contemporary technical communication workplace writing spaces are remote, collaborative, content-focused, usability-driven, and strategic, involving multiple structures. Literacies include knowledge of tools along with understanding the concepts behind the tools as the tools themselves continue to change. Soft skills, especially listening and practicing empathy, are critical to communicate and work well in teams.

In contrast to the recent research of Andersen and Hackos (2018) and St.Amant and Melonçon (2016), none of these 20 technical communication leaders mentioned a "major divide" between this academic research and their needs for research in their jobs or that this academic research did not apply to them. All asked to be engaged as part of their commitment to building the profession. We credit such engagement to these leaders' service as members of our TCAB. TCAB began in 2014, and all but two of the original members have chosen to continue service throughout this time. Lora Anderson (2019), in her call for proposals for this edited collection, writes that while "a smattering of journal articles have examined workplace writing in the 21st century . . . no sustained engagement (i.e., monograph or edited collection) has been produced on workplace writing since 2000." In our case, TCAB members exemplify sustained industry-academia engagement for the purpose of student success and professional development.

However, we note that an important limitation of our study is that our participant sample is not random. Because all participants are also members of our advisory board, participants may be already predisposed to academic environments. Said differently, we cannot claim that our participant responses are representative of the larger technical communicator population. Yet, our participants engage in technical communication work across a range of companies and organizations (and some are self-employed), and our interviews suggest that technical communication has evolved by its practitioners becoming active partners in these respective workplaces. According to these participants, the future involves understanding technical communication as a highly collaborative profession which affects identity and literacies. Amidst the exigency of a pandemic, this study provided us with a chance to reduce confusion and illuminate our understanding of writer identity, literacy, and collaboration for 2020 and beyond. A clear implication of this study is that sustained collaboration with advisory board members is key to bridging the gap between academia and industry. This sustained collaboration may include continued discussions with advisory board members and mentor programs to continue connections with students, and finding ways to foster reciprocal relationships that benefit both advisory board members and students in our programs is critical.

The insights we received through these interviews have helped us see the future of technical communication; that is, students have to see themselves as entering a profession with multiple roles. Collaboration is a professional imperative as is understanding technical communicators as strategic business partners. We will apply the insights of these findings to develop and strengthen curricula and professional development opportunities that foster multiple literacies and collaboration to prepare students for the future writing workplace.

■ Epilogue

We wish to provide an epilogue regarding the killing of George Floyd, which occurred on May 25, 2020 as we were working on this project. In fact, we conducted focus groups two days after George Floyd's death, before protests began in Minneapolis. As many people in this study live and work in the Minneapolis area, we are aware of the profound impact George Floyd's death has had on our community. We struggle to understand unjustifiable acts of violence toward Black Americans that have occurred in our own community and across the country. After the conclusion of our interview project, we began to have discussions with some TCAB members about integrating social justice more meaningfully into the work and partnerships with TCAB, such as inviting more people of color and focusing on ways to reach out to students of color in our programs. We will continue these discussions and work together with TCAB members to identify ways we can address social justice in our work. We also support statements by our national organizations, including the Association of Teachers of Technical Writing, Council of Programs in Technical and Scientific Communication, and the National Council of Teachers of English.

So, has technical communication arrived as a profession? No, not yet. Again, our interviews suggest that technical communication has evolved by its practitioners becoming active partners in respective workplaces. However, intense scrutiny of the past and present is necessary so as to work toward a future of greater diversity, equity, and inclusion, of greater social justice across our profession. In December 2019, our Department of Writing Studies approved an Equity and Diversity Statement; this is the opening paragraph:

The Department of Writing Studies at the University of Minnesota-Twin Cities recognizes that equity, diversity, and inclusion must be addressed on individual and group levels. The Department is also aware that relations of privilege and oppression are institutionalized on a systemic level but commits the principle of social justice for all. The Department recognizes that society is often unjust but that the Department (and its individual members) can play important roles in mitigating these injustices and become a space that better embodies equity, diversity, and inclusion. Thus, the Department encourages equity, diversity, and inclusion in representation as well as development of personal awareness, and the Department actively seeks to engage in creating socially just learning and workplace environments and opportunities.

Amidst the exigency of a pandemic and the trauma of racism, we know that TCAB members will continue to guide, to direct our profession and its workplace writing identities, literacies, and collaboration. As we continue to build the profession, we will strive to "arrive" at a socially just writing workplace.

■ Acknowledgements

We cannot thank these TCAB members enough; they provide exemplary networking and experiential learning opportunities for students, enriching the curriculum and visibility of our programs and students. They both ground us and provide direction for continuous improvement and evolution of our field.

■ References

Allen, Nancy, Atkinson, Dianne, Morgan, Meg, Moore, Teresa & Snow, Craig. (1987). What experienced collaborators say about collaborative writing. *Journal of Business and Technical Communication, 1*(2), 70–90. https://doi.org/10.1177/105065198700 100206.

Anders, Abram. (2016). Team communication platforms and emergent social collaboration practices. *International Journal of Business Communication, 53*(2), 224–261. https://doi.org/10.1177/2329488415627273.

Andersen, Rebekka & Hackos, JoAnn. (2018, August 3). *Increasing the value and accessibility of academic research: Perspectives from industry* [Paper presentation]. SIGDOC'18, Milwaukee, WI, United States.

Anderson, Lora. (2019). Call for Proposals—Rewriting work. [CFP].

Anderson, Paul V., Brockmann, R. John & Miller, Carolyn R. (Eds.). (1983). *New essays in technical and scientific communication: Research in theory and practice.* Baywood.

Behles, Jessica. (2013). The use of online collaborative writing tools by technical communication practitioners and students. *Technical Communication, 50*(1), 28–44.

Blythe, Stuart, Lauer, Claire & Curran, Paul G. (2014). Professional and technical communication in a Web 2.0 world. *Technical Communication Quarterly, 23*(4), 265–287. https://doi.org/10.1080/10572252.2014.941766.

Breuch, Lee-Ann. K. (2002). Thinking critically about technological literacy: Developing a framework to guide computer pedagogy in technical communication. *Technical Communication Quarterly, 11*(3), 267–288. https://doi.org/10.1207/s15427625tcq1103_3.

Breuch, Lee-Ann K. (2008). A work in process: A study of single-source documentation and document review processes of cardiac devices. *Technical Communication, 55*(4), 343–356.

Breuch, Lee-Ann K., Duin, Ann H. & Gresbrink, Emily. (2022). Real-world user experience: Engaging students and industry professionals through a mentor program. In Kate Crane & Kelli Cargile Cook (Eds.), *User experience as innovative academic practice*. The WAC Clearinghouse; University Press of Colorado. https://doi.org/10.37514/TPC-B.2022.1367.

Brumberger, Eva R., Lauer, Claire & Northcut, Kathryn. (2013). Technological literacy in the visual communication classroom: Reconciling principles and practice for the "whole" communicator. *Programmatic Perspectives, 5*(2), 171–196.

Burnett, Rebecca E., Cooper, Andrew & Welhausen, Candice. A. (2012). What do technical communicators need to know about collaboration? In Johndan Johnson-Eilola & Stuart A. Selber (Eds.), *Solving problems in technical communication* (pp. 454–478). University of Chicago Press.

Software Advice (n.d.). *Find the best collaboration software*. Retrieved June 9, 2020, from https://www.softwareadvice.com/collaboration/.

Cook, Kelli C. (2002). Layered literacies: A theoretical frame for technical communication pedagogy. *Technical Communication Quarterly, 11*(1), 5–29. https://doi.org/10.1207/s15427625tcq1101_1.

Cross, Geoffrey A. (2001). *Forming the collective mind: A contextual exploration of large-scale collaborative writing in industry*. Hampton Press.

Duin, Ann H. & Hansen, Craig J. (Eds.). (1996). *Nonacademic writing: Social theory and technology*. Lawrence Erlbaum Associates.

Duin, Ann H. & Palumbo, Giuseppe. (2021, July 8). *Redesigning TAPP for developing critical understanding for managing Global Virtual Teams* [Paper presentation]. AELFE-TAPP International Symposium, Barcelona, Spain.

Duin, Ann H. & Tham, Jason. (2018). Cultivating code literacy: A case study of course redesign through advisory board engagement. *Communication Design Quarterly, 6*(3), 44–58. https://doi.org/10.1145/3309578.3309583.

Duin, Ann H., Tham, Jason & Pedersen, Isabel. (2021). The rhetoric, science, and technology of 21st century collaboration. In Michael J. Klein (Ed.), *Effective teaching of technical communication: Theory, practice and application* (pp. 169–192). The WAC Clearinghouse; University Press of Colorado. https://doi.org/10.37514/TPC-B.2021.1121.2.09.

Equity and diversity statement. (2019). Department of Writing Studies, University of Minnesota.

Fluckinger, Don. (2019). AI in enterprise collaboration platforms: A comparison. Tech Target Network. https://www.techtarget.com/.

Gourlay, Lesley & Oliver, Martin. (2016). It's not all about the learner: Reframing students' digital literacy as sociomaterial practice. In Thomas Ryberg, Christine Sinclair,

Sian Bayne, and Maarten de Laat (Eds.), *Research, boundaries, and policy in networked learning* (pp.77–92). Springer.

Hart-Davidson, William. (2013). What are the work patterns of technical communication? In Johndan Johnson-Eilola & Stuart A. Selber (Eds.), *Solving problems in technical communication* (pp. 50–74). The University of Chicago Press.

Hovde, Marjorie R. & Renguette, Corinne C. (2017). Technological literacy: A framework for teaching technical communication software tools. *Technical Communication Quarterly, 26*(4), 395–411. https://doi.org/10.1080/10572252.2017.1385998.

Johnson, Tom. (2018, August 9). If writing is no longer a marketable skill, what is? *I'd Rather Be Writing.* https://idratherbewriting.com/2018/08/09/writing-no-longer-a -skill/.

Joint Information Systems Committee (JISC). (2019). *Jisc digital capabilities framework: The six elements defined.* http://repository.jisc.ac.uk/7278/1/BDCP-DC-Framework-Individual-6E-110319.pdf.

Jones, Scott L. (2007). How we collaborate: Reported frequency of technical communicators' collaborative writing activities. *Technical Communication, 54*(3), 283–294.

Kellogg, Katherine C., Orlikowski, Wanda J. & Yates, JoAnne. (2006). Life in the trading zone: Structuring coordination across boundaries in postbureaucratic organizations. *Organization Science, 17*, 22–44. https://doi.org/10.1287/orsc.1050.0157.

Lay, Mary M. & Karis, William M. (Eds.). (1991). *Collaborative writing in industry: Investigations in theory and practice.* Baywood.

Martin, Allan & Grudziecki, Jan. (2006). DigEuLit: Concepts and tools for digital literacy development. *Innovation in Teaching and Learning in Information and Computer Sciences, 5*(4), 249–267. https://doi.org/10.11120/ital.2006.05040249.

Maxwell, Joseph A. (1997). Designing a qualitative study. In Leonard Bickman & Debra J. Rog (Eds.) *Handbook of applied social research methods* (pp. 69–100).

Northcut, Kathryn M. & Brumberger, Eva R. (2010). Resisting the lure of technology-driven design: Pedagogical approaches to visual communication. *Journal of Technical Writing and Communication, 40*(4), 459–471. https://doi.org/10.2190/TW.40.4.f.

Odell, Lee & Goswami, Dixie. (Eds.). (1985). *Writing in nonacademic settings.* Guilford.

Palumbo, Giuseppe & Duin, Ann H. (2018). Making sense of virtual collaboration through personal learning networks. In Birthe Mousten, Sonia Vandepitte, Elisabet Arno & Bruce Maylath (Eds.), *Multilingual writing and pedagogical cooperation in virtual learning environments* (pp. 109–136). IGI Global.

Pringle, Kathy & Williams, Sean. (2006). The future is the past: Has technical communication arrived as a profession? *Technical Communication, 52*(3), 361–370.

Rude, Carolyn. (2009). Mapping the research questions in technical communication. *Journal of Business and Technical Communication, 23*(2), 174–215. https://doi.org /10.1177/1050651908329562.

Saldaña, Johnny. (2013). *The coding manual for qualitative researchers* (2nd ed.). Sage.

Selber, Stuart. (2004). *Multiliteracies for a digital age.* Southern Illinois University Press.

Society for Technical Communication. (n.d.). *Defining technical communication.* Retrieved November 14, 2023, from https://www.stc.org/about-stc/defining-technical -communication/.

Spilka, Rachel. (Ed.). (1993). *Writing in the workplace: New research perspectives.* Southern Illinois University Press.

Spilka, Rachel. (Ed.). (2009). *Digital literacy for technical communication: 21st century theory and practice*. Routledge.

St Amant, Kirk & Mclonçon, Lisa. (2016). Reflections on research: Examining practitioner perspectives on the state of research in technical communication. *Technical Communication, 63*(4), 346–364.

Stordy, Peter. (2015). Taxonomy of literacies. *Journal of Documentation, 71*(3), 456–476. https://doi.org/10.1108/JD-10-2013-0128.

Thompson, Isabelle. (2001). Collaboration in technical communication: A qualitative content analysis of journal articles, 1990–1999. *IEEE Transactions on Professional Communication, 44*(3), 161–173. https://doi.org/10.1109/47.946462.

Turnley, Melinda. (2007). Integrating critical approaches to technology and service-learning projects. *Technical Communication Quarterly, 16*(1), 103–123. https//doi.org/10.1080/10572250709336579.

Volini, E., Denny, Brad & Schwartz, Jeff. (2020). *Superteams: Putting AI in the group*. Deloitte Insights. https://www2.deloitte.com/us/en/insights/focus/human-capital-trends/2020/human-ai-collaboration.html.

Wilson, H. James & Daugherty, Paul R. (2019). Collaborative intelligence: Humans and AI are joining forces. *Harvard Business Review, 96*(4), 114–123.

Winsor, Dorothy A. (2003). *Writing power: Communication in an engineering center*. State University of New York Press.

6. Functional Flexibility: Cultivating a Culture of Adaptability for the Work of Professional Writing

Mark A. Hannah
ARIZONA STATE UNIVERSITY

Chris Lam
UNIVERSITY OF NORTH TEXAS

Abstract

Contemporary workplaces are constantly evolving and complex and require professional writers to have a breadth of expertise and skill sets that enable them to adapt and take on multiple roles in and across diverse work units and teams. Rather than reaffirm the need for adaptability, this chapter provides a new way of thinking about workplace adaptability through theorizing a model of functional flexibility that describes how professional writers collaborating on teams can be adaptable in light of the relational, oftentimes tacit, barriers that precede and spur the need for adaptation. The authors assert that developing insights about such barriers is an essential first step to developing any model about how professional writers can be adaptable and work effectively, efficiently, and economically—that is, to be functional—in dynamic workplace cultures so as to participate in the rewriting of work rather than be rewritten by it.

Keywords

adaptability, collaboration, teams, organizational communication, workplace culture

Contemporary workplaces are constantly evolving and simultaneously global and local (Spinuzzi, 2007). They are temporally diverse, distributed, and ad hoc in nature (Spinuzzi, 2007, 2014). They require employees to have broad expertise and skill sets that enable them to perform multiple roles in and across diverse units and teams (Dusenberry et al., 2015; Hart & Conklin, 2006; Ranade & Swarts, 2019). In essence, workplaces are unstable and pose unique challenges to employers and employees alike. To respond to this workplace reality, employers strive to build a workforce of individuals with broad technical (e.g., tools, languages, development and design) and interpersonal (e.g., communication, collaboration, creativity, empathy) skills flexible enough to keep pace with or even outpace the forces of change that shape the contours of work (Brumberger & Lauer, 2015; Lanier, 2009; Lucas & Rawlins, 2015). Professional writers (PWers) have been identified as just the group of professionals well-suited to this new workplace reality. Despite the positive recognition, there is an underlying awareness and tension, what some may call an anxiety, amongst PWers that they cannot keep pace with persistent, evolving workplace demands. Evidence of this anxiety manifests in continuing calls for PWers who can continuously adapt and respond to these very demands (Henning & Bemer, 2016; Johnson-Eilola & Selber, 2012). For many, adaptability is the lynchpin of success, the core capacity for getting things done and participating meaningfully in the knowledge work that defines contemporary workplaces (Dusenberry et al., 2015, Henning & Bemer, 2016, Myers, 2009).

We enter this conversation motivated to develop new ways of thinking about workplace calls for adaptability. Rather than reaffirm the need for adaptability, we want to develop a model that expresses how to be adaptable in the face of evolving work. To think through the *how* question, we use as a case study Mark's experience working as a PWer on a cross-disciplinary/boundary team adapting to emergent work demands.[1] The cross-boundary team included individuals with differentiated expertise in deep Earth and surface Earth geoscience, and it was assembled to examine the conditions in Earth's early history that gave rise to the oxygenation of the Earth's atmosphere, a phenomenon known as the Great Oxygenation Event (GOE). Mark's expertise in this team was as a PWer who can diagnose and develop applied solutions to team communication problems. As such, his experience mirrors many workplace contexts wherein PWers are seen as performing secondary support roles. During his research, Mark invited Chris to work as a sounding board collaborator and help him think through the emerging research findings as he developed a shared language model.[2] It was in these interactions that the theorizing work introduced in this chapter occurred.

In this chapter, we develop a model of "functional flexibility" and illustrate its use in an organizational context that involves the features of contemporary workplace contexts. First, we establish the groundwork upon which calls for adaptability are built. We then use this background to support our theorizing and building of a functional flexibility model and follow with three vignettes from Mark's work and his reflective memoing (Birks et al., 2008; Razaghi et al., 2020) and sounding board conversations with Chris to illustrate how the model can support adaptability in teaming contexts. We close by discussing the model's implications to PWers.

---

1.   Mark's work was supported by the National Science Foundation Frontiers in Earth-System Dynamics program under Grant 1338810 ("The dynamics of earth system oxygenation").

2.   The basis for our collaboration stems from previous research we conducted about social media usage in professional writing contexts (see Hannah & Lam, 2017; Lam & Hannah, 2016, 2017). Of particular relevance to this chapter was our research documenting disparate knowledge dissemination practices between practitioners and academics that fostered a disconnect between the two communities (Hannah & Lam, 2016).

◼ Adaptability in Professional Writing

Adaptability, in many respects, is the calling card of PWers' workplace abilities. Employers increasingly require it, and successful performance depends on it. The significance of adaptability is most evident in the continuing interest practitioners and scholars have in documenting and predicting the skills and expertise needed to keep pace with continuously evolving workplace demands (Brumberger & Lauer, 2015; Lanier, 2009, 2018; Whiteside, 2003). Implicit in each of these evaluative efforts is an awareness that trying to keep pace will prove insufficient. There always will be an unbridgeable gap between what is deemed important now and what will be deemed important in the future. Working in this gap thus requires a new kind of learning, a kind of adaptable, flexible intelligence or metis (Scott, 2008). This new way of thinking guides PWers' decision-making and reconfiguration of existing skills to match new workplace requirements. Through drawing on metis, PWers can cultivate the capacity to "learn how to learn" in novel environments and pivot in and between existing and incipient skills, i.e., adapt, in order to perform effectively (Dusenberry et al., 2015; Johnson-Eilola & Selber, 2012; Saidy et al., 2011). Ultimately, in calling for the ability to "learn how to learn," PW practitioners and scholars reframe their expertise as emergent (Hannah & Arreguin, 2017; Henry, 1998), which reveals not only that PW expertise is dynamic and unstable (Henry, 1998) but also that the potential value of that expertise is unknowable to themselves and collaborators.

Dynamic yet unknowable expertise has implications for teaming and case-making. As Allen Brizee (2008) argues, the ability to work in teams is paramount, and within teaming contexts, there is a persistent need for PWers to case-make their expertise (Hannah & Arreguin, 2017) and locate themselves as creative, productive problem-solvers (Bekins & Williams, 2006). Doing so successfully helps PWers craft their ethos and an attendant sense of legitimacy amongst team members, which ultimately enables PWers to take on leadership roles and mediate between competing project needs. In these roles, PWers draw on a willingness and ability to engage with inchoate project conditions (see Dusenberry et al., 2015) and identify and name the tacit and explicit communication barriers that limit the team's work. Implicit in all of this work is the adaptability and flexibility that facilitates workplace success.

Across these conversations, it is clear how PWers have come to bear the moniker of "masters of contingent flexibility" (Coppola, 2006), which suggests an always-ready openness and responsiveness to emergent workplace factors. While valuable for a resultant breadth of adaptability in the face of uncertainty, we also see the breadth of contingent flexibility as simultaneously narrowing through its centering of contingency at the individual level, an interior adaptability characterized by questions such as "What must I, the PWer, do to adapt?" "How do I reconfigure my skills and practices to align with emergent work demands?" and "How do I re-describe the nature of my work and its value to team members?"

Though an essential starting point for responding to the unstable conditions of contemporary work, questions like these limit considerations of the value of adaptability to individual workers at the expense of broader, relational processes of adaptability that involve the local, social factors of teaming environments. Examples of relational factors include a team's language use practices, interpretive models, and value systems which underlie and predispose how team members work. Such factors involve various tacit ways of doing work that unintentionally create barriers that constrain the ability to conduct work effectively, efficiently, and economically. Arguing for the centrality of such factors in any articulation of adaptability, we offer our functional flexibility model to give form to the relational practices needed to participate in and shape new forms of work.

■ Introducing Functional Flexibility

As outlined in the literature review, much scholarship has alluded to a somewhat narrow construct of adaptability. Specifically, calls for adaptability are typically at the individual level with the onus to be adaptable on the PWer. Though we agree about the importance of individual adaptability, our model responds to a growing need to build group-level flexibility in teams. And, rather than putting the onus primarily on PWers, the model suggests ways for all team members to recognize, grow, and foster flexibility. In naming our model, we chose "flexibility" rather than "adaptability" for one key reason. Namely, flexibility acknowledges the inherent value each individual brings to a team, but it also requires each member to bend their ideas, language, and practices to create a new team culture.

PWers are encouraged to be adaptable in and across workplace contexts; however, little work has defined and delineated necessary skills to foster and maximize adaptability. To work in this space and organize our theorizing about flexibility, we developed the construct of *functional flexibility*, which we define as team members' ability to function effectively, efficiently, and economically within the subcultures of a group, unit, or team. We use the term *subculture* because subcultures have distinct languages, practices, and values. Therefore, we argue that being functionally flexible is more than schooling yourself in a particular content area. Rather, functional flexibility requires deep understanding of workplace subcultures. Our model uses common boundaries faced by cross-boundary work units; however, instead of framing these as boundaries, we present them as opportunities for PWers to be functionally flexible.

■ Cross-Boundary Teams and Knowledge Diversity

Cross-boundary work is a relatively new academic area of study but has been applied in a variety of industries to spur innovation. Cross-boundary work units are defined as teams that comprise members spanning traditional organizational boundaries. Therefore, cross-boundary teams comprise members that come from diverse backgrounds. Team diversity has been defined in two primary ways: surface-level diversity and deep-level diversity. Surface-level attributes are "readily detectable" differences like age, gender, race, or ethnicity. In contrast, deep-level attributes involve less visible differences like team members' knowledge, functional, and educational backgrounds (Harrison et al., 1998). Amy C. Edmondson and Jean-François Harvey (2018) refer to deep-level diversity as "knowledge diversity," which we also use throughout this chapter.

There are challenges associated with cross-boundary teams with high levels of knowledge diversity. Edmondson and Harvey (2018) divide knowledge diversity into three categories: *separation, variety,* and *disparity.* Examples of separation diversity include opinions, beliefs, values, and attitudes. Variety diversity includes content expertise, functional background, network ties, and industry experience. Disparity diversity includes differences in pay, income, prestige, status, authority, and power. The authors argue that these diversity types are "entangled and confounded" in practice (Edmondson & Harvey, 2018, p. 348). Specifically, the authors argue that examining knowledge diversity from a cognitive perspective, where knowledge is reduced to information sharing, does not explain the challenges of truly knowledge diverse teams. That is, if knowledge is solely cognitive, overcoming challenges of knowledge diversity involves sharing information so that all parties have the information. In contrast to a solely cognitive view of knowledge, Edmondson and Harvey (2018) argue for a "practice lens," which relies on practitioners' "ongoing and situated actions as they engage with their environment" (p. 348). Further, understanding how cross-boundary teams can thrive depends on what team members *"do . . .* and not only at the expertise they *possess."* (Edmondson & Harvey, 2018, p. 348).

If knowledge diversity is contextually bound to practice, what, then, are the unique boundaries that cross-boundary teams face? According to Edmondson and Harvey (2018), they relate these boundaries to "transferring, translating, or transforming" embedded knowledge. The challenges to cross-boundary teams are related to diverse "languages" associated with communities of practice. This work of transferring, translating, and transforming seems perfectly catered toward PWers' skill sets, yet PWers often find themselves as outsiders in cross-boundary teams, wordsmiths brought in during the final project phases to document knowledge that was created. Therefore, as we develop our functional flexibility framework, we will focus on a deeper, contextual, and more embedded view of developing "shared languages" earlier in a cross-boundary team's project work.

Borrowing from linguistic categories, Edmondson and Harvey (2018) define three primary boundaries to knowledge diverse teams: *syntactic, semantic,* and *pragmatic.* Syntactic boundaries refer specifically to the lexicon differences between team members. For example, product designers may refer to product features very differently than marketing communicators. Syntactic boundaries are relatively thin and easy to overcome compared to semantic or pragmatic boundaries. Semantic boundaries, which refer to how knowledge is interpreted, call for "common meanings to be developed through shared mutual involvement around problems" (Edmondson & Harvey, 2018, p. 352). Pragmatic boundaries are differences in competing motivations, interests, or agendas, and they exist because individuals from various communities of practice have potentially vast differences in what they deem valuable in the process and outcomes of their workplace team.

Research has shown how these boundaries can positively or negatively impact team outcomes. Teams inhibited by syntactic boundaries, for instance, struggle with communication accuracy and information sharing (Kotlarsky et al., 2015). Groups that struggle with communication accuracy also exhibit higher levels of slacking and lower levels of team performance (Lam, 2015). Additionally, groups with wide pragmatic diversity—i.e., they have widely different interests or values—find team members with competing interests untrustworthy (Williams, 2001). A lack of trust leads to a variety of negative outcomes, including inhibiting knowledge sharing (Andrews & Delahaye, 2000). On the other hand, teams high in trust exhibit greater perceived task performance, team satisfaction, relationship commitment, and lower stress levels (Costa et al., 2001).

A Model of Functional Flexibility for Technical Communicators

Our model (see Figure 6.1) is inspired by the prior literature on cross-boundary teams and knowledge diversity coupled with our observations and contextual experiences as PWers working on cross-boundary teams. The model has three stages and follows a typical theoretical model. We visualize the input with three concentric circles, each representing a barrier as outlined by Edmondson and Harvey (2018). The outer circle represents pragmatic opportunities, the middle circle semantic opportunities, and the inner circle syntactic opportunities. As the visualization suggests, the outermost circle encompasses the two inner circles. If team members develop skills or literacies to address pragmatic opportunities, they also inherently have addressed the two inner rings.

Syntactic opportunities refer to ways team members may develop shared lexicons within cross-boundary teams. As the inner circle of our model, this is a foundational opportunity for PWers to facilitate.

Semantic opportunities refer to ways that team members might develop shared interpretations of knowledge within cross-boundary teams. While there is no one-size-fits-all approach to addressing this opportunity, one way is through developing visual models.

Pragmatic opportunities refer to ways that team members might better understand and appeal to underlying values and motivations within cross-boundary teams.

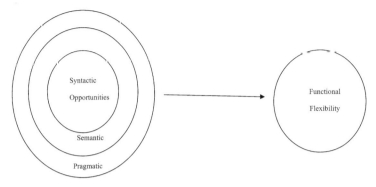

Figure 6.1. Functional flexibility model.

■ Vignettes From a Cross-Boundary Organization

To describe the model in fuller detail, we provide vignette examples from diary entries, reflective memoing, and experience reports taken by Mark as a researcher on the GOE cross-boundary team. Mark's sounding board conversations with Chris inform the vignettes. Please note, we include the vignettes only to provide context for our theorizing and not to represent results from an empirical analysis.

▌ Example 1: Overcoming Syntactic Boundaries by Developing a Shared Lexicon

An important antecedent to becoming a functionally flexible PWer is the ability to develop a shared lexicon with team stakeholders. Often, in cross-boundary teams where PWers are not the majority, so-called subject matter experts (SMEs) rarely think it is necessary for the communication expert to share in the SME's lexicon. However, as research has shown, this may inhibit the SME's ability to trust and/or respect the communication expert to complete meaningful work (Lee & Mehlenbacher, 2000). In these cases, it may be up to the communication expert to learn, practice, and integrate a specialized lexicon. This was Mark's experience, as exemplified by his approach to developing a shared lexicon.

Mark's research objective was to build a corpus of the most frequently used oxygen-related terms and then design a survey that asked collaborators to disclose their familiarity with and confidence level in using the terms. Mark wanted to document the wide breadth of understanding between the collaborators about oxygen-related concepts, and it was through visualizing this gap that he hoped to identify the need for shared language development as well as foster a corresponding commitment amongst team members to do so.[3] Providing a detailed

---

3. For more detailed descriptions of the survey-building process, see Hannah, 2018 and Hannah & Simeone, 2018.

account of Mark's research practice for securing this commitment is not possible here; however, there were particularly revealing talk contexts created through his practice wherein we can surmise the operation of syntactic barriers and how they potentially delimited the team's efforts to develop shared language.

One such moment stemmed from Mark's adopting an ethos of naïve outsider at team meetings. Specifically, to fine-tune his understanding of the terminology, Mark frequently asked clarifying questions about the terms being used so he could hear how team members differently defined them, but most importantly, he wanted to hear how they drew connections between terms. For example, when discussing a concept like degassing, what other terms did the team member use in relation to it? How team members responded to Mark's questions offered insight into attitudes about language use. Specifically, the responses showed a willingness to teach. Admittedly, that willingness could be dominated by a desire to communicate to rather than communicate with (Hannah, 2011), but the instinct to teach is important for demonstrating what we characterize as a disposition towards language use, namely team members' default approaches to framing oxygen-related content. Team members responding to Mark's questions might resist being labeled as teachers, but in responding to his questions, they initiated an encounter wherein they assumed an explanatory role and sought to achieve a modicum of identification with him and, indirectly, with other meeting attendees. How these teachers responded to follow-up, clarifying questions was telling about their potential adaptability. For example, if unable to offer relevant, satisfying answers in an initial response, could the teacher reconfigure their approach to language selection and identify terminology more suitable for addressing the questioner's information needs? Often, when researchers performing the teacher role suspected they did not communicate clearly, they would initiate their adaptation by innocuously asking, "Does that make sense?" In moments like these, Mark observed teachers' efforts to develop anchoring points. For example, the teacher might refer back to a comment made earlier in the meeting that had been well understood, e.g., "Remember when we discussed weathering earlier today? Thinking about your question in that light, I would say . . ." Though we are hesitant to infer too much about the adaptive capacities of teachers in such instances, we see grounds for identifying potential allies, i.e., individuals who can move in and between competing knowledge frames through successful translation. The relevance of ally identification to addressing syntactic barriers lies in the constitutive capacity of modeling in team environments. Specifically, after identifying team members who are adept at teasing out language nuance, the PWer can tap those people as models and consistently engage them in meeting settings to generate nascent conditions for others to learn and become teachers themselves. The payoff for modeling here stems from the opportunity to spread the onus for adaptability throughout the teaming environment. For the PWer, model identification, thus, is a foundational move for activating incipient conditions for cultivating a culture of functional flexibility in which all participants share the onus for securing a commitment to shared language development.

Attendant with the teacher role, Mark witnessed team members engage in what he characterized as play and exploration that signaled a willingness to experiment with language and participate in needed translation work. At team meetings and the on-site interviews Mark conducted to observe language use in a one-on-one research setting, he witnessed various team members let their guard down when speculating about the potential impact of language on their work. This experience of speculative play was clearest with the deep Earth researchers, who were the most skeptical about the usefulness of studying the impact of shared language. Drawing on this sense of play, Mark presented his findings at a team meeting wherein the team confirmed that the corpus accurately represented how the team thought about and used oxygen-related language. Of particular note in the meeting were the arguments team members made regarding inclusion and exclusion criteria about what words would populate the corpus. While some arguments were made forcefully, the most interesting were arguments made in jest, hedged with statements like "this may sound strange ... which isn't hard to believe." In such instances, attendees would offer a quick laugh and smile knowingly while nodding their heads that something unique was about to be expressed. Jesting like this example typically encouraged more responses from team members, which gave shape to a considered conversation, as opposed to the halting, fleeting discussions that followed a forceful argument.

In sounding board conversations about the experience of jesting, we recognized a power dynamic at play in these exchanges, not power over, but a power to claim which terminology is most useful and thus valuable to the team. For example, offering up for play a difficult conceptual term like *fugacity* secured a temporary commitment to explore that term. Fugacity, which is a measure of how easily gases permeate into geological substances, is a tricky concept because the deep and surface Earth researchers understood it in conflicting ways—e.g., surface Earth researchers understood fugacity in terms of partial pressure, whereas deep Earth researchers understood it in terms of ideal gas laws—and these differences invited vastly different responses from team members. Through focused conversation about these competing understandings, the term thickened and took on more significance and clarity. Importantly, the thickness became an anchor through which emerging connections between disparate deep and surface Earth ideas about fugacity could be made. Though this claim about thickness may seem obvious, team members who offered challenging terms up for play culled credibility as translational, hybrid deep/surface Earth experts through the clarifying work they performed when new conceptual connections were made. Ultimately, this credibility enabled them to set the agenda for future research meetings and thus shape the team's continuing work.

As in our previous discussion of ally identification, we are hesitant to infer too much into what motivated the articulation of various inclusion and exclusion criteria or why a team member framed an argument in a certain way, but we see grounds for understanding the constitutive role of play and its converse, resistance, in team environments, namely how play spurs team members' willingness to let their guard down and think about their language operating in new ways. Resistance and openness are directly linked to addressing syntactic barriers because they can reveal locations for building shared language. It is from those opportunities where team members enact their adaptive practices and respond to team members' communicative needs. As with modeling, identifying these locations is a first step in initiating the spread of responsibility for adapting away from an individual to the shared team environment. Ultimately, it is upon the sharing of responsibility that PWers can secure the team's commitment to drawing from what is shared between their work rather than what divides it.

Example 2: Overcoming Semantic Boundaries by Developing Methodological Literacy

Semantic boundaries can be more difficult to overcome because they rely heavily on understanding how team members interpret and apply information in their contexts of practice. In our model, we suggest that developing methodological literacy is particularly important for PWers in overcoming cross-boundary semantic boundaries. By methodological literacy, we refer to a baseline understanding of the methods and approaches that team members take to interpreting information and solving novel problems within *their own* communities of practice. This involves not only identifying particular methods, but it also requires understanding *how* and *why* particular methods or approaches are selected *over* others and what the end goal of such methods and approaches ultimately is. This methodological literacy gets to the heart of how individuals interpret and apply knowledge within their communities of practice.

Underlying shared language development are relational semantic concerns about competing interpretive practices that shape a team's work. For Mark, this semantic tension appeared most clearly in team discussions regarding the crafting of a knowledge domain for the deep and surface Earth research interests to merge, a middle Earth space. Thinking through this middle Earth space began from a common starting point for all team members, namely their shared commitment to the scientific method. But that shared sense quickly dissipated when they instantiated their individual interpretive practices within the general scientific method. The site of those instantiations was a tried-and-true method in the geoscience community, namely cartoon drawing. This method visualizes relationships between key concepts and offers the opportunity to distill complex information into accessible language for expert and lay audiences. Readers of this collection would understand cartooning as mapping (Sullivan & Porter, 1997), and in team discussions, Mark frequently witnessed members doodle images that demonstrated their understanding of interactions between the Earth's surface and interior environments. Through sounding board conversations, we recognized doodling as a "think aloud" protocol team members used to share their interpretive perspective and create a space for others to link their thinking. Typically, doodles had a lifespan ranging from a few to twenty minutes, but sometimes a doodle developed a stickiness that kept the figure alive across meetings.

Proposed themes for cartoons included an archipelago, a blind person with their hand on an elephant, and a record player, each suggesting some sense of simultaneous connection/disconnection, and the team settled on the image of a synthesizer (see Figure 6.2) for its ability to visualize how different geological materials and/or processes as inputs (slide bars/knobs) led to different oxygen accumulations in the atmosphere (sounds).

The team members commended the model for how it enabled them to use terms/phrases like turning the inputs up or down. Translated into geoscience terms, the inputs from the Earth's interior included iron, sulfur, heat, time, etc. and how their combination at different levels led to the output of oxygen (O_2) to the atmosphere. It is beyond the scope of this chapter to discuss the intricacies of how the synthesizer was used to link differentiated understandings of how changed input levels affected O_2 production, but the basic operations of the model lay a foundation for describing how varied interpretive practices manifested in the team's process of developing and using the synthesizer cartoon. For example, when discussing the role of oxides—e.g., FeO, Fe_2O_3, MgO, MgO_2—in redox operations, team members often would default to using one particular form of oxide to frame their understanding of its influence on O_2 production; i.e., a surface member may always start with iron, and a deep member may always start with magnesium.

Of note for the team was the especially high value the deep Earth researchers placed on cartoons. Specifically, because of the inaccessibility of the Earth's interior (core, mantle, crust), deep Earth research relies on speculative modeling based on estimated control variables across different modeling scenarios. Deep Earth researchers' model use was a knowledge production practice rather than a tool for synthesizing the team's findings for dissemination. Of course, deep Earth scientists also rely on cartoons to improve the messaging of their findings, but the difference in principal orientation to cartooning evinced an underlying interpretive knowledge-making practice that operated as a barrier and divided the team's deep and surface Earth subcultures. Specifically, the different orientations led to distinct ways of framing research findings. Deep Earth framing was speculative but closed, whereas surface Earth framing was explicit yet open, and these framing practices created fundamentally different discourse spaces for collaboration. To a fault, the deep Earth members resisted answering exploratory questions. Instead, they often shifted a discussion by asserting assumptions that were built into a particular model, e.g., "The model's timing assumptions don't allow me to answer your question [about the relationship between degassing and magnesium content]." Any follow-up questions also were redirected to those very assumptions, e.g., "Can we revise your question in light of the model's timing assumptions?"

The surface members' explicit framing, on the other hand, attempted initially to restrain the team to consider only that which was framed, yet it was dynamically open to expansion. As soon as anyone posed a question in the framing's context, the surface members invariably would offer a quick response—e.g., "That's interesting

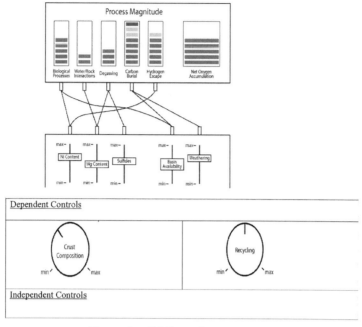

Figure 6.2. GOE synthesizer cartoon.

... what if we also asked about hydrogen escape? ... Does this tie back to our question about carbon burial?"—and then move on to what seemed like endless hypothesizing about scenarios they developed when referencing the synthesizer cartoon. Most important, the surface Earth researcher who established the initial framing question willingly participated in the hypothesis exploration—e.g., "That framing changes our approach to carbon burial as an input. What do we see now?" Such willingness in effect certified the interpretive space as open for business and necessary to the synthesis work performed in anticipation of disseminating the team's findings. In sounding board conversations, we saw the difference in framing as revealing an always already interpretive tension that prefigured a semantic barrier to the deep and surface subteam interactions, a tension that further extended the conceptual distance between the deep and surface subcultures.

From these anecdotes, we identified two conceptual practices as useful lenses for thinking about how to foster a culture of functional flexibility: knowledge orientation and knowledge framing. These practices go hand in hand in invention work, yet their conceptual separation is important for understanding where and how semantic barriers develop in invention. Knowledge orientation is attitudinal and readily discernible by how one talks about work, i.e., the terminology that shapes the syntactic barrier in our model. Knowledge framing is the follow-up, explicit instantiation of the attitudinal that sets the grounds for work and its desired impact. Being attentive to and informally documenting talk provides PWers a roadmap for alerting themselves to where the major discursive throughways are on the team, where dead ends and detours exist, and most notably, where new knowledge construction is taking place. It is this last example where the syntactic and semantic merge and the need for flexibility arises. Informing any needed flexibility are the insights gleaned from assessing language use—does language and attendant tone signal passiveness and tentativeness or conversely, overconfidence about the team's work? Does language signal a playfulness or spirit of innovation and willingness to take risks to heighten the impact of the team's work? We are not suggesting that answers to these questions lead to one-to-one determinations that "this person is (or is not) disposed to conservative approaches to interpretation and knowledge making." Rather, we are asserting that the syntactic here leads to a surfacing of the semantic. The language, of which an absence of shared usage reveals syntactic barriers, likewise surfaces locales where the always already interpretive tensions between team members pulse the loudest in invention. It is in these reverberations where the work of surfacing pragmatic barriers begins.

Example 3: Overcoming Pragmatic Boundaries by Developing Socioemotional Literacy

Our final example covers the most difficult barrier to overcome in cross-boundary teams—pragmatic boundaries. As described previously, pragmatic boundaries relate to individual and team-based values and motivations, which have significant potential to disrupt team productivity when values are misaligned. While the United States Congress is not a team per se, the lawmaking body of the U.S. government is a clear example of how competing partisan values and motivations stifle cooperation and productivity. On the other hand, when teams align, or even reconcile, values and motivations, pragmatic barriers can become building blocks for a shared vision. When teams work together in the framework of shared vision, they can accomplish deep and meaningful work. So, while pragmatic boundaries are the most significant and difficult to overcome, overcoming such boundaries is most rewarding.

PWers overcoming pragmatic boundaries is unique because the nature of their typical roles in cross-boundary teams is so unique. PWers are rarely the producers of the final subject-matter-specific deliverable. For example, on a cross-boundary team developing a digital product, PWers often are only responsible for developing essential communications about the product for a variety of stakeholders and users. In these instances, there may be a mismatch in values and motivations of, for example, a product engineer and a PWer. The PWer may place a higher emphasis on the product's end user, while the product engineer may place a higher emphasis on the product itself. But these different emphases rely on much deeper values that are shaped through professionalization, personal experience, and a host of other factors. Product engineers operate under a set of specific ethical guidelines that is developed through experience within the context of a particular discipline. The same is true for PWers. To get to the heart of the differences between values and motivations on teams, we must develop socioemotional literacy and attempt to understand the social and emotional connections between an individual's values and their work/interactions on a team. Developing understanding of someone's emotional and social ties to their work provides further insight and context into other areas of our model, namely methodological frameworks and shared lexicons.

Values abound in work contexts, and as our model intimates, how values operate as barriers stems from how language passes through and/or shapes syntactic and semantic barriers. Values initially shape responses to the *how* and *why* questions that inform and motivate work, but thinking beyond these starting moments requires an ability to identify the persistence of values, namely how and where values continuously shape subsequent collaborative work. For Mark, an example of thinking beyond arose when observing his collaborators discuss how to formalize their work for publication. In those conversations, Mark witnessed the collaborators make arguments about the value and importance of publication venues. For example, questions like the following signaled values orientations about the impact researchers want from their work:

- Do we submit to a more macro journal that has the potential to reach a range of geoscientists?
- Do we submit to a specialized, sub-disciplinary journal that will help us craft the middle Earth research space?
- Do we submit to a popular press outlet to cultivate public understanding about how the world was/is oxygenated?

Central to each of these questions was a concern with audience. Was it attendees at a national or international conference? Readers of a particular journal? Scholars at peer institutions or research teams studying adjacent GOE content? Through sounding board conversations, we came to realize that through the question-asking processes, Mark witnessed the activity of formal practice, specifically, the instantiation of the norms, rules, guidelines, and tacit practices—i.e., the values—that made up and informed his collaborators' professional disciplinary training. Significant to the recognition of formal practice here was how it signaled the ways team members were habituated to work, in particular the doing of work and how they perceived its impact. In recognizing the duality of doing and perceiving, Mark developed a nascent awareness of how values shaped his collaborators' views about what "ought" to be done. More specifically, whenever he heard the word "ought," Mark was cued as to where to look and assess how pragmatic, value-based barriers might surface and delimit the team's work. For example, as the team's project was funded by a National Science Foundation grant, there were expectations that publications would focus on broad dissemination to geoscience research communities and the public. The surface and deep Earth researchers were clear about this expectation, but at times, they diverged about how to meet it. For instance, the perceived opportunity to craft a middle Earth space was appealing to surface Earth team members to break what in many respects was new ground in their geoscience subfields. Much time was spent discussing whether they ought to pursue the opportunity to innovate through publications that centered interactions between different oxygen related content e.g., hydrogen, carbon, iron, and oxygen—or to simply develop publications that traditionally focused on one geological content area—e.g., hydrogen. In contrast, deep Earth team members' conversations about publishing expectations were incrementalist in tone. They hewed closely to their desire to address a specified research gap and not speculate two or three steps down the road about what new research terrain their work might open, i.e., what they ought not do. Ultimately, the preference for incremental impact over transformative impact signaled a difference in values orientations regarding how to address the grant funder's preferences. Now, this is not to say that deep Earth researchers forever eschewed any interest in positioning their work as innovative. Rather, we simply want to direct attention to the oppositional relationality of values orientations in those moments during the grant period when team members preferred different, and at times, competing approaches to achieving the team's overarching goal to develop a unified deep/surface Earth theory that explained how the Earth was oxygenated. The persistence of the pragmatic barrier in this instance played a significant role in what Mark perceived as the deep Earth researchers' diminishing desire to collaborate and publish with their surface Earth colleagues. For example, their presence at weekly in-person research meetings declined in favor of the infrequent team listserv discussions. Opportunities for sustained conversations to tease out the difference in publishing motivations diminished too, thus leaving pragmatic barriers in place.

Attendant with the venue and impact conversations were other attitudes wrapped up in audience analysis, which we again recognized as part of the team members' habitual formal practice. During the grant period, there were publications by a noted researcher who was not a member of the team but was well known by the surface Earth collaborators. In venue selection discussions, these team members frequently referenced the researcher's work and its potential relationship to the team's interest in oxygenation. For the team's deep Earth researchers, there also were notable papers published by outside researchers, yet in venue conversations, those papers were only mentioned in passing. During sounding board conversations, we recognized that the difference in attention to contemporaneous publications revealed conflicting motivations for engaging research peers. More specifically, surface Earth researchers evinced a maximalist tendency towards audience engagement, speculating about how they could interact with research peers not just as readers but as proxies who could spread and amplify their research findings and knowledge to other relevant audiences. Parts of these conversations involved strategizing about how to frame their findings as a roadmap for outside peers to link up their own findings, an implicit "here's how to join our work" expression. Notably, the prospect of proxying was not similarly apparent in deep Earth researchers' discussions. Their interest in noteworthy findings in contemporary publications was limited to "that's interesting" or "that's valuable" statements and did not extend to any consideration of how to amplify their findings through the activation of particular peer researchers. Ultimately, we recognized the sustaining tensity of publishing motivations as an example of pragmatic barrier entrenchment that contributed to the deep Earth researchers' diminishing interest in co-publishing.

Translating the insights from these anecdotes to the workplace, how might PWers think about formal practice as locales for surfacing pragmatic, values-based barriers that initiate a need to adapt? Habits are the locus of adapting. They arise from formal practice and are what people must move away from—i.e., pivot—when they adapt to emerging workplace demands. Helping others recognize the constitutive force of formal practice is a pathway to spreading the onus of responsibility for adaptability. Specifically, making visible those habituated practices through attending to the disruptions of formal work practices between workers and their decision-making superiors culls awareness about the latent barriers that can stunt a team's success.

■ Moving Forward with Functional Flexibility

Creating a culture of functional flexibility is not easy. It requires a reorientation to adaptability as not something everyone says you need to do—i.e., an exterior phenomenon—but rather as an acceptance of professional responsibility to distribute and share—i.e., an interior phenomenon. It is not possible to level all the barriers in our model, but we can heighten our awareness of their influence as a provocation to empathize with team members as they work through language use. We can center empathy as a necessary practice for creating conditions needed for spreading the onus of responsibility for adaptability throughout the teaming environment. Our flipping of adaptability as a cultural concern rather than an individual one forges a new pathway for rethinking work and positioning PWers for success in rewriting work rather than being rewritten by it.

■ References

Andrews, Kate M. & Delahaye, Brian L. (2000). Influences on knowledge processes in organizational learning: The psychosocial filter. *Journal of Management Studies, 37*(6), 797–810. https://doi.org/10.1111/1467-6486.00204.

Bekins, Linn K. & Williams, Sean D. (2006). Positioning technical communication for the creative economy. *Technical Communication, 53*(3), 287–295.

Birks, Melanie, Chapman, Ysanne & Francis, Karen. (2008). Memoing in qualitative research: Probing data and processes. *Journal of Research in Nursing, 13*(1), 68–75. https://doi.org/10.1177/1744987107081254.

Brizee, H. Allen. (2008). Stasis theory as a strategy for workplace teaming and decision making. *Journal of Technical Writing and Communication, 38*(4), 363–385. https://doi.org/10.2190/TW.38.4.d.

Brumberger, Eva & Lauer, Claire. (2015). The evolution of technical communication: An analysis of industry job postings. *Technical Communication, 62*(4), 224–243.

Coppola, Nancy W. (2006). Guest editor's introduction: Communication in technology transfer and diffusion: Defining the field. *Technical Communication Quarterly, 15*(3), 285–292. https://doi.org/10.1207/015427625tcq1503_1.

Costa, Ana Cristina, Roe, Robert A. & Taillieu, Tharsi. (2001). Trust within teams: The relation with performance effectiveness. *European Journal of Work and Organizational Psychology, 10*(3), 225–244. https://doi.org/10.1080/13594320143000654.

Dusenberry, Lisa, Hutter, Liz & Robinson, Joy. (2015). Filter. Remix. Make. Cultivating adaptability through multimodality. *Journal of Technical Writing and Communication, 45*(3), 299–322. https://doi.org/10.1177/0047281615578851.

Edmondson, Amy C. & Harvey, Jean-François. (2018). Cross-boundary teaming for innovation: Integrating research on teams and knowledge in organizations. *Human Resource Management Review, 28*(4), 347–360. https://doi.org/10.1016/j.hrmr.2017.03.002.

Hannah, Mark A. (2011). *Theorizing a rhetoric of connectivity* (Publication No. 3479493) [Doctoral dissertation, Purdue University]. ProQuest Dissertations.

Hannah, Mark A. (2018). Objects of O2: A posthuman analysis of differentiated language use in a cross-disciplinary research partnership. In Kristen R. Moore & Daniel P. Richards (Eds.), *Posthuman praxis in technical communication* (pp. 217–234). Routledge.

Hannah, Mark A. & Arreguin, Alex. (2017). Cultivating conditions for access: A case for "case-making" in graduate student preparation for interdisciplinary research. *Journal of Technical Writing and Communication, 47*(2), 172–193. https://doi.org/10.1177/0047281617692070.

Hannah, Mark A. & Lam, Chris. (2016). Patterns of dissemination: Examining and documenting practitioner knowledge sharing practices on blogs. *Technical Communication, 63*(4), 328–345.

Hannah, Mark A. & Lam, Chris. (2017). Drawing from available means: Assessing the rhetorical dimensions of Facebook practice. *International Journal of Business Communication, 54*(3), 235–257. https://doi.org/10.1177/2329488415572788.

Hannah, Mark A. & Simeone, Michael. (2018). Exploring an ethnography-based knowledge network model for professional communication analysis of knowledge integration. *IEEE Transactions on Professional Communication, 61*(4), 372–388. https://doi.org/10.1109/TPC.2018.2870682.

Harrison, David A., Price, Kenneth H. & Bell, Myrtle P. (1998). Beyond relational demography: Time and the effects of surface-and deep-level diversity on work group cohesion. *Academy of Management Journal, 41*(1), 96–107. https://www.jstor.org/stable/256901.

Hart, Hillary & Conklin, James. (2006). Toward a meaningful model of technical communication. *Technical Communication, 53*(4), 395–415.

Henning, Teresa & Bemer, Amanda. (2016). Reconsidering power and legitimacy in technical communication: A case for enlarging the definition of technical communicator. *Journal of Technical Writing and Communication, 46*(3), 311–341. https://doi.org/10.1177/0047281616639484.

Henry, Jim. (1998). Documenting contributory expertise: The value added by technical communicators in collaborative writing situations. *Technical Communication, 45*(2), 207.

Johnson-Eilola, Johndan & Selber, Stuart A. (Eds.). (2012). *Solving problems in technical communication*. University of Chicago Press.

Kotlarsky, Julia, van den Hooff, Bart & Houtman, Leonie. (2015). Are we on the same page? Knowledge boundaries and transactive memory system development in cross-functional teams. *Communication Research, 42*(3), 319–344. https://doi.org/10.1177/0093650212469402.

Lam, Chris. (2015). The role of communication and cohesion in reducing social loafing in group projects. *Business and Professional Communication Quarterly*, *78*(4), 454–475. https://doi.org/10.1177/2329490615596417.

Lam, Chris & Hannah, Mark A. (2016). Flipping the audience script: An activity that integrates research and audience analysis. *Business and Professional Communication Quarterly*, *79*(1), 28–53. https://doi.org/10.1177/2329490615593372.

Lam, Chris & Hannah, Mark A. (2017). The social help desk: Examining how Twitter is used as a technical support tool. *Communication Design Quarterly Review*, *4*(2), 37–51. https://doi.org/10.1145/3068698.3068702.

Lanier, Clinton R. (2009). Analysis of the skills called for by technical communication employers in recruitment postings. *Technical Communication*, *56*(1), 51–61.

Lanier, Clinton R. (2018). Toward understanding important workplace issues for technical communicators. *Technical Communication*, *65*(1), 66–84.

Lee, Martha F. & Mehlenbacher, Brad. (2000). Technical writer/subject-matter expert interaction: The writer's perspective, the organizational challenge. *Technical Communication*, *47*(4), 544–552.

Lucas, Kristen & Rawlins, Jacob D. (2015). The competency pivot: Introducing a revised approach to the business communication curriculum. *Business and Professional Communication Quarterly*, *78*(2), 167–193. https://doi.org/10.1177/2329490615576071

Myers, Elissa Matulis. (2009). Adapt or die: Technical communicators of the twenty-first century. *Intercom*, *56*(3), 6–13.

Ranade, Nupoor & Swarts, Jason. (2019). Humanistic communication in information centric workplaces. *Communication Design Quarterly*, *7*(4), 17–31. https://doi.org/10.1145/3363790.3363792.

Razaghi, Naghmeh, Abdolrahimi, Mahbobeh & Salsali, Mahvash. (2020). Memo and memoing in qualitative research: A narrative review. *Journal of Qualitative Research in Health Sciences*, *4*(2), 206–217.

Saidy, Christina, Hannah, Mark & Sura, Tom. (2011). Meeting students where they are: Advancing a theory and practice of archives in the classroom. *Journal of Technical Writing and Communication*, *41*(2), 173–191. https://doi.org/10.2190/TW.41.2.e.

Scott, J. Blake. (2008). The practice of usability: Teaching user engagement through service-learning. *Technical Communication Quarterly*, *17*(4), 381–412. https://doi.org/10.1080/10572250802324929.

Spinuzzi, Clay. (2007). Guest editor's introduction: Technical communication in the age of distributed work. *Technical Communication Quarterly*, *16*(3), 265–277. https://doi.org/10.1080/10572250701290998.

Spinuzzi, Clay. (2014). How nonemployer firms stage-manage ad hoc collaboration: An activity theory analysis. *Technical Communication Quarterly*, *23*(2), 88–114. https://doi.org/10.1080/10572252.2013.797334.

Sullivan, Patricia & Porter, James E. (1997). *Opening spaces: Writing technologies and critical research practices*. Greenwood.

Whiteside, Aimee L. (2003). The skills that technical communicators need: An investigation of technical communication graduates, managers, and curricula. *Journal of Technical Writing and Communication*, *33*(4), 303–318. https://doi.org/10.2190%2F3164-E4Vo-BF7D-TDVA.

Williams, Michele. (2001). In whom we trust: Group membership as an affective context for trust development. *Academy of Management Review*, *26*(3), 377–396. https://doi.org/10.2307/259183.

7. Entry-Level Professional Communicators in the Workplace: What Job Ads Tell Us

Kelli Cargile Cook, Bethany Pitchford, and Joni Litsey
TEXAS TECH UNIVERSITY

Abstract

Job ads provide entry-level job seekers key insights into professional communication workplaces; for example, ads can reveal what professional behaviors are expected, where work occurs, and how coworkers interact. Reading ads to see what they reveal offers job seekers a snapshot of the internal workings of these workplaces. This chapter provides such a snapshot through a content analysis of 176 job ads posted over two months on four internet job search websites. The findings presented in this chapter provide an overview of workplaces that employ professional communicators and insights into employers' expectations for entry-level professional communicators they intend to hire.

Keywords

entry-level jobs, entry-level skills, employer expectations, job success

Graduates of professional communication programs are frequently taught to read job ads for qualifications they should highlight when applying for their first position. These entry-level job seekers match ad keywords to their own skills to demonstrate their qualifications. Read in this way, the ads are externally directed away from the employer toward the applicant. The ads' message is clear: "Here's the employee we need; now you tell us how well you fit our needs." These same job ads, however, can be read with an internal focus, providing job seekers key insights into workplaces they'd like to join; for example, ads can reveal what professional behavior is expected, where work occurs, and how coworkers interact. Reading ads to see what they reveal can offer job seekers a snapshot of the internal workings of professional communication workplaces. This chapter reports such a study, a content analysis of 176 job ads posted over two months on four internet job search websites. In doing so, it provides further insights into the professional communication workplace, extending the work of Eva Brumberger and Clarie Lauer's (2015), Sally Henschel and Lisa Melonçon's (2014), and Melonçon and Henschel's (2013) studies.

To report our findings, our chapter is divided into three parts. In the first part, we explain how we collected and coded the job ads. In the second part, we

DOI: https://doi.org/10.37514/TPC-B.2023.2128.2.07

provide a snapshot of the applicants and qualifications these ads request. In the final part, we focus on the workplace itself and the expectations these employers have for professional communicators. With this focus, we provide advice on how to leverage academic knowledge into workplace know-how.

■ Selecting Ads for the Snapshot

We began our research collecting ads posted from July 1 to August 31, 2019, on Glassdoor, Indeed, LinkedIn, and Monster. We chose these four search engines because their search features allowed us to search by date and job title. To locate ads, we used six *position* keywords: "corporate communication," "corporate communicator," "business communication," "business communicator," "professional communication," and "professional communicator."

We chose these terms for several reasons, which are institution-specific:

- Our newly founded department is called Professional Communication, and our primary reason for conducting the research was to discover where our graduates might find entry-level positions.
- Our department's degree, also newly approved, is called Digital Media and Professional Communication.
- Our core faculty were from a business communication program, which was moved to our department at its founding.
- Our primary organizational affiliation is with the International Association of Business Communicators (IABC), and corporate communication is used synonymously with business communication in its descriptions.
- Having chosen these adjectives ("professional," "business," and "corporate") for these reasons, we searched with both "communication" and "communicator" as the modified noun.

We did not include the terms "technical communication" or "technical communicator" in this list because these designations belong to another campus department with which we are not affiliated.

Within the search results, we then narrowed our focus by applying *required experience* keywords: "entry level," "bachelor's degree," "BA," or "BS." Job ads that included position and required experience keywords were added to the sample. If a job ad appeared in more than one search engine, we added it only once and recorded it as located in the search engine where it was first posted. However, if a job was listed twice with the same title and description but located in different cities, we counted both ads because two different positions were advertised. We collected a total of 176 job ads from the four search engines. We found 78 ads (44%) on LinkedIn, 58 (33%) on Indeed, 23 (13%) on Monster, and 17 (10%) on Glassdoor. Figure 7.1 provides a breakdown of the number of ads found in each search engine.

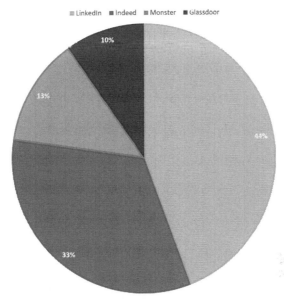

Figure 7.1. Percentage of job ads found in each search engine.

■ Coding the Ads

After collecting ads and saving copies, we uploaded all ads into NVivo to begin our open coding. To develop a provisional list of codes, two coders independently coded ten percent of the collected ads. We then compared codes and conducted a manual card sort exercise to identify commonly included information in these ads. Our card sort revealed five categories of content on these ads, which we labeled degree and experience, hard skills, soft skills, physical attributes, and other domains. We define these categories below:

- **Degree and experience:** We used this category to confirm that all jobs included a degree or entry-level designation and to quantify prior experience requirements.
- **Hard skills:** We coded skills that are measurable as hard skills. Examples include writing, reading, math, and computer program use.
- **Soft skills:** Soft skills are personal traits that cannot easily be measured. Examples of soft skills mentioned in the ads include etiquette, flexibility, leadership, teamwork, and time management.
- **Physical attributes:** We used this code to note job requirements and responsibilities that had physical implications, such as working long hours and travel.
- **Other domains:** Many job ads required specific domain knowledge, such as communication, business, and information technology. We used this category to track specific domains that job ads required or requested.

With these categories identified, we then conducted a second card sort to create subcategories to use for coding. Some categories had only a few subcategories. Table 7.1 lists each category and major subcategories we identified. Some subcategories, such as those in hard skills, were further divided into sub-subcategories.

With these codes in place, two coders divided the remaining 90 percent of the ads and coded in increments of 12–24 ads per week. Each week, coders met to discuss coding, check for agreement, and reach consensus on codes.

Table 7.1. Category and Subcategory Codes

Degree & experience	Hard skills	Soft skills	Physical attributes	Domains
Degree	Genres	Personal traits	Age	Communication
Prior experience	Project management	Teaming traits	Long hours	Business
	Grammar or language		Travel	Information technology
	Research or planning		U.S. work authorization	Healthcare
	Technology			Other
	Rhetoric			
	Promotion			
	Marketing			
	Visual design			

■ Viewing Job Requirements as a Workplace Snapshot

The content analysis we conducted revealed a snapshot of the job requirements, responsibilities, and duties of entry-level professional communicators. This snapshot tells us, in general, what employers are seeking from their applicants, ranging from years of experience to hard skills and soft skills that are required. Table 7.2 provides an overview of the major categories we considered in this section and the frequency of mentions within the ads.

The first column in Table 7.2 lists the five major categories we identified in our sample, the second column lists the number of ads that contained at least one code within the category, and the third column lists the total number of codes in the sample. For example, hard skills were listed in all 176 ads we examined; within those 176 ads, 3,379 hard skills were coded, the most of any category. The rest of this section briefly describes what these codes tell us about the professional communication workplace where our majors might find employment.

Table 7.2. Category Code Frequency in Ads

Category	Number of ads included in this category code	Number of codes within this category
Physical attributes	51	99
Domains	154	382
Degree and experience	171	341
Soft skills	171	1,233
Hard skills	176	3,379

A professional communication workplace is one where an employee may typically create content for specific, known audiences rather than unknown, mass audiences (Faber, 2002). Since this communication is tailored to the reader, the various soft and hard skills identified in this study may contribute to the success of the new graduate in this type of environment. This may differ from mass communication in terms of the skills and experience needed. Mass communication involves providing information to a large general audience. Although the mediums for providing communication may be similar, such as digital or print, professional communication in the workplace draws out specific characteristics as described in the following categories, which are discussed from least to most frequently included.

Physical Attributes

Only fifty-one ads included physical requirements, the least of all categories. Twenty of these ads posted commonly found physical requirements related to sitting, standing, and lifting—all activities typically required in office settings. Two physical attributes, however, tell us more about work expectations. Nineteen ads mentioned that employees work long hours, including nights, weekends, and holidays. Even more ads (29) stated that applicants must be able to travel. Travel requirements were typically listed as 5–15 percent of the job. Travel locations were primarily within North America; only three ads mentioned international travel. While physical attributes were the least frequently discussed categories, they tell us that entry-level professional communication workplaces sometimes require overtime and may require employees to spend time away from friends and family.

Domains

Eighty-eight percent (154) of all job ads mentioned specific domains (or types of knowledge) that an applicant should possess. Domains are comparable undergraduate majors and minors. Figure 7.2 provides a breakdown of the specific domains. The domains identified in the ads give us insight into the industry sectors where professional communicators are employed. Four specific domains were frequently mentioned: communication, business, information technology, and healthcare.

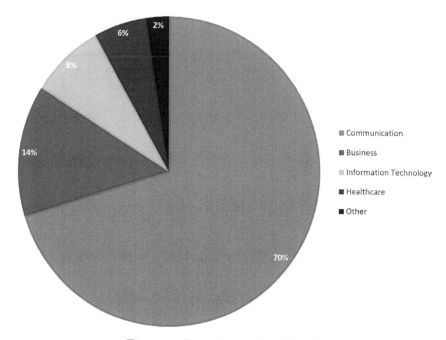

Figure 7.2. Domains mentioned in ads.

Communication was, by far, the most common; 70 percent of the 154 ads listed communication as a required domain. Within communication, job ads specified three specific areas: business and corporate communication, public relations, and media relations. The most frequently mentioned business subcategory was management. Domains listed in job ads offer two kinds of information: They tell us the major focus of the job being advertised, but they may also indicate the type of business the company does. For job seekers, this information suggests that communication knowledge is most valued in these jobs, but some background in a secondary field, such as business or information technology, is also considered a plus.

▌ Degrees and Experience

All 176 job ads required some type of bachelor's degree; however, the type of degree (BA, BS, or other) was rarely stated. Only nine ads specifically requested a Bachelor of Arts degree (BA) and six, a Bachelor of Science degree (BS). Requirements for years of experience ranged more widely. One hundred and forty-seven ads listed prior experience as required. Eighty percent of the ads required applicants to have two or more years of experience, with almost one third (32%) requesting at least two years of experience. Two to three years of experience were required by over half of the ads. Table 7.3 summarizes the years of experience listed and the percentage of ads requesting this experience.

Table 7.3. Years of Experience Requested in Ads

Years of experience	Percentage of ads
1 year	18%
2 years	32%
3 years	22%
4 years	6%
5 years	18%
6+ years	2%
No experience	1%

While many employers accept a degree as two to three years of experience, 88 percent (151) ads required both a degree and experience. This combination suggests that applicants need to gain experience as early and often as possible, even while pursuing a degree. Internships, for example, can provide opportunities that allow students to gain experience and fulfill degree requirements.

Soft Skills

Soft skills were the second most frequently coded category in the job ads. Soft skills were coded into two subcategories: the ability to work well alone (personal traits) and the ability to work well with others (teaming traits). We identified 11 different personal trait categories in Table 7.4.

Table 7.4. Frequency of Personal Traits in Ads

Personal trait	Percentage of ads
Time management	70%
Relationship building	68%
Drive, motivation, or work ethic	40%
Able to work independently	38%
Flexibility	27%
Problem-solving	27%
Creative	21%
Leadership	21%
Positive attitude or enthusiasm	19%
Open to learning	13%
Handle ambiguity	9%

Table 7.5. Frequency of Teaming Traits in Ads

Teaming Trait	Percentage of ads
Working across teams	75%
Working within a team	56%
Supporting administration	44%
Supervising others	14%
Supporting staff	8%

These 11 traits appeared in 97 percent (171) of ads; many ads had multiple references, for a total of 710 personal traits. As Table 7.4 illustrates, the abilities to manage time and to build relationships were included by almost 70 percent of all ads. Several of these traits also connect easily to other categories. For example, the abilities to be flexible and manage time were frequently mentioned along with the physical requirement to work long hours. Teaming traits were mentioned in 90 percent (159) of the ads, but they appeared less frequently (522 times) than personal traits. Teaming traits were divided into five subcategories, with working across teams (75%) and working within a team (56%) being most frequently mentioned. Entry-level professional communicators often provided administrative support but only rarely provided staff support or supervised others. Table 7.5 provides a breakdown of these traits.

█ Hard Skills

Hard skills were unquestionably the most frequently mentioned requirements for professional communicators. The 176 job ads listed hard skills 3,379 times, for an average of 20 hard skills listed per job. These skills were coded into eight categories. Table 7.6 identifies the eight categories, defines each, and lists the percentage of ads that included the category.

As Table 7.6 illustrates, almost all professional communicators are responsible for developing content and managing projects. Their soft skills prepare them to work alone on deliverables or to work with a team on larger projects. They communicate using both written and spoken language skills, and they use technology frequently in their work. They will need to have a firm understanding of workplace communication, but a secondary knowledge drawn from business, information, or health care domains is helpful for landing a job in a specific industry. A degree in communication can provide some of this knowledge, but prior experience, such as internships, is helpful and often required to enter these jobs. These entry-level jobs also require long hours occasionally and sometimes travel. These components comprise the snapshot of the professional communication workplace. In the next section, we delve more deeply into the ads to offer advice on how entry-level job seekers can turn their academic knowledge into workplace know-how.

Table 7.6. Frequency of Hard Skills in Ads

Category	Definition	Percentage of ads including this category
Genres	Creating specific deliverables or types of professional communication the job requires. Includes print, electronic, and oral deliverables.	97%
Project management	Organizing, tracking, reviewing, scheduling projects	94%
Grammar or language	Demonstrating effective writing and speaking skills (often generic). Includes style guide knowledge and foreign language fluency.	85%
Technology	Knowing and using information technologies, including specific software, media applications, and hardware, such as digital cameras and video equipment.	78%
Research or planning	Supporting or conducting research. Includes research methods, such as interviews and data analytics.	71%
Promotion/ marketing	Promoting services, products, and organizations	57%
Rhetoric	Analyzing audiences, adapting content for different audiences, and developing strategies	56%
Visual design	Knowing and applying graphic design, layout, and design principles	12%

Leveraging Academic Knowledge into Workplace Know-How

Using job ads to read the professional communication workplace offers the opportunity to see what communicators do, but how can entry-level job seekers spin what they've learned in classrooms into workplace gold? This section looks more closely at the specific words and phrases employers use in these ads to describe workplace activities: how and where work is performed, who does it, and who works with who. This section also connects these activities to work professional communication students have completed. It is divided into two subsections: First, we focus on hard skills described in the ads; second, we discuss soft skills.

Hard skills, as we noted earlier, are activities that can be seen, counted, or measured. Included in this group are six categories: communicating content, managing projects, using grammar and language, learning and using technologies, researching and planning, and persuading and promoting. Soft skills are less easily measured; they are personal traits that one exhibits through actions. Included in this group are four subcategories: working well with others, working independently, being flexible, and being creative. We discuss these skill sets from most frequently to least frequently identified in the job ads.

■ Communicating Content

Approximately 97 percent of the job ads identified specific content, or genres, a professional communicator must create on the job. Table 7.7 presents a summary of many of the genres included in these job ads.

As Table 7.7 illustrates, workplace writing genres in these jobs are multiple and varied. Business or corporate communication genres were the most noted, appearing in 76 percent (134) of the job ads. Within business and corporate communication genres, internal communication genres were mentioned in 64 ads. Internal communication genres include announcements, employee messaging, and reports. For example, a communication coordinator job ad for a job placement company listed "research and prepare proposals to help identify and prioritize goals/situations" as an internal communication responsibility. Another ad for a communication specialist for a finance company noted that "planning, developing, executing internal communication strategies across the enterprise" was expected. External communications, such as "press releases, marketing materials, executive backgrounders, scripts and award submissions," were also commonly identified. The previously mentioned job placement company ad included "write and assemble business proposals"—the same genre but directed to an external audience. Many ads stated that professional communicators were required to write both internal and external communications, such as one from a medical organization, which required professional communicators to "develop content for corporate announcements and member communications, including newsletters and social media posts, and tailor for distribution across internal and external channels while ensuring consistency of message and editorial quality." As these examples illustrate, communicating content is a critical responsibility of professional communicators. While students may not have had experience writing all genres required by a job, they may have had experiences throughout their college career that can show a potential employer their abilities to learn and use different genres. For example, have they prepared a proposal or created an outline for a paper or project for a class? Have they taken a creative writing class or any upper-level writing course where they had to write a short story or create a podcast?

Some entry-level jobs required genres that are more journalistically focused, as seen from 82 of the job ads. Although press releases (45%) or video or multimedia (43%) accounted for the top genres, an interesting third was storytelling (30%). Storytelling has become an important part of organizational communication strategies as the workforce became more diverse (Barker & Gower, 2010).

Table 7.7. Genres Mentioned in Ads

Genre	Percentage of ads including this genre	Examples
Advertising	33%	Graphics, ads, promotions and signs
Business or corporate communication	76%	Internal communication, communication calendar or schedule, and reports
Correspondence	44%	Newsletters, emails, and e-blasts
Journalism	47%	Press release, video or multimedia, storytelling and photography
Digital social media	40%	Social media content, engagement, channels, and campaigns
Digital web content	47%	Web content, blogs, and training documents
Plans	38%	Communication, marketing, crisis
Public relations	23%	PR campaigns, award submissions, and announcements
Presentations	35%	Presentations, speeches, and talking points

One senior communications coordinator job at an R1 university listed "use storytelling techniques in an effort to effectively reach diverse audiences and further promote key messages and deliverable outcomes in support of . . . priorities." Storytelling can help employees engage more in the workplace (Gustomo et al., 2019). Another ad for a communications and outreach specialist for an insurance company listed one responsibility as "recommending and creating impactful storytelling content for ongoing communications that align with the social impact strategy." To help remember how to tell an impactful story, remember PLOT: plain, light, obvious, and tight (Guiliano, 2000). Keep it simple, easy to understand, relevant to the topic, and short. Most importantly, practice. Entering the job market, job seekers may have a short window of opportunity to talk about their story. They may only have a few hundred words in a press release to convey a message. To practice this skill, students should think of how to tell an impactful story in a short amount of time and practice retelling and refining that story. Finally, as they begin to tell their own story, entry-level job seekers should be sure to discuss genres produced and to describe experiences learning new genres. These details could be keys to entering a new workplace. Another sought-after skill set in any entry-level communication job is project management (PM) skills. Of the 176 job ads reviewed, 94 percent (167) listed some type of project management skill as a duty or responsibility. Although initially associated with construction projects, PM as a field has found its way into businesses because of the benefits, such as the ability for organizations to be more efficient and effective (Pinto, 2002). PM "is the application of knowledge, skills, tools, and techniques to project activities to meet the project requirements" (Project Management Institute, 2012). PM activities are typically categorized into five groups: "initiating, planning, executing, monitoring and controlling, and closing" (Project Management Institute, 2012). When it comes to entry-level communication jobs, PM is a key skill set employers desire in successful candidates. Managing is less about managing other people and more about managing multiple priorities and deadlines. Many of the job ads examined included duties and responsibilities such as managing "complex projects to meet goals," "multiple projects simultaneously," and "competing priorities." Another ad from the food and beverage industry required "careful management of files to ensure edited and final files are saved accurately." PM requires an understanding of processes as well; an ad from a philanthropic division of a manufacturing company required knowledge of "design processes to maintain communications assets and documents, and ensure compliance from team."

Entry-level applicants may think they don't have any PM skills, but they don't need any special training or certification to possess skills that could be useful in the workplace. They have likely already managed many different projects during their college career. Managing multiple items is complicated when transitioning between tasks. Sophie Leroy (2009) found a negative impact when transitioning from one task to the next, depending on the amount of time required to complete the previous task. However, experience and practice ease the transition. Extending the definition of a project to include college experiences allows entry-level job seekers to talk about projects completed in an interview. A project could simply be a semester of classes. For registration, students may have reviewed which courses were available. They planned their schedules around those courses, along with any jobs or internships for the semester. An applicant could also discuss tools and skills used to keep track of everything to make the schedule work. A project could also be a group paper they've had to write. For example, many students can recall taking an online course over the summer, not knowing anyone in the class, and having to write a group paper with complete strangers. In a very short time, they get to know each other, learn each other's strengths and opportunities, and work together to write a cohesive paper. These could be examples of "competing priorities" and "gather[ing] resources for projects" as listed in the job ads. In a professional setting, the same skills would apply. Students often find themselves prioritizing work based on a number of factors, including when the work is due, who they engage or consult with, and which other tasks need to be completed at the same time.

■ Delivering Messages with Correct Grammar and Language Skills

Being able to manage projects and communicate in multiple genres requires strong language skills. Possessing strong grammar and language skills may seem obvious requirements for professional communicators. In fact, this skill set was third most frequent in the ads we examined, with 85 percent (149) mentioning them. Although seemingly obvious, entry-level job seekers should understand specifically what employers look for when job ads request either written communication skills (141) or verbal communication skills (114) in their ads. One ad for a corporate communications specialist wanted someone who could "cultivate a consistent voice . . . across multiple platforms." Another ad for a human rights campaign communications coordinator asked for a candidate who "possess[es] solid writing skills as well as communication skills necessary to elicit the right information from a variety of sources." A third ad for a communications coordinator searched for "highly developed written, verbal, and interpersonal skills with the ability to work effectively in a large culturally diverse environment." Many ads identified offered more general descriptions, such as one requesting "superior ability to communicate effectively with others at all levels, orally and in writing," while others were more specific about situations that require language skills, such as one from a recruiting agency that requested the "ability to communicate complex situations clearly and simply by listening actively and conveying difficult messages in a positive manner." Whatever the situation, knowing how to speak and write clearly in a variety of workplace settings is another key expectation. Professional communication students likely have had many occasions where they have practiced writing and speaking skills in classes. Whether they were creating deliverables in multiple genres, delivering a speech, or engaging in a mock job interview, they were building grammar and language skills that will be important in the professional communication workplace.

▋ Learning and Using Technology

Technology is a broad category, and 78 percent of the job ads looked for a variety of different technology experiences and skills. Managing and engaging through social media (e.g., Instagram, Facebook, LinkedIn, X [Twitter], YouTube) may be part of an entry-level job's responsibilities. Even if the job seeker doesn't have a presence on these platforms, they may be asked to manage their new company's social media presence. If their job involved PM as we described previously, they may find PM software, such as Asana, Basecamp, and Workamijig, mentioned in job ads. Many ads also included familiar programs or applications like Microsoft Office, Google, and Adobe Creative Cloud software suites. Industry-specific tools, such as Cision and PR Newswire/Businesswire, or business management software tools like NetSuite are common in the ads. The key with technology is not necessarily having experience with different platforms, but rather being able to learn how to use the different technologies to get the job done. While entry-level job seekers may not be proficient in every technology mentioned, they can describe what technologies they know as well as how they learn technologies to demonstrate that acquiring technology skills is something they know how to do.

▋ Researching and Planning Strategically

In the job ads, we categorized activities that required supporting or conducting research as research and planning. We found these activities mentioned in 71 percent (126) of ads. Like the genres category, research and planning included a broad range of activities. For example, some ads identified specific research methods that the professional communicator should know, such as surveys, interviews, and data analytics. An ad from a technology company was quite specific about the kinds of research activities required: "target audience research . . . [through] eMails, surveys, video, blogs, virtual events, events/campaigns." A data analytics firm required interview skills to create articles on "industry professionals (internally as well as externally)." In other ads, research was used internally for strategic planning. These ads required applicants to be able to conduct "communication audits" and "research business trends." A financial company searched for someone who could "translate marketing/business plans, competitive research and information into effective, efficient and innovative communication strategies that support business unit goals." Similarly, a medical insurance company looked for research skills, such as "evaluat[ing] communications programs and processes; identify[ing] lessons learned and recommend[ing] changes for future campaigns based on results (e.g., apply metrics to determine success of the process)." While job seekers may have experience with some of these research methods, like interviewing, the more strategic research requirements—communication audits, metrics, and program evaluations—may seem unfamiliar. These particular research activities are commonly discussed online and in business trade magazines, like *Forbes* and *Fortune*. When job seekers encounter the unfamiliar in ads, they can apply the information-gathering research skills they have to learn more. A communication audit, for example, is a study that looks at how communication occurs within a communication organization in order to recommend change: How do managers communicate with their employees, what channels are used, and under what circumstances are they conveyed? When job seekers understand what research the task requires, they will discover that they already know how to ask questions and get answers. These skills are, to put it simply, more focused on specific types of research that students in professional communication classes already learned to do.

▋ Using Messages to Persuade and Promote

A final hard skill we consider in this section includes information we categorized as "rhetoric" and "promotion." Rhetoric relates to how communication impacts the audience. Specifically, we coded responsibilities as rhetoric if they involved analyzing, adapting content, and developing strategies for specific audiences. Similarly, promotion responsibilities involved marketing services, products, and organizations to specific audiences. While it may seem odd to connect an ancient practice like rhetoric to promoting or marketing, both categories referenced "persuasion" and "audiences," so we felt they were suitably combined into a single discussion here. Of the 57 percent (100) of ads that listed rhetoric as a hard skill, the audience was a frequently identified component, appearing in 44 of the ads. Job duties and responsibilities included examples of both, such as "communications experience with proven experience simplifying concepts and convey them to audiences," "creative storytelling across a variety of formats and channels," or "ability to tell a story that appeals to different audiences". Other skills could include "translating business strategies to comprehensive corporate communication strategies," having a "comprehensive understanding of marketing and communication channels including digital, print, direct, email, social media and more," and supporting "strategic employee communications." Ads that focused on promotion often involved public relations and community engagement, such as this ad from a digital security firm, which required the applicant to be able to "generate, curate and publish daily content that extends our reach, builds meaningful connections and encourages followers to take action." Media relations was another common aspect of promotional activities. These activities were sometimes as simple as "maintain[ing] lists of media contacts" or as complicated as working in a team to "increase the average number of press hits by 15% per quarter by building and maintaining monthly communications with reporters with press pitches, drafting and sending press releases, and managing the logistics of media requests." Whatever the activity's complexity, entry-level job seekers will need to draw on lessons they have learned about audiences, situations, and strategies for persuasion to exhibit these skills. One way that they could translate their experience is to think back to a time when they had to explain a concept or a topic to a class or in a paper. Oftentimes this requires the skills to comprehend the details of a paper, journal article, or book chapter and then summarize it for a broad audience. The audience may have been familiar with the topic, but the student had to find a way to clearly and concisely explain it.

▮ Teaming or Working Well with Others

With this section, we transition from hard skills that are measurable to soft skills that are more personal. Teaming or working well with others was the most frequent soft skill we found in the job ads, appearing in 90 percent (159) of the ads. Students have likely worked with others during coursework, but if not, now is the time to learn to work in teams.

As seen in Table 7.8, for this category, we included three sub-nodes—working across teams, working within teams, and relationship building—because they all apply to working well with others. Forty-eight percent of the ads include skills for working across teams. Twenty-four percent of the ads mention skills for working within teams. Another 24 percent of the ads ask for relationship-building skills. Therefore, 96 percent of the ads include skills related to teaming or working well with others.

Table 7.8. Percentage of Teaming or Working
Well with Others Soft Skills in Ads

Sub-nodes in the Teaming or Working Well with Others category	Percentage
Working across teams	48%
Working within a team	24%
Relationship building	24%

Clearly, applicants must be skilled at teamwork. As for working within teams, one ad for a communications coordinator notes that applicants must have "the ability to collaborate and work effectively with individuals." The same ad explains that applicants must "support project coordination and daily workflows by engaging with cross functional teams." These cross functional teams may be within or outside of the professional communicator's organization. As for relationship building, the job ads note that professional communicators must "possess strong interpersonal skills at all levels" and have a "proven ability to build relationships with diverse groups."

Similarly, building relationships with a departmental team, other cross-departmental teams, external teams, clients, and members of the community is essential. For example, one job ad for a public relations and communications coordinator explains that applicants must "develop and maintain successful relationships with key reporters." Building positive relationships with reporters makes it easier to plan press conferences, field reporters' questions, and maintain a positive image for the organization. Another ad for a communications coordinator job mentions how applicants should "maintain contracts and relationships with consultants and external entities providing services to the Communications Department." Building positive relationships with consultants leads to smoother project management.

Students should practice teamwork and relationship-building skills before searching for their first entry-level position. To practice teamwork, they might volunteer for group projects at work, school, or a local charity. Even playing a small role will help them gain more experience. They can practice relationship building by actively adding new people to their network. A good place to begin this work is getting to know their instructors. Chances are their instructors will be willing to introduce them to other working professionals. Second, they can use tools like LinkedIn to reach out to communication professionals and ask if they have time to talk about their professional lives. Third, students can ask communication professionals at their jobs if they have time to talk about their work. However students grow their network, they should remember to express thanks to a person who is willing to take time to meet with them—a handwritten thank-you note shows appreciation and increases the likelihood of being remembered when applying for a job with a new contact's company after graduation.

▌ Working Independently

Although this category may seem contradictory, given that the first soft skill is teaming, it is equally important to be able to work well independently. Like several other categories, this one is broad. It includes personal traits that students possess, like good time management, a strong work ethic, and a positive attitude, but it also includes how well students can make decisions as a leader of a group or as a supervisor. Although these last two activities do include working with others, they often require an individual to make independent decisions about teams and their work. The frequency of these traits in the job ads is illustrated in Table 7.9.

When discussing time management, the ads explain applicants should be "a master juggler of multiple projects" with a "demonstrated ability to work well under pressure." Furthermore, applicants will be asked to manage and prioritize "competing deadlines" in a "fast paced environment" while creating high-quality work. Successfully managing multiple projects may help new employees to move up the corporate ladder. Employers also seek driven professional communicators who are able to work alone. For example, one ad for a communications specialist explains applicants should be "be assertive, and take ownership" when working on projects. A different ad for a communications coordinator notes applicants should be able to "work independently with little day to day guidance."

Companies also seek applicants who show strong leadership and who are, according to one ad for a corporate communications coordinator, "tactfully relentless to get what is needed to make progress." Possessing this quality creates the momentum to sustain long-term projects. One example of leadership comes from an ad for a communications specialist who works with mergers and acquisitions (M&A) integration. The ad explains how the person in this position must "be the M&A integration and change management communications subject matter expert in the Integration Management Office, ensuring industry best practices are being deployed through all integration projects." On the job, entry-level professional communicators may be asked to lead a team because of their expertise in a specific area, whether in communication or a different domain. Having a positive attitude is also key. One ad for a corporate communications specialist notes that applicants must "bring passion and enthusiasm to every project, every interaction, every day." An ad for a communications and engagement specialist explains that applicants should be "energetic, positive and outgoing, while able to maintain a professional demeanor." Having a positive attitude may not always be easy, but it helps to build stronger relationships with coworkers and clients. Last, new employees may be asked to supervise others in a leadership role. Specifically, they may be supervising an internship program. Or they might be coaching an administrative assistant. Other possibilities include supervising student interns, content managers, web consultants, contractors, faculty, or volunteers. While the group being supervised depends on the company and the position, leadership always requires supporting others, not just telling others what to do.

Table 7.9. Percentage of Working Independently Soft Skills in Ads

Sub-nodes in the Working Independently category	Percentage
Time management	24%
Drive, motivation, or work ethic	10%
Able to work independently	10%
Leadership	6%
Positive attitude or enthusiasm	5%
Supervising others	5%

Working independently is also a skill students can practice. First, they might take opportunities to lead in group projects for class or for projects in their current job. Second, they should consider volunteering for a local non-profit whose mission they believe in. Volunteering will give them an opportunity to add more people to their network and allow them more chances to take on leadership roles, even if it is something as simple as teaching incoming volunteers how they can help.

Being Flexible

A third category that appeared in our analysis of the job ads was the importance of being flexible. In this category, we combined sub-nodes on flexibility, openness to learning, and handling ambiguity because they all related to flexibility. As Table 7.10 indicates, six percent of the ads mention flexibility. An openness to learning is included in three percent of the ads, and two percent of the ads note applicants' ability to handle ambiguity.

When discussing flexibility, job ads described the ideal applicant as one who can "shift gears and acclimate quickly" to accommodate changes in schedules, project plans, and corporate environments. For example, one job ad for a communications specialist explains applicants must have "the ability to shift across multiple mediums in a fast-paced environment." One minute, they might find themselves working on an email to a client. The next minute, they are finishing a call for proposals for contract work. They'll likely be asked to switch between writing in a variety of genres, which may include emails, podcasts, and communication plans, to name a few.

Table 7.10. Percentage of Flexibility Soft Skills in Ads

Sub-nodes in the Being Flexible category	Percentage
Flexibility	6%
Open to learning	3%
Handle ambiguity	2%

This flexibility also applies to acquiring new knowledge on the job. Many of the job ads mentioned how applicants should be open to learning. Examples include learning new technology and professional development. No matter where they work, entry-level professional communicators should keep in mind that there is always something new to learn. They can practice this openness by teaching themselves how to use a technology that's new to them. For example, they could learn a new software like Adobe InDesign using books, YouTube videos, and online classes. Learning new technologies will also strengthen future job applications in the long run.

Last, applicants must "deal with ambiguity" and "unexpected changes" on the job. For example, one ad for a marketing communications project coordinator noted applicants must show they "can effectively cope with change; can shift gears comfortably; can decide and act without having the total picture." Furthermore, the company needs someone who "isn't upset when things are up in the air; doesn't have to finish things before moving on" and "can comfortably handle risk and uncertainty." The key to operating in ambiguity is to remain calm. Find a healthy coping mechanism that is useful in uncertain situations. What these final responsibilities suggest is that, in the moment, flexibility isn't always easy. But with the rapidly evolving nature of a professional communicator's environment, it's a necessary skill.

Being Creative

A final soft skill worth noting is creativity. As seen in Table 7.11, for this category, we combined the problem-solving and creativity sub-nodes of the soft skills section because they both apply to creativity. Six percent of the ads mention problem-solving skills. Creativity is included in five percent of the ads.

The first form of creativity to consider is problem-solving creativity, and the second is design creativity. Problem-solving creativity, or creativity in motion, focuses on "creativity and initiative in solving problems." Design creativity includes tasks like generating new ideas and storytelling in ways that engage audiences. The ideal candidate has the "ability to use innovative and creative techniques that drive effective organizational communications." Two examples help illustrate this point. As for problem-solving creativity, one ad for a communications and engagement specialist notes applicants must be able to "continuously look for ways to improve." Chances are students have already been problem-solving creatively in their current jobs, but don't realize it. Are there ways in which coworkers could be communicating more effectively? Is there a process that could be running more efficiently? When's the last time someone claimed "this is the way we've always done it" when asked why an inefficient process is done a certain way? That would be an excellent place to make change. Students should not wait until their first professional communication job to start practicing these skills. Professional communication training helps a student look at problems and processes from a different angle.

Table 7.11. Percentage of Creative Soft Skills in Ads

Sub-nodes in the Being Creative category	Percentage
Problem-solving	6%
Creativity	5%

As for design creativity, one ad for a senior specialist in corporate communication notes applicants should be a "highly creative writer experienced in crafting compelling messaging, stories and narratives." Often, part of an entry-level job is translating complex technical information into accessible formats for a diverse range of audiences. The power of narrative can help. Practicing these two types of creativity as a student is possible. For problem-solving creativity, or creativity in motion, students who work should consider solving problems in their current workplace. For design creativity, they can practice explaining what they are working on for a class or work project to a friend or family member who doesn't know the topic. Books and online classes can also assist when learning design principles. Two excellent books on design include *The Non-Designer's Design Book* by Robin Williams (2015) and *100 Things Every Designer Needs to Know About People* by Susan Weinschenk (2011). *The Non-Designer's Design Book* provides an easy-to-follow guide for the basic design principles of contrast, repetition, alignment, and proximity. *100 Things Every Designer Needs to Know About People* explains why people react to design the way they do. Websites like LinkedIn Learning and MasterClass offer online classes for a variety of new skills. Creativity is essential to finding solutions for design and practical problems.

Knowing these soft skills can assist entry-level professional communicators. Working well with others, working independently, being flexible, and engaging their creativity will help them grow these skills. While their first professional communication job may seem like it is many years away from now, practicing these skills as a student provides the foundation for getting and succeeding in an entry-level position.

■ What We See and What We Don't See in Job Ads

The job ads we've discussed in this chapter have allowed us to see commonalities of the professional communication workplace. It is a fast-paced, exciting environment where professional communicators will work closely with others, whether they are planning a project or managing a team. Professional communication jobs are located across multiple industries, but their focus is almost always on communicating with both internal and external audiences. This communication may take many forms, but the organization's story will be a constant touchstone that professional communicators will tell and retell in multiple media and genres.

Yet these ads cannot tell us what is going on behind the scenes. Once hired, professional communicators may find that their entry-level position is not as glamorous as they had hoped. They may also find that jobs with the same title are not created equal. This is where reading through the responsibilities listed in each job ad will provide a better understanding of whether the job may include administrative or even clerical duties. One communications coordinator job ad was straightforward and stated, "administrative duties include answering phones, scheduling meetings, travel and appointments, managing department meetings, reporting expenses, and filling out check requests." In another communications coordinator job, administrative tasks included "assisting the SVP, Corporate Communications, with scheduling, managing budgets and invoices, scheduling meetings, answering phones, leading brainstorm sessions, creating agendas and meeting recaps, and other activities."

Supporting senior administrators can be beneficial in the long run even if it's not an ideal job to start. Assisting and getting to know these administrators may help the professional communicator move up the ranks in their company when a new opening surfaces. Making phone calls and schedules may not be fun, but it gives new employees the chance to demonstrate their work ethic, which administrators notice. New employees should also keep in mind that while they are providing support and assisting senior leaders within an organization, this work can prove beneficial depending on their long-term career goals.

Finally, professional communicators unquestionably find themselves in workplaces full of energy and sometimes pressure. These workplaces demand people skills and emotional labor that can wear employees down, whether they are working alone or with others. Such workplaces, we believe, require another important kind of attention not found in any job ads we examined: making time for self-care. In a fast-paced environment, it can be easy to move forward to the next item on the to-do list instead of taking a break after hours of screen time. For this reason, our last advice, wherever professional communication students find that entry-level position, is to take care of themselves as much as they help take care of everyone else.

■ Acknowledgments

We would like to thank Geraldine Lingnau for her effort in gathering the job ads.

■ References

Barker, Randolph T. & Gower, Kim. (2010). Strategic application of storytelling in organizations. *Journal of Business Communication, 47*(3), 295–312. https:/doi.org/10.1177/0021943610369782.

Brumberger, Eva & Lauer, Claire. (2015). The evolution of technical communication: An analysis of industry job postings. *Technical Communication, 62*(4), 224–243.

Faber, Brenton. (2002). Professional identities: What is professional about profession-al communication? *Journal of Business and Technical Communication, 16*(3), 306–337. https://doi.org/10.1177/1050651902016003.

Guiliano, Peter. (2000). Spinning yarns. *Successful Meetings, 49*(8), 64–65.

Gustomo, Aurik, Febriansyah, Hary, Ginting, Henndy & Santoso, Imelia M. (2019). Understanding narrative effects: The impact of direct storytelling intervention on increasing employee engagement among the employees of state-owned enterprise in West Java, Indonesia. *Journal of Workplace Learning, 31*(2), 166–191. https://www.emerald.com/insight/content/doi/10.1108/JWL-07-2018-0088/full/html.

Henschel, Sally & Melonçon, Lisa. (2014). Of horsemen and layered literacies: Assess-ment instruments for aligning technical and professional communication undergrad-uate curricula with professional expectations. *Programmatic Perspectives, 6*(1), 3–26.

Leroy, Sophie. (2009). Why is it so hard to do my work? The challenge of attention residue when switching between work tasks. *Organizational Behavior and Human Decision Processes, 109*, 168–181.

Melonçon, Lisa & Henschel, Sally. (2013). Current state of US undergraduate degree programs in technical and professional communication. *Technical Communication, 60*(1), 45–64.

Pinto, Jeffrey K. (2002). Project management 2002. *Research Technology Management, 45*(2), 22–37. https://www.jstor.org/stable/24134511.

Project Management Institute. (2012). *A guide to the project management body of knowledge (PMBOK® Guide)*. Project Management Institute.

Weinschenk, Susan. (2011). *100 things every designer needs to know about people*. Pearson Education.

Williams, Robin. (2015). *The non-designer's design book: Design and typographic principles for the visual novice*. Pearson Education.

Contributors

Lora Anderson is Associate Professor in technical and professional writing at the University of Cincinnati. Her research focuses on technical communication pedagogy and medical rhetoric. Her book *Living Chronic: Agency and Expertise in the Rhetoric of Diabetes* was published in 2017 by The Ohio State University Press.

Janel Bloch is a faculty member at Northern Kentucky University, where she teaches business and professional communication. Her work has appeared in *Business and Professional Communication Quarterly*, *Technical Communication*, and *Journal of Management Education*.

Kelli Cargile Cook is Professor and Founding Chair of the Professional Communication Department at Texas Tech University. Her research focuses on professional and technical communication pedagogy, program development, and assessment. Her most recent co-edited collection is *User Experience as Innovative Academic Practice*.

Lance Cummings is Associate Professor of English in the professional writing program at the University of North Carolina Wilmington. In addition to researching histories of rhetoric, he explores rhetoric and writing in technologically and linguistically diverse contexts. His work has appeared in *Business and Professional Communication Quarterly*, *The Routledge Handbook of Comparative World Rhetorics*, and *Rhetoric, Professional Communication, and Globalization*, among others.

Brian Fitzpatrick is Associate Professor at George Mason University, where he teaches composition. His research is primarily focused on workplace writing, as well as online and hybrid pedagogies. He is the co-founder of the Archive of Workplace Writing Experiences and was recipient of the Conference on College Composition and Communication's Emergent Researcher Award for 2017-18 and a CCCC Research Initiative Grant in 2021-22. His work has appeared in *Effective Teaching of Technical Communication: Theory, Practice, and Application*, as well as *Performance Improvement Quarterly*, *WPA Journal*, *Academic Labor: Research and Artistry*, and *Double Helix*.

Ann Hill Duin is Professor of Writing Studies and Graduate-Professional Distinguished Teaching Professor at the University of Minnesota. Her recent books, together with Isabel Pedersen, are *Writing Futures: Collaborative, Algorithmic, Autonomous* (Springer, 2021) and *Augmentation Technologies and Artificial Intelligence in Technical Communication: Designing Ethical Futures* (Routledge, 2023).

Mark A. Hannah is Associate Professor of English at Arizona State University, where he serves as Director of Writing, Rhetorics, and Literacies. He publishes widely on the intersections of law, rhetoric, and expertise in professional communication.

Lee-Ann Kastman Breuch is Professor in the Department of Writing Studies at the University of Minnesota, where she serves as department chair. Her essays on rhetoric, digital writing, and technical communication have appeared in *Technical Communication Quarterly*, *Journal of Technical Writing and Communication*, *Computers and Composition*, and *Technical Communication*. She is past president of the Council on Programs in Technical and Scientific Communication (CPTSC) and former co-editor of the CPTSC journal, *Programmatic Perspectives*, with Lora Anderson.

Chris Lam is Associate Professor of technical communication at the University of North Texas. He specializes in statistical methods and experimental design and publishes widely on communication in team projects and the professionalization of technical communication.

Joni Litsey is a Ph.D. student at Texas Tech University in the College of Media and Communication and a member of the Innovation Diffusion Lab. While completing the program part-time, she works full-time as a process manager for a Fortune 100 company, where she has been for the past 20 years. Her research interests focus on how opinion leaders can model innovative change within organizations.

Jessica McCaughey is Assistant Professor in writing at The George Washington University. She is also co-founder and co-director of the Archive of Workplace Writing Experiences (www.workplace-writing.org), a collection of interviews and resources about workplace writing in America. Her research focuses primarily on the transfer of writing skills from the university to the professional realm.

Lisa Meloncon is Professor of technical communication at the University of South Florida. Her research focuses on programmatic issues in technical and professional communication, user experience, research methodology and methods, and the rhetoric of health and medicine.

Bethany Pitchford is a recent graduate from the College of Media and Communication at Texas Tech University, where she completed her doctoral program. Her work has been featured in *Survive and Thrive: A Journal for Medical Humanities and Narrative as Medicine*, the *Journal of Communication Inquiry*, and *Health Communication*. Her research focuses on how journalists frame mental illness when reporting on mass shootings and how creativity helps people cope with mental illness and traumatic experiences.

Jeremy Rosselot-Merritt is a lecturer in writing & communication at Carnegie Mellon University, where he teaches courses in technical, professional, and first-year writing. A specialist in workplace communication practice, he has authored or co-authored work in publications such as *Technical Communication*, *Journal of Technical Writing and Communication*, and *Business and Professional Communication Quarterly*.